Karen Dewey is a Senior Producer for The Midday Show on the Nine Network. In 1992 and 1993 she produced Angry's Soapbox segment, before taking maternity leave in 1994. Karen is a BA Communications graduate from Mitchell CAE, and in 1984 was awarded the National Journalism Education Award (Broadcast Journalism). Karen has also worked previously as Senior Line Producer for Good Morning Australia, on the Ten Network and as a columnist for the Riverina Leader. She lives in Sydney with her husband Kieran "Spud" Murphy, and their daughter, Billie.

ANGRY

SCARRED FOR LIFE

KAREN DEWEY

"AJ"
Stay young
Grow Strong

Angry

IRONBARK

First published 1994 in Ironbark by Pan Macmillan Australia Pty Limited
63-71 Balfour Street, Chippendale, Sydney

National Library of Australia cataloguing in-publication data:

Dewey, Karen
Angry: scarred for life

ISBN 0 330 27372 8

1. Anderson, Angry 2. Rose Tattoo (Musical group)
3. Rock musicians - Australia - Biography. 4. Rock music - Australia
1. Title

780.92

Design and type by Philippa Jenkins of In Visible Design

Photographs:
Thank you to all of the photographers whose work appears in this book. Chrystene Carroll generously gave us access to her extensive collection of photographs of Angry Anderson and contemporary portraits of the Anderson family. We especially thank her for her luminous photography of Angry's tattoos used throughout this book. Thanks also to Rosemay Roach and Lindy Anderson who both allowed us to use precious family photos from their personal albums. The dramatic Reading concert shots are by Robert Ellis along with the London portraits and all are courtesy of Albert Productions. Thanks to Bob King for his concert shots in Australia and for access to his impressive files on Angry. Serge Thomann took the photograph of Angry in *Jesus Christ Superstar* and the film stills from *Mad Max Beyond Thunderdome* are courtesy of Kennedy Miller and Warner Brothers. To any photographers we have been unable to identify, despite our considerable efforts, we thank you too.

Printed in Australia by McPherson's Printing Group

*To the survivors...all those who inspire through their strength,
their courage, and their determination.*

Acknowledgements:

*Firstly, thanks to Deborah Wood at Pan Macmillan for all her
support and encouragement, and to Rory Callaghan for being
the bridge that made this book possible. Special thanks to
Rosemay Roach, Robbie Williams and Lindy Anderson for
their help in relating the story. To Philippa Jenkins for her
imagination and enthusiasm, to all the photographers,
particularly Chrystene Carroll, for their wonderful work and to
Hilary Innes for painstakingly gathering all the visual material.
Thanks to Ray Martin for the foreword (and the rest!), and to
Sylvia Dewey for her regular progress reports. Of course, love
and thanks to both our families; Lou, Roxy, Galen, Blaine,
Liam, Kieran, and Billie.*

CONTENTS

FOREWORD

Angry Anderson is a dangerous cocktail.

Simple recipe. Just mix passion and opinion. Stir a lot. Add heat. Whammo! It's highly combustible stuff.

What's worse is that people quickly get a taste for Angry. They keep coming back for more. That makes it even harder to shut him up! Occasionally you have to slap a hand over his mouth, grab his microphone and get four hefty goons to carry him off stage. Angry doesn't yet understand that in commercial TV you occasionally have to STOP for commercials! With Angry stopping is a problem when he's in full stride. (Although to be accurate, for a human dynamo of Angry's stature, "full stride" is more like a manic flurry of small steps! He'll hate me saying that.)

Having worked with Mrs Anderson's golden-haired boy (can't resist it) for ten years I recognise Angry as a performer who likes the sound of what he says. But then, so do an awful lot of other people. We put him on a soapbox at "Midday" last year. Literally. Angry absolutely loved it. Especially when we made the box so big he needed an extension ladder to get up on it. He insisted that it merely lifted him to the rarefied heights he was intended to be. Predictably, from those alpine reaches he proceeded to tip a bucket on everybody below. Certainly, he revelled in dumping on a wide range of arrogant and pretentious buffoons. But, he does that from whatever height he happens to be!

Angry gets mad as hell and refuses to take it anymore, as Peter Finch once said. It's quite amazing to watch an audience as Angry starts to cut up rough. You can see them reach for their handbags, (even the women), prepared to storm whatever citadel Angry is attacking. Angry breathes fire and fury and gets a standing ovation. He'd have been a hit in the French Revolution, I tell you.

I stand there and shake my head in awe. Just when I think I've got a handle on his politics and opinions he comes out in favour of guard dogs and lax gun laws. Or something else I don't expect! Angry, the card-carrying Lefty, has suddenly developed a seige mentality! But, that's Angry. Put him in a box and he busts out of it!!

The simple truth is Angry Anderson is a great communicator. Don Burke is, too. And John Singleton. Paul Keating can be. No doubt about Kerry Packer. But, there aren't many on the top shelf. Angry sits comfortably up there.

Now it's obvious you can't communicate, or sell something unless people want to buy what you're offering. Or you must convince them that they need it! Angry does. He is absolutely fair dinkum. And people know it. Like Fred Hollows was.

He gets right-up governments (especially local governments) and public servants and racists. He's merciless, too, with those fridge and washing machine servicemen who mess up our lives. They never come when they promise and never fix it first time. He hates, with a passion, selfish drivers who take those shopping centre parking spots that are marked for wheelchairs. It comes as one helluva shock to idiot drivers to see this bald-headed motor-mouth, festooned with tattoos and sporting a black, red and ochre-coloured Koori t-shirt, aim both barrels at them. For the kids' sake it's a good job he does. But then kids' causes and kids' welfare are a personal crusade of Angry Anderson's. Remember he and his lovely Lindy have four kids themselves. At last count.

I remember clearly the first "Midday" story Angry did. It was about a couple of cancer kids, including a beautiful little girl named Annie. Bravely, Annie, for a while, beat the odds but finally the cancer won. When Angry sat in our studio, with the lights down and in front of an audience of a couple of hundred people, we watched Annie's story unfold. Tears streamed down his cheeks. This is a man who feels deeply for others and wears his emotions in public. As loud and obvious as his tattoos. This is a wild rock and roller who used to head-butt and try to scale chicken-wire protective fences to get at the animals in the audience. No wonder they snared him for the *Mad Max* movie. He had attitude, long before it was trendy.

Now, Angry is a good mate of mine. He's warm and loyal and persistent. And decent. His energy and commitment to charity work and battlers, especially where kids are at stake, is extraordinary. At times over the years, his professional and family fortunes have suffered because he's a "soft touch" when someone needs a helping hand. But then, he wouldn't be Angry Anderson if he acted differently.

He's been molested, protested and probably arrested. But, I doubt he's been bested many times.

Angry is a most extraordinary bloke. I hope this life story helps us know him even better. I already know I like him.

RAY MARTIN
JUNE 1994

'EVERYONE KNOWS I CAN SMILE ... BUT THIS IS REALLY ME'

ANGRY

Angry on the release of RAPS condoms aimed at 12-16 year olds:

'Our children are experiencing life, and sex is part of life, at a younger age, in a more adventurous way. Now, the thing is, there are children out there who are going to make up their own minds, without you and I, and without influence from parental guidance or whatever. They're going to make up their own minds against our better wishes. They're going to make up their mind, and they're going to have sex. Now, if they're going to do it – a responsible society is going to protect them.'

FROM 'THE MIDDAY SHOW' WITH RAY MARTIN, 18TH MARCH 1993

It's a typical Angry rave. There's no discipline, and he misses the point as many times as he hits it, but somehow his message gets through. He has a knack. He rolls every sentence into one, but he always makes sure you know how he feels.

Unless he's tired, Angry won't bring a conversation to an end. He'll go on all night if you let him, from one subject to the next. That's the kind of person he is. He loves to talk. He is an enigma, totally exasperating and totally appealing.

He's a man full of contradictions - a self-confessed former chronic drunk and drug taker with a violent history, who has been made a recipient of both an Advance Australia Award and an Australia Medal for his services to the community. A sexually, physically and mentally abused child who broke the brutal family pattern to become a besotted, devoted father of four.

When people are introduced to him, they usually shuffle and stutter over his name. For most people trying to say "Oh nice to meet you Angry" is a bit like trying to say "Oh nice to meet you Fierce" or "Irate" or "Indignant" or something. Eventually though, everyone gets used to it and calls him Angry, except his mum Rosemay. For a whole host of motherly reasons, she's always called him by the name she gave him, Gary.

He is bald, tattooed, and five foot two inches tall. His teeth are broken at the front, leaving a kind of triangular shaped gap which, if he's tempted, can look menacing. He has an obsession for Fisherman's Friend cough lollies and he sucks them constantly, squeezing a new one out of the packet before the old one's even finished.

He likes to wear clothes that clash, and he's almost always in a T-shirt with a slogan. He wears seven rings in his ears, four in the left and three in the right, because to Angry "seven is a magical number".

When I asked him to choose which photograph captures him best, he chose the cover shot. It's typical...he's brooding, letting you know somehow that he's come a long way. He doesn't like to smile for photographs. He has a more romantic view of himself with a scowl. He says "Everyone knows I can smile...but this is really me." His wife has another story. She says he doesn't like to smile because he exposes his double chins. If you could meet him, this is how you'd see him. You can almost read in his expression that although he's capable of it, he hasn't thumped anyone in years.

HEN ANGRY FIRST MADE HIS MOVE TO STARDOM THERE WAS ONLY ONE
THING THE REVIEWERS COULD AGREE UPON ... THAT HE WAS A SURPRISING PERSON. THAT HE
WAS MORE INTELLIGENT THAN HE MADE OUT, THAT HE WAS DEEPER THAN HE CARED TO LET
PEOPLE KNOW, AND THAT HE WAS MUCH MORE THAN JUST A MORONIC BRAWLER.

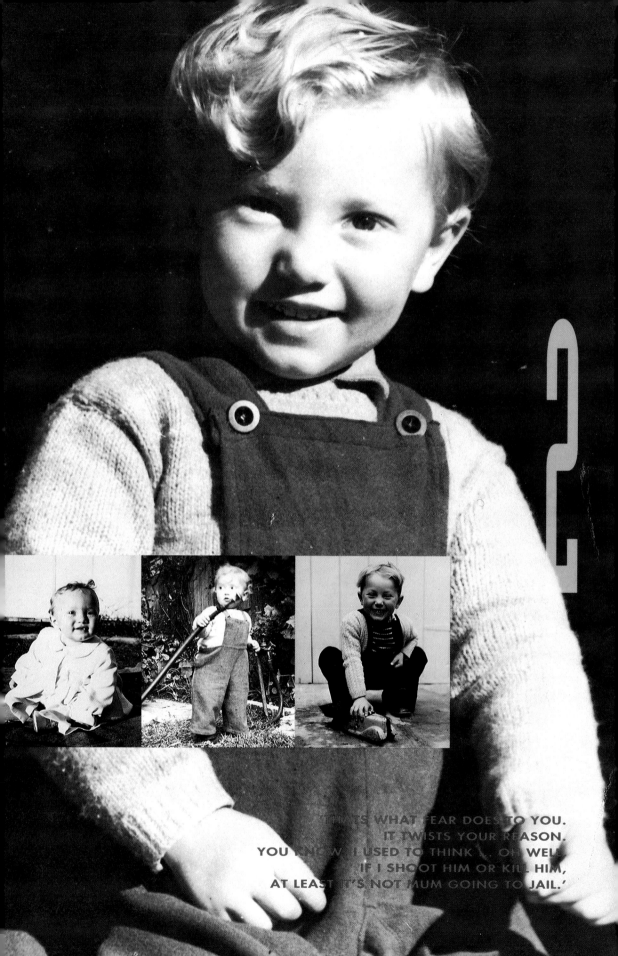

'THAT'S WHAT FEAR DOES TO YOU.
IT TWISTS YOUR REASON.
YOU KNOW, I USED TO THINK ... OH WELL,
IF I SHOOT HIM OR KILL HIM,
AT LEAST IT'S NOT MUM GOING TO JAIL.'

ALWAYS THE INDIAN

In his mid forties, Angry Anderson booked himself in for therapy with a psychiatrist. "The Doc", he called him. By then, he was a husband and a father, suffering under the weight of the demons tormenting him since childhood. He had two major problems. The first was his almost overwhelming fear of following the family cycle — the abused becomes the abuser. He'd seen it happen to his father, and his father before him, so he knew what he was capable of. Every day was a struggle with the fear that something would spark off this awful inherited bent, and he'd suddenly find himself hurting his wife or his children.

His other major problem was recall. Many of his memories, much of his childhood had been locked away in "safe boxes". It was the only way he knew to protect himself. **LEO THE LION** The years of fear, the events and their details, had all been put away in different parts of his memory. Some things he'd just blocked out completely, and others he'd softened to the point where he could live with them. As Angry says, "When certain things happen you suppress them. You can actually visualise rooms where you put things, or where you go to get away from them."

He'd lost years and years of his childhood, and the job of trying to go back to face all the fears was huge. One of the toughest things was making a distinction between the dreams, the creations of a frightened child, and the actual events. As he says, he needed help from a therapist. He didn't think he could do it alone. "If you try to unlock memories, you're trying to open doors, or see through walls or open boxes. You've got to be very careful that it's a true and legitimate recollection. It takes a lot of time. That's why it's important to have someone who can say 'What makes you think that happened?', 'Are you absolutely sure?'. "

Even after a year on the psychiatrist's couch, for Angry there's still work to do. There's never any sense of nostalgia when he looks back at his childhood, like there would be looking back on the "bad old" somehow "good old" days. For him, the earliest years were just bad. It's as simple as that.

He once had to ask his mother if there was ever any normal period in their family life, if they ever just sat around the dinner table, or watched the television together, because he couldn't remember a single time when they were just a family - Mum, Dad, and the kids. He thought maybe he'd forgotten. But he hadn't. The happy times were few and far between, and the normal times were nonexistent.

Angry's father, Colin Anderson, was a jockey...high profile and flamboyant. He'd been virtually forced into the profession by his family. He had two older brothers, one in the army and the other in the air force. Colin was small and athletic, perfect jockey material, and as far as his father could see, he was good for little else.

As a young man he wore the hats and the 200 dollar suits of a dandy, and drove around town in fast cars. He was a real glory boy. In his best gear he looked like James Cagney, his hero. At the track, people said he'd made and lost a fortune more than once, but however his luck held, he always looked the part.

It was on the island of Mauritius that Colin met his future wife. He was in his early twenties, and he and some of his other jockey mates had been offered an opportunity to ride in Durban and Madagascar. They jumped at the chance. The African racetracks were trying to lift their profile, so they were keen to fly in overseas jockeys, and he was just the right kind of bloke for the job. Working in Africa meant regular holidays in exotic locations, and the little island of Mauritius quickly became a real favourite.

At the time, Rosemay Louis was just a wide-eyed schoolgirl, sheltered and spoiled. She was only seventeen, one of a family of nine children - seven girls and two boys. She was the daughter of a wealthy island baker, who over the years had managed to bake his way into a sweet fortune with his sensational cakes. In 1945, by the time Colin arrived on the island, Rosemay's father owned the major tourist hotel and was part of the syndicate that owned the island racetrack. The deal was that the jockeys would be well looked after in the hotel for their holidays, just as long as they rode at the local race meetings.

Many Mauritian families in those days lived like royalty, with an army of servants to run their households. Rosemay had always been waited on hand and foot. She'd never done anything for herself, so to her, Colin was like a breath of fresh, dangerous air. He was fast and flashy, and he swept her off her feet like a whirlwind.

It was only six months before they were married, but for Rosemay, it was not a happy day. Her father didn't approve. It wasn't that he didn't like Colin. He just wasn't sure of his background.

As Rosemay says, "I hardly knew him, but of course, you know what children are like. Dad kept telling me that I didn't know what kind of person he was. But I thought I did. I had no idea."

Within hours of taking the wedding vows, Rosemay decided she'd made an enormous mistake. With the words "I do" she'd stepped out of her protected childhood, and into life as an abused wife. As she discovered, her new husband was a volatile and aggressive man who suffered terrible tempers. He was a bully. It was as if there were two distinct sides to his character. He was sometimes charming, sometimes fierce. He could play the witty ladies man, or he could be a rogue. "He was like a Jekyll and Hyde" says Angry "There were things I didn't find out until I was a grown man. Mum never told me, because she was introduced to Mr Hyde basically once the marriage ceremony had taken place."

COLIN AND ROSEMAY'S TORN WEDDING PHOTOGRAPH (COLIN'S BEEN RIPPED FROM ALL THE FAMILY PHOTOGRAPHS)

Although Rosemay almost immediately regretted her walk down the aisle, she felt there was no turning back. She was bewildered. She'd always been taught that when you married, it was forever. She was only nineteen, but she knew she'd made a decision that was for life. The times, her religion, her family, and her conscience demanded she stood by her vows, no matter what.

For her, the move to Melbourne, one year later, was an almost greater jolt because this time she was alone, pregnant, and heading for a country with a different language and a different culture. Colin's family also got a jolt. They didn't know much about their son's new bride. To them, it was as if he'd gone off on holiday to a foreign island, and suddenly lost his head. "When Dad bought her home the family were very taken aback," says Angry "She was an islander for a start. She was Roman Catholic, had long dark curly hair and she spoke French."

BABY GARY (ANGRY)
BEFORE HIS FIRST BIRTHDAY

There wasn't much Colin's father could do about Rosemay's race or language, but he made sure he fixed what he could about the religion. As soon as Rosemay arrived in Australia she was absolutely forbidden to attend church, or talk about her religion. She had no comeback, and certainly her husband didn't stand to defend her.

Colin's father was more than just anti-Catholic. He had a real bent against the religion. No one could remember precisely the history of his hatred, but its intensity was well-understood.

The family abuse pattern began long before Angry. When his father was a boy he also took regular beltings, so although Colin Anderson spent many years as the perpetrator of abuse, he also spent many years, to some extent, as the victim.

In Angry's grandfather's house, the family code called for strict discipline, and that meant liberal use of the strap. Neighbours used to whisper over their back fences about the terrible noises that came from the Anderson shed. They'd say they were forced to turn up their radios and televisions to try to block it out. In those days, though, people kept to themselves, so no one ever did anything. There were no anonymous phone calls to the police or community services. It was a time when there were unwritten rules about 'family business'.

Whatever happened outside the perimeters of your own fenced yard, was simply not your concern, so you didn't get involved.

Besides, Colin's father was not a man anyone ever argued with. Colin himself only tried to take him on when he was feeling particularly aggressive or brave, and he always lost. There were times even as a grown teenager when Colin would come home from the stables and say he wasn't going back, but his father would thrash him so badly that, next morning, he'd be out with the horses again.

In some ways Colin was a chip off the old block, but not all his aggression was inherited from his father. In his earliest days as a jockey he rode steeplechase, and had a series of horrendous falls. He took some real knocks to the head, and the family always believed they contributed to his quick tempers. He was punch-drunk or something similar. Angry is still bitter. He won't accept any excuses for what happened, but Rosemay has more sympathy. "There were times when Colin was nice, and he was good, but perhaps he just couldn't help himself. Sometimes I think he just didn't know what he was doing."

From the very beginning, for Rosemay and Angry, living with Colin was like living with a time bomb. One minute he was a loving husband and father, the next he was blind with rage. Whenever he was around, arguments erupted from nowhere, and quickly became violent.

As a child, Angry was lonely and frightened. In his innocence, he was baffled by the arguments. The relationships were so fragile, it was like balancing a tightrope. Instead of waiting anxiously for his father to come home from work, he waited in fear. To him, his father was like a monster who could turn the nicest day into a disaster. When he was very young the yelling always took place around him and above him, but as soon as he was big enough, he'd get involved, either trying to protect his mother or just trying to claim some peace.

Some days, the family would be together happily, and everything would be all smiles. Then, suddenly, Colin would snap, and the whole scene would turn ugly. The music would stop, and the family would cower. Within minutes, Colin would be hurling wild insults. Through the calm of a Saturday afternoon chairs would be thrown, and glasses

AS A CHILD, ANGRY WAS LONELY AND FRIGHTENED. IN HIS INNOCENCE, HE WAS BAFFLED BY THE ARGUMENTS. THE RELATIONSHIPS WERE SO FRAGILE, IT WAS LIKE BALANCING A TIGHTROPE.

would be broken.

Like Angry, Colin Anderson was short. He barely stood taller than 1.5 metres (five foot), but what he lacked in height he made up for in pure ferocity. He was a teetotaller, and, as a doctor once told Rosemay, it was the only good thing about him. Alcohol would have magnified the rage, and the results would have been terrifying.

Even without a drink, he was frightening enough. He was the sort of man who picked fights in the street. If someone said the wrong thing or did the wrong thing, he'd flatten them. There were occasions when he'd accuse total strangers of having affairs with his wife. He'd believe it vehemently, and demand a fight there and then. Angry can remember times when they'd go riding on the bike together. Within minutes, if anyone so much as looked sideways at him, Colin could turn a happy Sunday bike ride into a brawl. He was hotheaded and irrational. He'd blow things totally out of perspective, and react furiously.

"I don't know whether he was just clever and he only ever picked on people that he knew he could frighten or beat," says Angry,

ANGRY WITH MUM, ROSEMAY

"but I always knew that my old man wasn't anyone to be fooled with. He was a very strong person. You know, you've got to be strong to ride horses, physically strong. But you see, another thing too, he was big. He wasn't tall, but he was big. He wasn't wiry like a lot of jockeys. I remember his chest. His chest was really big. I remember his shoulders, from the back they were big. And he had big arms and big legs. He was very solidly built."

When Colin hit out at the family it wasn't always with his fist...often he used the strap or his open hand. He never hit Rosemay in the face, he always hit her on the arms or the upper body. As Angry says, "He didn't beat Mum senseless like some men bash their wives. I don't think any of us would have survived that. I think I would have killed him, or something else would have happened. But he certainly used to knock her around a bit". When he hit Angry it was often across the back, or the lower part of the legs. He didn't really start to use his fists until Angry was big enough to challenge him.

Colin used to be cagey and cunning about the abuse. He'd sometimes follow Rosemay into another room after an argument, so he could hit her or yell at her with no one watching.

For Angry though, the violence was as much emotional as it was physical. As he says, "To be threatened by him...for him to threaten me or her, to see him in that Neanderthal sort of state was terrifying, and to live with the knowledge that any one minute of the day when he was around he could just click...and bang, it was all over, for no reason at all."

'TO BE THREATENED BY HIM...AND TO LIVE WITH THE KNOWLEDGE THAT ANY ONE MINUTE OF THE DAY WHEN HE WAS AROUND HE COULD JUST CLICK AND BANG, IT WAS ALL OVER, FOR NO REASON AT ALL.'

Everyone would tiptoe around him, trying to say the right thing, or do the right thing, but there was no pleasing him.

He did strange things. He was threatening and dangerous. He used to tell Rosemay that if he ever caught her in a Catholic church he'd kill her. Rosemay took him at his word. It's a sad thing for her looking back, because she realises how naive she was when she first got married. She believed, not only that Colin would support her religion, but that he'd actually convert to it. She had dreams of having her children christened, and of regular visits to the local priest, but from the moment she arrived in Australia, she would never have dared.

Colin also had bizarre ideas about what was happening when he wasn't around. He used to watch Rosemay's every move, constantly suspicious. Sometimes he'd decide she was sleeping with another man, and he wouldn't believe the truth, no matter what Rosemay said or did to convince him. He'd even tell all the neighbours that Rosemay was having affairs, and get even angrier when they ignored his ranting. As Angry says, "The crazy thing about it was, he used to accuse Mum of infidelity, and he used to tell me that I wasn't his son. He told other people that I wasn't too, yet, he was disgustingly obsessed and disgustingly obvious about what he thought of women. The way he treated Mum too...you can't imagine what it's like to listen, to know, to hear. You just can't imagine what it's like."

Some of Colin's actions were completely irrational. Every few weeks he'd come home with a brand new car, but he'd never pay the lease. Inevitably, a month or so later, the repossession men would be there with their towtrucks. As soon as one car had been taken away, he'd bring home another.

Rosemay says she doesn't really know how she managed in those early years. She had no friends, and no way of making any, and to make matters worse, for many years she spent her time struggling just to cope with the language. Before she arrived, she could only say a few words in English. "For a long while I had no-one here in Australia. I'd left all my sisters, and my mother and father. I felt so alone. The Andersons were really good, but once things started to go bad between Colin and I they sort of brushed me away and didn't want to know me."

Rosemay devoted all her time and energy to Angry. He was her one saving grace, the most positive thing in her life, but even he couldn't adequately relieve her from her loneliness. "Gary and I were so close," says Rosemay. "When he was little, he had his cot next to my bed, and I used to feel so lonely at night. I just used to think...oh, if only Gary was older, and he could talk. Then I would have somebody to talk to. But he was just a little baby."

For the first few years Colin disappeared regularly for work. His father would organise for him to ride in some overseas race meeting, so he'd pack his bags and go without question. Sometimes he was gone for months at a time, but Rosemay was never consulted about how she felt, or whether she could cope alone with the baby. Sometimes she wasn't even told he was going. There'd just be a note.

But by the time Angry was five or six his father had started leaving the house for even longer periods, often missing Christmas and birthdays. These trips weren't always for work, they were often for pleasure. Years later, Angry found out that Colin was living two lives, one as a husband and father, and one as a high-flying bachelor boy. There were times when he spent months and months in de facto relationships with other women who presumably had no idea he was even married.

As Angry says, Colin's absences weren't the problem. He was

Angry

MUM ALWAYS USED TO SAY TO ME 'DON'T GET INVOLVED. DON'T SAY THOSE THINGS TO HIM, THEN HE WON'T TURN ON YOU'. BUT I REMEMBER THIS ONE DAY I STEPPED IN BETWEEN HER AND HIM. I ACTUALLY PUT MY HAND ON HIS CHEST AND I PUSHED HIM BACK, AND THEN I JUST REMEMBER HAVING CLENCHED FISTS. HE JUST LOOKED BACK AT ME. IT ALL HAPPENED IN A SECOND...HE JUST LOOKED AT ME AND SMILED, AND THE INSTANT THAT HE SMILED AT ME, I KNEW THAT IT WAS LIKE HE'D TRAPPED ME. AND THAT WAS THE LAST THING I REMEMBER, AND I WOKE UP ON THE FLOOR.

much happier when his father wasn't in the house. It was the homecomings that concerned him. "As I got older it just seemed the times that he spent away got longer and longer. I mean, I didn't really question why. I was just glad he went. The only thing was, that after he'd been gone for a long while, then set in this fear that, of course, sooner or later he'd walk through the door."

"You've got no idea what it's like to wait for someone to come home for weeks, if not months. It's incredible pressure on you," says Angry. "To think it's going to happen, I know it's going to happen...you're always ready to duck, or you're always ready to confront this thing."

Whenever his father did come home, Angry and Rosemay would be expected to act like nothing had happened. They just had to go on, without questioning him about where he'd been, or what he'd been doing. Life was supposed to go back to usual. If Rosemay tried to argue, or tell him to leave, he'd just yell, and say that he could come and go as he pleased. "This is my house," he'd tell her. It was his favourite saying.

This pattern went on for years, and it never got any easier. "I remember coming home one day," says Angry, "and I'm pretty sure I was working at the time, and I knew. I just knew as soon as I walked through the door that he was back. I could feel him in the air, that's what it was like. I just felt the energy and the presence, and I walked in, and Mum just sat there, and I looked at her, and she said 'Your father's back'. He'd gone out somewhere, and the period from the time I'd got home till when he got back was just...it was hell. It was like waiting for the hammer to fall. It was awful. I thought to myself — How much time have I got? Where can I go? What can I do?"

ANGRY AND HIS MOTHER WERE EXTRAORDINARILY CLOSE. THEY WERE A LITTLE TEAM, STICKING UP FOR EACH OTHER WHENEVER COLIN WAS AROUND. THEY WERE PARTNERS.

Angry and his mother were extraordinarily close. They were a little team, sticking up for each other whenever Colin was around. They were partners. Even when Angry was only eight or nine years old, he filled in all the gaps, he was the man of the house, the responsible one, his mother's protector. Slowly Rosemay began to rely more and more on Angry. He was the only person she could really relate to. He was the only thing that was really hers.

"What was happening to me," says Angry, "was that I was taking on the parental role. It's a classic syndrome. If you've got a parent that's either a drunk or an abuser or a neglecter, what happens, usually with the oldest child, is they become what therapists describe as the little mother or the little father. And that's what happened to me."

The relationship between Rosemay and Angry infuriated Colin. He turned on Angry jealously, and treated him as a competitor for Rosemay's attention. They were more like combatants than father and son. They'd go for days and weeks without speaking, without even acknowledging each other. Whenever they were forced to speak, it would always be with great reluctance and bitterness.

Rosemay tried to pacify Colin by keeping a distance from Angry. She didn't want to spark the jealousy or the rage of her husband, so she held back in her relationship with her son. She stopped hugging him or kissing him, and she pulled back during some of their conversations. She forced a change in their relationship so that Colin would never walk into a room to find them laughing or talking together.

To Angry, it was a crushing withdrawal. He needed affection from his mother. He didn't understand or want to cater for his father's jealousy. He felt terribly alone and abandoned. Although his mother was acting in what she felt were his best interests, he was hurt by the rejection.

Whenever Angry tried to discuss the situation with Rosemay, she avoided the subject. She thought he was too young to understand. He'd often come home from school and find her crying, but whenever he asked what was wrong, she'd try to smile and tell him nothing. "He says I always pushed him away," Rosemay says, "but I thought I was doing the right thing. He was just a little boy. I didn't want to burden him. But perhaps he really needed to know what was going on."

When Angry was nine years old, Rosemay had another child, Rodney. It was a wonderful day for her, but a strange day for Angry. She remembers what a shock he got when he found someone else had come in on their team. "I remember the day I came home from the hospital, and he was standing there. He had his little yellow T-shirt on, and he said 'You won't love me anymore now, will you?' I said 'Of course I will'. He was the only one in my life, so he must have felt terribly alone then."

ANGRY WITH ROSEMAY AND UNCLE IVAN

Rodney never became a target of Colin's abuse, because he was basically too young. Rosemay was the main target, and Angry seemed to cop the rest. Most of the abuse came in the form of intimidation. It was one of Colin's greatest crafts. He would threaten and insult Angry to the point where Angry was sometimes too frightened to speak. As he says now, "My old man was one of those sadists who meters out their physical punishment to the point where the fear is worse than the actual blows, so I never really suffered much at Colin's hands by being beaten or kicked or punched. The real suffering, the suffering that's lasted all this time, is the fear."

As a child Angry was very resourceful. He learned to develop his own forms of therapy, his own means of escape. He was totally obsessed by radio. He used to hide himself in it. When he was only four or five years old, before Colin and Rosemay had a house of their own, the family all lived in the sewing room in Colin's father's house. Colin's younger brother Ivan was still living at home and he used to sleep in a room off the verandah. It was called the sleepout, and it was Angry's haven.

AS A CHILD ANGRY WAS VERY RESOURCEFUL. HE LEARNED TO DEVELOP HIS OWN FORMS OF THERAPY, HIS OWN MEANS OF ESCAPE. HE WAS TOTALLY OBSESSED BY RADIO. HE USED TO HIDE HIMSELF IN IT.

Uncle Ivan was only a young man at the time, but he was, and still is, a hero to Angry. "He committed the two cardinal sins of the Anderson household...he drank and he smoked," says Angry. "He also rode a motorcycle, which is how I eventually got hooked on motorcycles, and he played drums in a swing band."

Whenever he was home, Ivan would have the radio playing, and Angry would go and hang around outside the door waiting to be noticed and asked in. It was the very early 1950s, so the music would be straight off the Pop Parade. Rock and roll hadn't made it yet. It was just around the corner, so Angry grew up listening to things like Rosemary Clooney, Patsy Cline, Doris Day and Frank Sinatra. "It was the music I loved...I used to lose myself in it, and every time Uncle Ivan was home, I used to stand at the door and wait for him to invite me in."

The radio obsession continued through his whole childhood. He listened to anything and everything. As he says, "The radio was a friend I could rely on. Every time I wanted it, just boom...click, it was there. You know I buried myself in serials. I used to listen to 'The Shadow' and 'Biggles' and 'Tarzan' and all the dramas. Also, I loved all the comedy...'Dad and Dave', 'The Goons', all the English stuff."

"MY HEROES WERE ALWAYS THE INDIANS, NOT THE COWBOYS. THE OTHER KIDS ALL BARRACKED FOR THE CAVALRY, BUT I ALWAYS LOVED THE INDIANS...THEY WERE PAINTED AND HALF-NAKED."

The cinema was also part of a regular pilgrimage. Every Saturday Angry would head off to the pictures. He loved the Boys Town series, but his favourite actor was Spencer Tracy and his favourite movie was *Captain Courageous*. Angry's mum says she can still remember the first time Angry saw *Captain Courageous*, because he came home in tears. He still remembers the story...all about a spoiled little rich kid, full of airs and graces, who's forced to learn the lessons of life on a tuna boat. As Angry says, "I just bawled. It really affected me."

The other big favourites on the screen were the westerns. Angry loved them. "My heroes were always the Indians, not the cowboys. The other kids all barracked for the cavalry, but I always loved the Indians...they were painted and half-naked. I loved the feathers, and the horses, and the buckskins, and the teepees. When we played cowboys and Indians in the street, I was always the one everyone wanted to play with because they'd say, 'Gary will be an Indian. He dies great'. You know, I died all day."

From his position as an Indian supporter, Angry didn't get to see many movies with happy endings. That was until General Custer made his last stand. As he says, he was the only one in the cinema cheering. "You've got no idea the feeling I felt the first time that

Hollywood depicted Custer as the loser. That, to me, was a real personal feeling of victory."

Just as he was the only one who wanted to be an Indian, Angry was different at school too...by then he was mixed-up and rebellious. He was no more of a fighter than anyone else, but he did have problems. He couldn't concentrate in class, and academically he fell behind quickly. The only subjects he could manage were art and English. The rest were disasters.

THE SECOND GRADE SCHOOL PHOTO (ANGRY IS SECOND FROM LEFT IN THE FRONT ROW)

He was popular at school though, and never short of friends. He was always playing the clown, talking when he was meant to be listening, joking with his mates. "There were some kids in the school who were troublesome because they were thugs," Angry says, "but I was never a thug. There were other kids in the school who were troublesome because they had problems with discipline. I was one of them. I had problems with discipline. As far as schoolyard behaviour went, even though I do remember being involved in fights and being blamed, it wasn't like I was the only one."

In about the fifth grade Angry cracked on to the idea of wagging classes, so that was something he did regularly. Although he wasn't really unhappy at school, he looked for any and every opportunity not to go. He only had one uniform and one pair of school shoes, so he developed a few tricks to convince Rosemay that he had to take the day off. He would roll in mud puddles, or walk in the wet gutters...anything that would force Rosemay to launder his uniform and keep him home while it dried.

He used to mastermind his excuses whenever his father wasn't around, because those were the times when it was nice to be at home. He was an expert at feigning illness, and had many more than his fair share of sick days. "I used to do great pains. I could roll around in bed, clutching my stomach, moaning about how much I really wanted to go to school. I did good coughs too."

Sometimes he wagged as often as two or three days a week because he hated being stuck in a classroom, behind a desk, listening to a teacher. He liked the atmosphere of primary school, but he didn't like the work, so he was constantly distracted and restless, waiting for the bell to sound.

HE WAGGED AS OFTEN AS TWO OR THREE TIMES A WEEK BECAUSE HE HATED BEING STUCK IN A CLASSROOM, BEHIND A DESK, LISTENING TO A TEACHER. HE LIKED THE ATMOSPHERE OF PRIMARY SCHOOL, BUT HE DIDN'T LIKE THE WORK, SO HE WAS CONSTANTLY DISTRACTED AND RESTLESS, WAITING FOR THE BELL TO SOUND.

Angry played all the sports at school from cricket to basketball to footy to handball, but he was never on any of the selected sides. He just sort of hung around and played for fun. He was a good all-round athlete, but he suffered from stress-related asthma, and was far too small to be a star player. Anyway, he and his buddies preferred different games. While the other kids were playing footy, Angry's group would be off at the back of the schoolyard playing with model cars and tanks and soldiers. And on weekends, they'd all be building and flying model planes.

All the local kids went to the same primary school, Coburg North, but when they were twelve years old, for their secondary schooling, they were divided into two groups. They were either sent to Coburg High School or Coburg Technical School. The girls all went to the high school, but the boys were separated depending on their marks.

Angry went to the Tech, a trade school for semiskilled and skilled labourers. There was traditional hatred between the two high schools. Coburg High had everything Tech didn't. They had girls for a start, and they also had bigger, better facilities. The boys from Tech were like the poor cousins. They didn't get the high marks, they didn't win the competitions, they weren't expected to carry on too far with their education. As Angry says, "I suppose all of us that went to Tech knew, or were made to feel, that it was because we weren't as good as everyone else. I know I certainly felt that. We thought; this is Tech. This is where all the dummies go, all the troublemakers, all the misfits. You know, we thought that if you've got a bunch of mess-ups, you put them all in one place."

In uniform - Coburg Tech

In the schoolyard he wasn't a ringleader, and he didn't hang out with the toughest group, but he still copped his fair share of the strap. That never bothered him though. In fact in a way, he found it kind of comforting to know that at school punishment was associated only with some sort of crime. There were clear-cut rules and guidelines, so at least he always knew when he was in trouble. More importantly, he always knew why. Compared to the wild rages he'd seen from his father, such regulated discipline was a relief. "I'd been knocked around enough physically and emotionally by the time I got to Tech that getting six cuts of the strap was nothing at all. It was like part of a game. When you got caught doing something you weren't supposed to do, you just copped it sweet. That was the way it was."

It was at technical school that Angry really discovered he was physically short. He'd always known he wasn't quite as tall as any of his mates at Coburg Primary, but he hadn't realised that he was actually one of the shortest boys in the whole school. He was still quite squat and strong, so he didn't really think about his height. It wasn't something that worried him.

It wasn't until he got into a more competitive environment where there were organised sports and activities that he realised he wasn't growing as far, or as fast, as anyone else. At the beginning of primary school, most of the kids had been around the same height, but by the first year at Tech, Angry was at least a foot shorter than some of the other boys. That in itself wasn't devastating, but combined with his other problems, it just added to his feelings of inadequacy. "The sport thing brings it home more than anything, because you've got to try harder."

He was given nicknames like "Mouse" and "Tiny", and was always the one who had to stand at the end of the line for school photographs so he didn't muck up the balance of the shot. He developed what he calls "little guy syndrome" - a big mouth, and a big chip on his shoulder. From a very early age he wanted to be thought of as dangerous, or somehow formidable. He didn't mind being short as long as people thought they shouldn't mess with him.

Height still means a great deal to Angry. Whenever a bunch of school kids run up to him in the street looking for his autograph, he always searches out the shortest one. Sometimes, if he finds a kid who's also overweight, he'll take them aside. He usually briefs them about fitness and health, and going to the gym. He tells them that just because they're short they're not weak. He really worries for them. He sees a little boy, and he sees the crumbling self-image, and he wants to jump in and save it.

Angry's great after-school pleasure was visiting the neighbours. There were lots of big families living in the same street, and he just loved hanging out. He was probably looking for the comfort of a lively, happy house. "One of the best friends I ever had lived right next door. He was one of the Harrisons. There was Fred and Betty, and Fred drove a cab. They had ten or eleven kids. Paul was the kid my age. He and his older brother, John, were two of the best friends I ever had. I've always been sorry that we lost contact."

ANGRY DESPERATELY SOUGHT A NORMAL FAMILY LIFE. HE LIVED IN A DREAM WORLD, CONSTANTLY IMAGINING HE WAS SOMEONE ELSE, LIVING IN SOME OTHER FAMILY.

As Rosemay says, she sometimes felt total despair as a mother. With Colin's bizarre entries and exits, she felt she couldn't possibly provide Angry with the security he needed. Although they were close, there was just nothing she could do to replace or make up for his father.

Angry desperately sought a normal family life. He lived in a dream world, constantly imagining he was someone else, living in some other family. There were many times when he'd say something or do something that would remind Rosemay of how important it was for him to have some semblance of normality at home. "He was friendly with the family down the street," says Rosemay, "and I remember I met the lady one day. She told me that she and her husband had been sitting on the couch, and her husband had his arm around her. She said Gary looked at them, and said that he'd never seen his mum and dad do that. That made me feel dreadful."

HE'D ALWAYS HAD THIS VAGUE KNOWLEDGE OF HIS OWN EXPERIENCE, BUT LIKE SO MUCH OF HIS CHILDHOOD, HE'D MANAGED TO BLOCK MANY OF HIS MEMORIES OUT

Over the years, Angry has talked many times about the physical and emotional abuse he suffered at home, although he's never given any details, but when he suddenly admitted on national television that he'd been sexually abused, he even surprised himself. He hadn't meant to say anything. He was discussing sexual abuse with Ray Martin on the 'Midday Show' and, before he realised what he was saying, he'd told Australia his biggest secret. It was something he hadn't even discussed with his family or his closest friends. He'd only ever really talked about it before in therapy, but on this day, it was like his mouth opened and the words came out before he even realised what was happening. It was like he was sitting somewhere else, watching someone else speaking. It was slightly unreal. But, he's adamant it wasn't a mistake. "I never really meant to talk about it in public. Now that it's done I don't regret if for a second. My brother was horrified ... he's never spoken to me about it since."

There were two incidents of sexual abuse in Angry's life. The first happened over a period of months when he was only six years old, the second when he was a young teenager. His full recollections were first triggered off when he became involved in community programs to help sexually abused kids. He says he started to see kids and meet kids, and he had this real affinity with them. He'd always had this vague knowledge of his own experience, but like so much of his childhood, he'd managed to block many of his memories out...either with drugs or alcohol, or rage.

"When it first used to come to me, I used to be horrified. It sent shivers down my spine. I thought no, that didn't happen to me, because you want to deny you were a participant. There's a certain amount of rejection there, but it's like one day someone just turned on the light, and I had this crystal clear recollection, and I thought, Oh Jesus, of course."

The first experience was with a male friend of his father. It's something Angry will always have trouble talking about. "I have vivid pictures of the room that it happened in. We used to go to this guy's house and there was another male there who used to take care of me. He'd entertain me and play with me. I remember sitting in an armchair...I can remember the room now, and if I walked into it tomorrow I'd say 'This is the roo'. I can remember sitting there and him talking or reading to me, and I would sit on his lap, and he'd be masturbating me...just playing with my genital area. I can remember his fingers rubbing up and down between the cheeks of my bum.

"I don't remember the sort of things a lot of kids remember, like being threatened with violence not to say anything. If I'm to sort of go back to that little boy, it's sad for me now, but I don't know if it was true sadness at the time. I was sort of resigned to it. This is very common with abused kids apparently...I'd just think 'What's the point?'"

The second case was more humiliating, and more confusing. Angry was a young teenager, about fourteen years old. To keep his mother happy he'd gone on a Christian camp with a big group of his friends. The organisers prided themselves on the fact they welcomed so-called troublesome and troubled youths, and Angry and his mates were perfect candidates. This particular trip was to Tasmania. The camp chaperones were in their late teens or early twenties, and they were all senior students in the church body.

Angry's group leader was a big clean-cut guy. He was well-built and seemed like a nice bloke. He was definitely a leading light in the bible studies group. That's why he had the job.

Angry had made a new mate on his first day at camp. A guy from another school whom he'd hit it off with immediately. After the first few hours they were firm buddies, becoming so involved with each other, they didn't really notice the extra attention they were getting from the group leader. Until one night. Angry woke to find his trusted group leader lying only inches from him. He was in a position

ON ASSIGNMENT FOR THE MIDDAY SHOW
... CHATTING WITH SOME OF THE INMATES AT COOMA JAIL

of authority, and the younger members of the group were meant to rely on him. He was talking like an old friend, being really soothing, but by the time Angry woke up, there was already a hand down his pyjama pants. Angry didn't jump up or yell or anything. He just froze. The group leader was asking him to touch him, to kiss him, to put his penis in his mouth, talking all the time in these soft tones. Angry just tried to ignore him. He was bewildered and petrified, and his heart was beating furiously. He lay there, holding his breath, and after a minute or two, the group leader went away.

It didn't end there though. He came back, doing the same sort of thing every night for a few nights. Angry went on trying to ignore him, and trying to ignore what was happening, but eventually he lost his temper. He told him to go, and he did go...but at the time Angry was embarrassed and confused.

The only person he told was his new mate. On one hand, he wanted to see if the group leader had visited him in the night as well, and on the other, he wanted to get it all off his chest. "I think I told him so we could make the group leader look like the jerk that he was, so we could get a laugh out of it. I needed to relieve any guilt associated with what had happened. There's a lot of guilt because you've participated in it. At the time you can't see it in terms of violation because it's not an unpleasurable thing. The onus of responsibility is on the person who is in control. The violence that's contained in the act is rape, regardless, because there's an age thing. It's an older person inflicting their own sexuality on a younger person. Now, at the instant that it happens, it might not necessarily be unpleasurable physically, but it is certainly unpleasurable emotionally."

In May 1988, Angry presented a report into child sexual abuse on "The Midday Show" with Ray Martin. It was ground-breaking television. He talked, on camera, to a number of kids who'd suffered sexual abuse, and then he talked with a group of convicted paedophiles at Cooma Prison. The story was so powerful it silenced the studio audience and sparked a huge response from the community.

IN MAY 1988, ANGRY PRESENTED A REPORT INTO CHILD SEXUAL ABUSE ON 'THE MIDDAY SHOW' WITH RAY MARTIN. HE TALKED TO A NUMBER OF KIDS WHO'D SUFFERED SEXUAL ABUSE, AND THEN HE TALKED WITH A GROUP OF CONVICTED PAEDOPHILES AT COOMA PRISON. THE STORY WAS SO POWERFUL IT SILENCED THE STUDIO AUDIENCE.

Midday's mailbag was full for weeks.

For Angry it was a very difficult assignment. He cried as the inmates at Cooma jail described their crimes. As they talked about their problems, and their rehabilitation, Angry had to keep excusing himself to wipe the tears away. They were all guys who'd pleaded guilty to sexual assault charges and were receiving treatment within the jail system. They had their faces darkened so they couldn't be identified and together they told Angry they were glad they were arrested. As one guy said, "Most of us who pleaded guilty had realised it was time to stop, time to change, time to do something about ourselves. I personally could never have gone through the court and said that I was innocent of what I did because I wasn't. I was guilty as hell. If I'd have done that, I could never have lived with myself."

OVER THE YEARS ANGRY'S DONE MORE AND MORE WORK WITH SEXUALLY ABUSED KIDS. AS HE SAYS, HE FEELS AN AFFINITY WITH THEM. ...THE CONFUSION AND THE GUILT, AND HE'S DESPERATE TO HELP VICTIMS.

Another guy told Angry the most important part of his treatment was to try to put himself in the position of the victim - to try to imagine what it was like for the child. He was a man who'd abused his stepsons, and been reported by his wife. As he said, it was heartbreaking for him to realise the damage he'd done to his own family. "To have to put yourself into a position where you realise what a mongrel you were...realise what you've done, to know you've destroyed love and trust, to know you've made your kids extremely confused. They want to please you, they want to make you happy, but they know that what they're doing is the wrong thing. And they're not able to go and tell Mum, because you've told them they can't tell Mum because this is our secret."

Although it was difficult for Angry to interview the perpetrators of sexual abuse, it was even harder for him to talk to the victims. He identified with some of the children to such a degree that he had trouble holding his composure through the interviews. One of the victims he spoke to was an eleven-year-old girl called Joy. She described her assault by a family friend with a chilling innocence. Her face was also masked to protect her identity, but it was impossible to hide the sadness in her voice. "Well, first of all he started tickling me under the arms. Then he realised that I wasn't ticklish. He said 'Oh, you're not ticklish', and he started going down my body till he got to my rude spot, and he came up behind me and he put his finger up."

After the assault Joy wrote a poem, a classic cry for help. She called it "My Feelings": "After this has happened I have felt strange about men. I have wanted to kill myself. I have tried several times. I have had poisons, sniffed glue, and run away. It is very embarrassing."

Joy was receiving counselling when Angry spoke with her, but she was still having trouble dealing with her feelings, and she was obviously copping a hard time at school. She told Angry the other kids laughed at her. She said they called her "AIDS", and "Slut", and taunted her, saying she was pregnant.

Over the years Angry's done more and more work with sexually abused kids. As he says, he feels an affinity with them. He's studied the syndrome, the confusion and the guilt, and he's desperate to help victims deal with it as quickly and as effectively as possible. The kids in the "Midday Show" story obviously felt they could talk to him, because they seem oblivious to the lights and cameras. And that's what Angry believes is important...talking. When he was abused, he felt ashamed. Like many victims, it was something he couldn't talk about until years after the event.

THE KIDS IN THE 'MIDDAY SHOW' STORY OBVIOUSLY FELT THEY COULD TALK TO HIM, BECAUSE THEY SEEM OBLIVIOUS TO THE LIGHTS AND CAMERAS. AND THAT'S WHAT ANGRY BELIEVES IS IMPORTANT...TALKING.

Back at school, after the camp, Angry tried to put the whole experience behind him. He was determined not to think about it. He didn't tell any of his mates because he was sure he'd somehow get the blame.

The boys at Coburg Tech were typical teenage boys. By their rules it wasn't "cool" to discuss personal problems, so Angry never talked about his home life either. Many of his friends actually knew what was happening to some degree because Angry's father's outbursts were always so public, but still, nothing was ever said.

Angry did everything he could to disguise the truth. He invented a fantasy father, a sort of superdad he could talk about whenever he was asked. He'd say he had this wonderful happy family, and lie about

Colin's profession. He often told people his father was only away on business so often because he was a commercial pilot, but he'd have many different stories to suit any occasion.

Angry became an expert at keeping his friends away from the house, so that they'd never meet his father. He tried only to invite mates home when he was certain Colin was away, but he was caught out on one occasion, and he still smarts at the embarrassment. As he says, "I had this friend at school and his father was a film projectionist. I don't know why, but I told him my father was a projectionist too. Then one day, there was this chance meeting when this friend came home with me. I didn't know the old man was there. Now, I don't know whether this kid was trying to trap me or if he just innocently blundered into it, but he started saying stuff to my father like 'My father is a projectionist, and Gary tells me that you are too'. So, of course, the old man proceeded to tell him what a liar I was, and how I never told the truth about anything. He completely belittled me. It was terrible. It was really humiliating."

At one stage, when he was around sixteen years old, Angry even plotted to kill his father. He was very serious. "I was going to shoot him with his gun. I knew where it was, and how to get at it. You see if I could have killed him and gone to jail it would have stopped the misery. It would have stopped him doing it, and it would have stopped me having to go through it. You've got to understand, that at that stage, at that age, spending ten or fifteen years in jail, as miserable as that would have been...it wouldn't have been as miserable as spending the next ten years with him. That's what fear does to you. It twists your reason. You know, I used to think...oh well, if I shoot him or kill him, at least it's not Mum going to jail. I don't want her to have to kill him because mothers shouldn't go to jail, sons should."

Angry even told his father he was going to shoot him, but Colin laughed. As Angry sees it, his father mocked him all the time, and that's why he feared him so much. He was never remorseful. There was no tenderness in him at all, no love, no affection.

Rosemay talked Angry out of using the gun when he told her what he was planning. As he says, "As soon as Mum sat there and tried to rationalise the whole thing with me, I backed off. You see, my fervour and my commitment fell apart under the scrutiny of good sense. It was a passionate thing, so when Mum talked rationally to me, basically I saw that it wasn't going to work."

For a few months though, he was really committed to the idea. He says it was the only way he could see through the fear.

The first time Angry really did strike out physically at his father, it was not with a gun, or even a fist. It was nothing more than a push, but it changed the whole tone of their relationship. His father welcomed it, like he'd finally found a more worthy opponent.

AS ANGRY SAYS, LOOKING BACK NOW IT'S SAD, BECAUSE HE'S REALISED HOW MUCH THE TECH BOYS HAD TO OFFER EACH OTHER IN THE WAY OF UNDERSTANDING AND SUPPORT.

"He'd been away for some time, and he'd come back and I walked in when he and Mum were arguing. He got up and he walked towards her, and I remember she shrank away from him. She was completely defenceless, and he grabbed her. She was really hysterical. He either hit her or pushed her, but she lost her balance and kind of fell. I was willing to let that go by, if that was where it was going to stop, but I just read that it was going to go on...Mum always used to say to me 'Don't get involved. Don't say those things to him, then he won't turn on you'. But I remember this day, I just got up, and I actually put my hand on his chest and I pushed him back, and then I just remember having clenched fists. He just looked back at me. It all happened in a second...he just looked at me and smiled, and the instant that he smiled at me, I knew that it was like he'd trapped me. And that was the last thing I remember, and I woke up on the floor. Mum and a neighbour were bent down over me, and I can remember the hissing of the gas fire next to my head. I can remember the fire clearly, as if it was yesterday, and I can remember the hissing."

Angry punched back many times after that, and he often went at him screaming or punching or kicking in frustration, but he never got on the better end of a fight. His father was too cool, and he was too angry.

As Angry says, looking back now it's sad, because he's realised how much the Tech boys had to offer each other in the way of understanding and support. As a teenager, Angry felt alone in his problems. He thought he was the first and only person in the world who was unhappy at home. But as an adult, he's realised that the same sort of thing was probably happening in the homes of many of the Coburg Tech boys, just as it was happening in the homes of many kids all over the country.

Even as he lists off his friends, and talks about what he knew of their lives back then, he recognises how bad things were for some of them. He had friends who were brought up by their big sisters, because their alcoholic mothers weren't around anymore. He had friends whose fathers were more physically brutal than his, and who came to school battered and bruised. He had friends whose homes were in complete chaos because the family unit had broken down years earlier, but no one knew how to clean up the mess. As he says, "At Tech, we were hundreds of boys from real basic, hard-case, working-class backgrounds. I know now there must have been a lot of other damaged kids there. There must have been a lot of kids there like me."

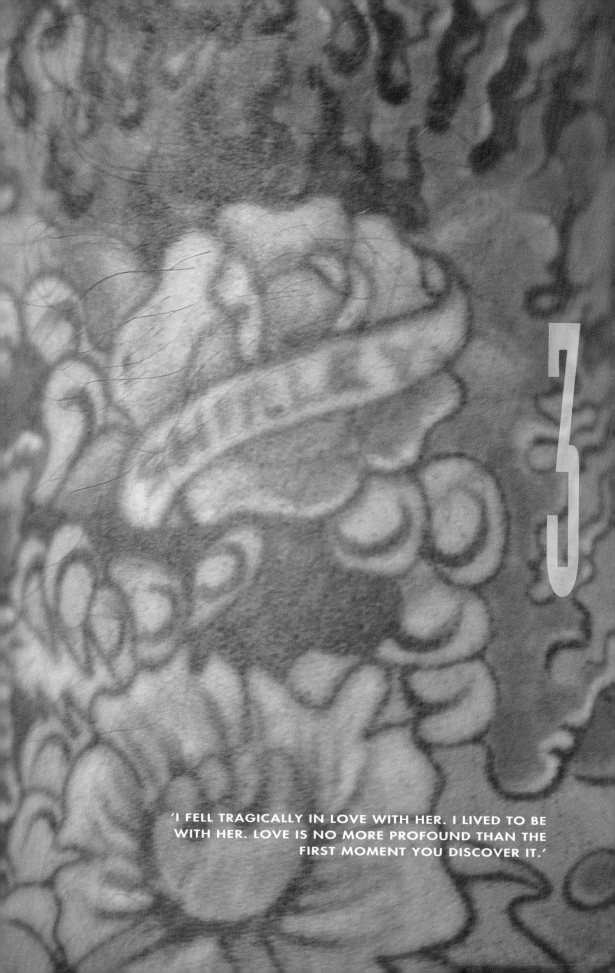

3

'I FELL TRAGICALLY IN LOVE WITH HER. I LIVED TO BE
WITH HER. LOVE IS NO MORE PROFOUND THAN THE
FIRST MOMENT YOU DISCOVER IT.'

SCARRED FOR LIFE

When Angry was about fifteen, his father was admitted to Royal Park Psychiatric Hospital for treatment. His tempers had become worse, and he'd been particularly unsettled after his mother's death a couple of years earlier. He'd been so bad, that at one stage, the police had come to the house to talk to Rosemay about his mental health. He'd been traced as the person sending strange love letters to a local girl. He didn't even know her. The police thought the notes sounded obsessive, and they felt he could be dangerous. They wanted to take him into custody for assessment, but Rosemay wouldn't sign the papers. Although she was frightened of Colin, she was convinced his problems were untreatable so she couldn't see any value in having him committed.

FOR SHIRLEY

Eventually though, he did go into hospital for treatment, and while he was there, Angry and Rosemay visited him on weekends. They used to make a regular trek across the city. "I used to despise him for it," says Angry "I despised him enough anyway, but it was even more of a reason. I used to think, like some people do, that insanity really is hereditary. I thought I was insane because he was insane."

"Visiting him in the hospital used to embarrass the shit out of me, because when the tram pulled up at the stop, and the people got off to visit the asylum, whether real or imagined, it always seemed everyone looked at you, and knew that you were going in to visit some loony."

Rosemay says the visits were terrible. Colin would rant and rave about everything, and he was still abusive. He'd call Rosemay and Angry names, and blame them for his hospitalisation. He'd be insulting and aggressive, and Rosemay now thinks it was a mistake to take Angry along with her at all.

For Angry it was a humiliating time. He still becomes furious when he talks about it. The entire neighbourhood knew Colin had been admitted to a psychiatric hospital. He was so notorious they knew everything about him. Angry was not only ashamed, he was constantly frustrated that the whole situation had anything to do with him. He considered his father an outsider, a gatecrasher who disrupted and complicated their lives. He couldn't see why Rosemay just didn't leave him in the hospital and forget him. As far as Angry was concerned, he was not part of the family, and his problems weren't their responsibility.

WHAT I REALISED IN MY HYSTERIA WAS THAT, ALL OF A SUDDEN, I WAS THE PURSUER. ALL OF A SUDDEN, THEY WERE SCARED OF ME. I HAD ABSOLUTE POWER. I WAS IN CONTROL.

At the hospital, Angry would sit in the corner of the room, as far away from his father as possible, and will the visit over. He'd spend the whole time trying to control himself, trying not to say a word, when in fact there were times when he was so frustrated and enraged about his predicament that he could have smashed everything in sight. His indignation bubbled under the surface, and he struggled just to hold himself together. He endured each visit in dark silence.

The local kids taunted him about his father being in the madhouse. They said he was mental, a lunatic, a crazy man. It wasn't a taunt they kept up for long, but still, it was enough to make Angry withdraw. "It was a really difficult time for me," says Angry. "Just to stay level because I thought at the time that I was crazy too. I mean really crazy. I think it must have been said to me, and I know it was said about me; 'His father's crazy...so is he'."

With every day Angry worried increasingly about his own state of mind. It was a major issue. He was terrified he was becoming more like his father as he got older. He knew he'd inherited his father's temper, because he'd already scared himself a couple of times. The first time he witnessed his own rage was when he was visiting his younger cousin's house. They'd all gone down to a local creek to play, but after a while a group of older boys had started hanging around. As Angry says, "We could tell they were real roughies, and my cousins said

'Quick, let's go!' We started to run and they started to chase us. They threw rocks at us, and I remember my cousin Joyce got hit in the back of the head, and one of my other little cousins also got hit. I just stopped and turned around, and just became something else.

"I just stood there, and I remember I was absolutely shaking. I was just hysterical. But, it was like I wasn't doing it...you know, I was with them in spirit. I was running. I wanted to get away. But I turned around, and just faced this gang of kids. There was about half a dozen of them, and I just ran at them. I mean, I was uncontrollable. And the thing about it was that they knew, and they ran. I remember this feeling of absolute superiority. You know, I could have fought those kids and beaten them all. When I turned on them, I was alone, but they all ran from me. What I realised in my hysteria was that, all of a sudden, I was the pursuer. All of a sudden, they were scared of me. I had absolute power. I was in control. I was at the point where I was the victor. I suddenly got to the point where I realised I wasn't scared of them. In fact, I wasn't scared of anything. I was crying, but these were tears of rage."

There was another time too, when a taunting game between Angry and his little brother suddenly turned serious. Angry snapped, and became furious, and something in his eyes or his expression warned Rodney the game was finished. Rodney took off at full speed, and Angry tried to catch him, but Rodney was smaller and faster. As Angry says, "I really think Rodney was just petrified. I really think he was so scared that he just couldn't let me catch him like other times when we'd wrestle and I'd punch him in the leg or something. I remember we ran in the house and around the house and I couldn't catch him, and he ran into the woodshed down the back. It was the little shed where all the wood and briquettes were stored. He ran in there and hid."

With Rodney hiding, Angry became even wilder. He remembers he was just incensed. As he says, "I chopped that shed down to get at him. I just ripped the whole thing to bits with my hands. I wrecked it. And I hurt myself so much trying to get at him that the pain dissipated the rage, because thankfully, I didn't do anything to him when I got him. That's when I really scared myself."

As Angry got older, his behaviour became more and more unusual. He was brooding and moody. At home, he was tearing himself apart. When his father was released from hospital, things went back to the way they'd always been. Colin just resumed the same lifestyle — away for a week or a month, then home for another. Often he was away for months at a time without explanation. He could have been off with another woman, he could have been working. For all Rosemay and Angry knew, he could have been living in the next suburb or sleeping on the streets. They had no idea where he went when he disappeared, and they were too frightened to ask him. He'd just turn up one day out of the blue and expect his dinner to be on the table.

AS ANGRY GOT OLDER, HIS BEHAVIOUR BECAME MORE AND MORE UNUSUAL. HE WAS BROODING AND MOODY. AT HOME, HE WAS TEARING HIMSELF APART.

Angry's role as the "little father" slowly became even more pronounced. He was there to take control, to do everything Colin was incapable of doing. Every time his father came home, Angry hated him more. He resented him, and felt he had no place in their lives. What had been fear when he was younger, turned into rage, and he became increasingly indignant that he had to have any relationship with his father at all. As he says, "I hated him, but hate is another word...is hate big enough? Is despise big enough? Do you really hate someone that you fear that much? I think hate is a word reserved for someone you have power over, and I think we need another word that goes beyond that."

Angry wanted desperately for them all to leave the house, so Colin could never find them. He kept begging his mother, telling her they'd be fine on their own. To him, anything would have been better than the suspense and the anticipation of knowing Colin could return home at any time. "It was like sometimes I'd come home from school," says Angry "and he'd be there, and I'd just feel like throwing myself under a car. When he was around I just didn't feel life was worth living. I just wished I was dead."

Angry pleaded with his mother for years to leave. As Rosemay remembers, "Gary kept saying, 'Mum let's go. We don't have to stay here.' But he didn't realise. Where would I have gone? I had no one. I couldn't work. I had no money. I had Rodney at home. It was really hard, but Gary didn't realise that because he was a child."

In his boldest moments now, Angry will still say he believes Rosemay should have taken more positive action. He admits he's not sure of the details — of how they'd have left the house, of where she'd have gone, or of what they'd have done, but he believes whole-heartedly they should have tried to get out of the situation. As he says, "Part of my anger now is my suppressed anger about why Mum didn't leave, even though I'd never reproach her for it. It's not a matter of having to forgive her. I don't think there's anything to forgive. I don't blame her, but I have to hold her responsible. She had good reasons, but I still have to hold her responsible because she was there, and she was in charge. My mother was trapped between isolation and her religion. "What do you mean get divorced? You don't get divorced." She was bought up to believe that you've got to sacrifice. Her church demanded it of her."

By his mid teens, all Angry was trying to do was block things out. He just wanted to push himself into oblivion. He started to use alcohol as an anaesthetic, sneaking bottles into the house whenever his mother wasn't looking.

He became rebellious, the kind of person who stood out in a crowd. He was the first one to grow his hair long, the first one to cut his hair short. He didn't dress like anyone else either. He went from one mad craze to another, and he loved to shock people with his outfits. He'd put on some outrageous shirt or coat, and try to pretend he was someone other than little Gary Anderson. As he says, "There were a few years where I became very disordered. My life inwardly was chaos, my emotions were just running wild, and there didn't seem to be any let up. So when I was aware, when I was awake and sober, and I knew where I fitted into things, I didn't like it. I didn't like my position in the scheme of things. I didn't like who I was. It was intense all the time, and when it goes on for years, it becomes like 'Just let me be like everybody else. I don't want to be like this.' I mean, I used to sit in class, day after day after day at school, and I'd just have my teeth and my knuckles clenched the whole time. I wanted to be somebody else. It was like, if that's what's

"THERE WERE A FEW YEARS WHERE I BECAME VERY DISORDERED. MY LIFE INWARDLY WAS CHAOS, MY EMOTIONS WERE JUST RUNNING WILD, AND THERE DIDN'T SEEM TO BE ANY LET UP."

happening to Gary, if that's what he's got to go through, then fine. I don't want to be him anymore, because you just want it to let up, and after a while, that feeling will twist you. It will make you say things you don't want to say, or be something you don't want to be, just for the relief."

He goes on to say that, over the years, he became better and better at disguising himself. "I desperately took the opportunity to become something else, because it was like that's Gary's life, and I don't like it, so I'll be someone else. You know, I won't dress like him, I won't think like him, I won't act like him. I'll be something else, and what I became, or what I grew into, was someone who didn't put up with any of the shit. Someone who went about their way in life, and people were afraid of what I was going to do, which was such a relief from all those years and years and years of me being afraid of what everyone else was going to do, particularly the old man."

Outside the home and away from school Angry found many distractions. He was into drinking, smoking, and most of all, girls. It didn't take much skill to be involved with the first two.

Girls were a different problem though. "I always had a really unhealthy interest in sex and girls", says Angry. "But then again I suspect all young boys do. We were always very much aware of them, but of course, I never did any good in the area. Again, that was a thing I came at the wrong way." He had one childhood sweetheart in primary school, and it went on for a little while, but his love life was really nothing more than dreams and fantasies until he met his first real love...Shirley.

He was fifteen, and he fell head over heels in love with her. She was a couple of years younger than him, and she went to Coburg High. Her parents had split up, and she lived with her elderly grandmother. They met at the Christian Youth Group, but she was there for all the same reasons as Angry ... she wasn't into all the religious talk, she just wanted somewhere to hang out.

It was the love affair with Shirley that gave Angry his first chance to turn his life around. "We were together for years, and I think if it hadn't been for Shirley, I probably would have been in real trouble. It was a very strong emotional relationship. It was also very stormy. Even though we had flirtations with sex prior to our monogamy, we truly discovered sex together."

Shirley and Angry had the kind of all-consuming love affair that inspired acts of incredible selflessness. If they'd argue, Angry would ring Shirley to apologise, then he'd run the three miles to her house to make up with her in person.

"I fell tragically in love with her. I lived to be with her. Love is no more profound than the first moment you discover it. I truly believe that. When your girlfriend goes away you don't miss her, you long for her. You pine. That's why it's so wrong for people to say 'you'll grow out of this'. That's not realistic, and it's far from an appreciation of what's going on."

The relationship gave Angry something stable and certain to cling to. Shirley loved him, and he'd talk to her about his fears and his anger. She knew he was a mess, but she knew he wasn't crazy, and she put up with all his obsessions.

They went out together for about three years, through the last year at Tech and the first years of work. They had a real bond, a real understanding of each other, and although Angry accepts it was young love, and it didn't last, he says it had a huge affect on him. Even now, he talks of her with great fondness, and they've always maintained the friendship.

As with all first loves, the break up was difficult. Angry was the one initiating the split, but he still found it hard. He felt it was almost out of his control, like they'd grown apart, and there was just nothing either of them could do to save it. "I knew it just wasn't right. The last couple of months of that relationship I knew it was going to end. I drove her away. I was really mean to her, and in the end, she just couldn't take it anymore. She gave me the opportunity to make good...you know it was like she was saying 'I'm going, aren't you going to stop me?' But I didn't. I regretted it for years. I really suffered over her."

Before he took the final step though, he made one everlasting tribute to Shirley. He got his first tattoo. "I think it cost me fifteen bucks, and I got a pierced ear for free. I really wanted something with

SHIRLEY AND ANGRY HAD THE KIND OF ALL-CONSUMING LOVE AFFAIR THAT INSPIRED ACTS OF INCREDIBLE SELFLESSNESS. IF THEY'D ARGUE, ANGRY WOULD RING SHIRLEY TO APOLOGISE, THEN HE'D RUN THE THREE MILES TO HER HOUSE TO MAKE UP WITH HER IN PERSON.

a scroll because I wanted to put Shirley's name in it. Although I knew it was over, I wanted to dedicate something to her.

"I thought, well I've got to get tattoos anyway, because you either had them or you didn't. I didn't want to be like the people who didn't get them. I'd always loved tattoos. I went out and got the rose and anchor, and I had her name put in it. But over the next few weeks, before she actually saw it, we broke up for good. The first time she saw it we were at a swimming pool, and everyone knew by then that I'd been tattooed, and that it was Shirley's name. So when she actually got to see it, we were no longer an item."

Rosemay didn't see the "Shirley" tattoo until months later when Angry let his cover slip. She knocked on the bathroom door one day, and he told her to come in, but he forgot that he wasn't wearing his shirt. When she saw the rose and anchor, she told him to wash it off. She thought it was just a transfer. He said, "Mum I can't. It's there for ever."

HE WAS TRYING
TO EXPLAIN THE
SYMBOLISM AND THE
TRIBUTE, BUT ALL
ROSEMAY COULD SEE
WAS AN UGLY TATTOO.
"I CRIED AND CRIED.
I TOLD HIM HE WAS
STUPID. I SAID HE WAS
SCARRED FOR LIFE."

Rosemay says it was a terrible night. She couldn't understand why he'd done it. He was trying to explain the symbolism and the tribute, but all Rosemay could see was an ugly tattoo. "I cried and cried. I told him he was stupid. I said he was scarred for life." The words rang in Angry's ears, and he later wrote a song called "Scarred for Life". He had no regrets about the actual tattoo though, he just regretted upsetting his mother.

Although he's spent many years covering his body with them, Rosemay says she's never come to terms with tattoos, and even now, to avoid upsetting Rosemay, Angry always wears long sleeves and high collars whenever they're out together. Her greatest horror came when she discovered many years later that he actually had tattoos on his legs. She says, "It worries me. I can't get used to them. I often wonder what his children will think when they grow up, because the other children's fathers don't have tattoos."

With the end of Technical school came the beginning of Angry's working life...an issue of huge concern to everyone but him. His final grades were so poor that they didn't qualify him for any sort of job, and it became clear that he wasn't going to get anywhere

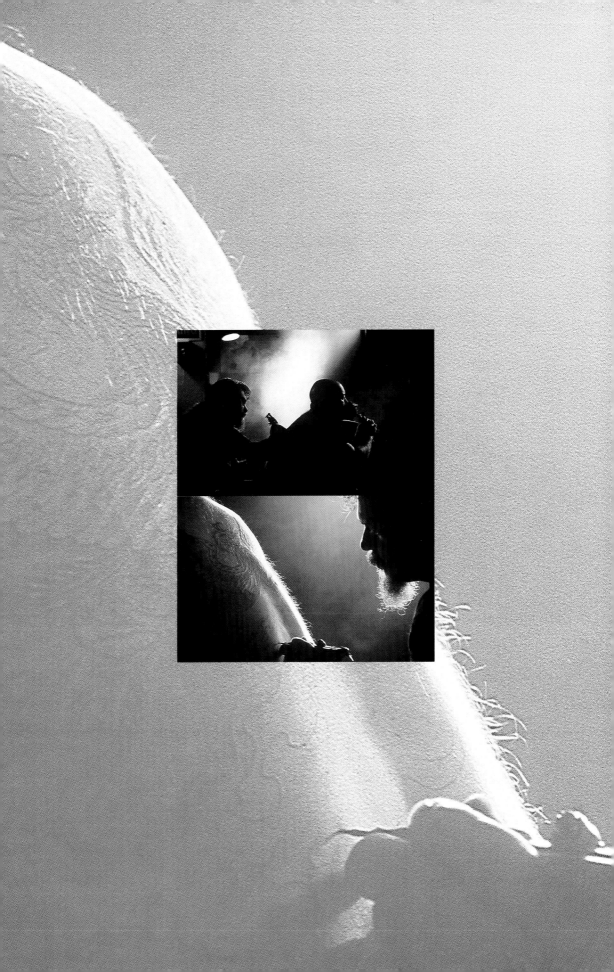

without someone pulling a few strings.

It was Uncle Jack who eventually came to the rescue. He was a panelbeater of great skill, who'd made a lot of money building boats and caravans and sports gear. In fact, a caravan of his was so revolutionary that it made him one of the most successful and most respected caravan builders in Australia at the time. Jack talked to one of his friends in a factory, and Angry was given a job as a fitter and turner. Angry took the job begrudgingly. At the time he had grand ideas of becoming a schoolteacher or an artist, so fitting and turning wasn't exactly the career path he was hoping for. As he says, "It certainly wasn't my choice, but I was starting to get a lot of 'You're going to turn out just like your father', and 'We know where you're headed'...that type of thing. I was abysmal at it, I hated it, but we needed the money so I stuck at it."

It was meant to be a four-year indenture, but Angry only lasted two years. Rosemay didn't ever really understand how Angry felt about the position. She thought he wanted to do an apprenticeship, and to keep her happy, he tried to play the part without complaining.

As Rosemay says, "After the first week at work he came home and he said 'I've got a present for you Mum.' It was in a brown paper bag. It had writing on it, and the writing said 'From your working son'. It was a box of chocolates. That's the type of boy he was. He did that apprenticeship for two and a half years, and one day he just came home and said he was giving it all away. I thought he was joking. I thought he'd get over it, and he'd go back. But he never did. He said he wanted to be a rock and roll singer, and that was it."

Through the years of the apprenticeship Angry and Rosemay's relationship became very strained. They could hardly see eye to eye on anything, and they were having lots of problems living together happily. Rosemay loved her house to be neat and tidy, but Angry loved his bedroom walls to be covered with posters and slogans. Rosemay loved peace and quiet, but Angry loved to hear his music turned up full bore. Angry would often bring home three or four mates at a time. They'd lock themselves in his bedroom and push the amps to their limits.

Angry says he slowly became morose and withdrawn. He was

trying to drink himself into oblivion, and at times he felt almost total despair. "I used to lock myself up in the room where my father used to develop photographs because he was a real photo buff. It was just this little room off the porch at the back of the house. It was just a door in with no windows because it was a darkroom. While he was away I used to knock the pins out of the hinges so I could come and go when I pleased. Of course, when the old man came back and found out I'd been in the room he wasn't too pleased. But, at the time I was writing a lot of dark poetry, and I started a lot of drawing and painting. I did lots of work in charcoals and thick black pencils. I was really into black and white...lots of smudges. I turned out some really disturbing stuff. I'd lock myself in the darkroom and I'd come out in the middle of the night, and not know it was the middle of the night. I used to take food in there and flagons of wine, and just be in there for days."

One of his few other pleasures at the time was music, and in his first summer as an apprentice, Angry made one of his most exciting discoveries. It was a new band, fresh from England. They were called The Beatles. To Angry, they were the most wonderful thing he'd ever heard in his life. When he first heard "Love Me Do", and "Please, Please Me", he was just thrilled. The music made complete sense to him. As far as he was concerned, it was the future of rock 'n roll. It was what music was all about.

ANGRY WITH HIS BEATLES HAIRCUT

As Angry says, "When we first heard the Beatles on radio, at the time I was becoming a fairly selective, but avid, record buyer. I went straight down to the shop and told them that there was this new English group soon to be releasing records here. I told them 'Whatever comes in, I want it'. I remember playing Beatles records. I used to open the windows to our house, and push the radiogram right up and sit out on the front porch, because I wanted people to know that I had a Beatles record. I'd play the Beatles, and kids from

Scarred For Life

I GREW UP FAST/ON WORKING CLASS STREETS
FIRST THING I LEARNED/WAS LIFE DON'T COME CHEAP.
TECHNICAL SCHOOL/ IT WAS A WASTE OF TIME
MAKING ROBOTS/ FOR SOME FACTORY LINE.

GOT MY FIRST TATTOO/ WHEN I WAS SIXTEEN
THE REBEL HAD LOST/ HIS TEENAGE QUEEN
I'D TAKEN A STAND/FOR AN OUTLAW'S LIFE
MY MAMA'S WORDS KEPT RINGING/ 'YOU'RE SCARRED FOR LIFE'.

SHE SAID/ 'YOU'RE SCARRED'
YOU'VE BEEN SCARRED/ SCARRED FOR LIFE.

I WORKED MY WAY/THROUGH THE TROUBLE AND STRIFE
I WAS SCARRED/SCARRED FOR LIFE.
MY REPUTATION/IT CUTS LIKE A KNIFE

I SPENT SOME TIME/A GUEST
OF THE STATE
I GOT OUT IN ORDER/TO GO
STRAIGHT
PEOPLE DON'T FORGIVE/THE
FORCE THEY DON'T FORGET
I WAS JAILED FOR CRIMES/I
DID NOT COMMIT
I WAS SCARRED/ I WAS
SCARRED
SCARRED FOR LIFE

I FOUGHT MY WAY/THROUGH THE TROUBLE AND STRIFE
MY REPUTATION/IT CUTS LIKE A KNIFE.
BEEN KNOCKED AROUND/I'VE HAD A HELL OF A LIFE
I FOUGHT TOOTH AND NAIL/EVERY INCH OF THE WAY
I'VE GOT SCARS TO PROVE IT.

I WAS IN LOVE/FOR KEEPS THAT TIME
BUT ROCK 'N' ROLL WAS ON MY MIND
STILL ON MY MIND/SHE WAS YOUNG AND TRUE
AND SO FULL OF LIFE/AND THE PAIN WENT DEEP
I WAS SCARRED FOR LIFE...

I WAS SCARRED/I WAS SCARRED
SCARRED
SCARRED
SCARRED FOR LIFE.

the street would come and sit on the porch and just listen. It was pretty bad when we had the singles because we just played them over and over, but it was when we got the album, because at least there were ten tracks."

Angry's obsession involved more than just listening to the Beatles. He wanted to dress like them too. He loved to look like all his heroes, so over the years he went through a dozen crazy fads. As Rosemay remembers, "First he'd have to get a suit like the Beatles. He'd have it made, so it looked just right. Then he'd have to wear his hair like the Beatles. Then it was the Rolling Stones. It went on and on. Then he had this leather jacket he wore all the time. I hated it. I really hated it. One day when he wasn't home I threw it out in the glad bag. He asked me what had happened to it, and I told him he must have left it somewhere. I've never told him I threw it out."

By the time he was eighteen, Angry already felt like he was some kind of freak, like there was something particularly wrong with him. He was damaged and bitter. But to make matters even worse, at around this time, the unthinkable happened. He had to face a new problem. He started to lose his hair.

He'd suffered psoriasis for most of his teenage years, which was made much worse by the stress he was under. He'd always scratched his head at night during his sleep to relieve the itch and irritation. He says one thing he remembers most clearly about being an adolescent was waking up in the morning, then going to wash his hands to get rid of the blood under his nails.

His hair loss was noticeable by the time he reached his birthday. He hadn't receded at the crown at all, but the areas around the temple were very thin. It was a maternal family trait. His father had always had a full head of hair, but all the men in his mother's family lost their hair early.

"It was just devastating," Angry says. "It just added to my feeling that I was really abnormal, that I just wasn't like anyone else. It couldn't have come at a worse time for me. I was a typical loser. I was short. I had an attention span of about twelve and a half seconds, I didn't retain anything that was supposed to be taught in school, I lived basically in a fantasy land, emotionally I was a wreck.

Then, to add weight to all of that, I started to lose my hair. I mean, I was a mess. You know I was absolutely devastated. I can remember the anguish I went through right up until my late twenties when it was obvious I was balding."

As soon as he realised what was happening, Angry tried everything. He'd go to the chemist to search the shelves for hair-loss products. He'd cover his head in creams and tonics or any kind of hair lotion he could find. When he saw ads on television talking about hair replacement therapy, he cringed, knowing that they were talking about him. Every time the TV voice-over man chimed in with the words "Are you losing your hair? Miserable? Looking twice your age?" he felt like he was being stung.

HE TALKS ABOUT THE DECISION TO LEAVE HOME AS ONE OF THE MOST GUT-WRENCHING OF HIS LIFE. IT WAS MUCH MORE THAN A HOUSE MOVE. IT WAS A DECISION WITH ENORMOUS SIGNIFICANCE.

All his friends noticed his hair loss. It was impossible not to, but as Angry says, to their eternal credit, they didn't give him a hard time. "I could never have coped with that. Everyone just pretended they didn't notice."

In his late teens, Angry decided to move away from home. He went to live with Ron, one of his mates. Before that he'd only taken short trips away, only for a week or so at a time, and he'd always come back.

He talks about the decision to leave home as one of the most gut-wrenching of his life. It was much more than a house move. It was a decision with enormous significance. Although Colin hadn't come home for a couple of years, Rosemay had taken no formal steps to block him out of their lives. As Angry saw it, unless they moved out of the family house, Colin could move back in whenever he felt like it.

The issue had become a major stumbling block between Angry and Rosemay. Angry would say they should pack their bags and go, and Rosemay would refuse. She was adamant that, if nothing else, her boys would have a roof over their heads. She was frightened of the future somewhere else, and felt it was just not possible to get out of the situation. She had no money, no job, no training, and no support. She was making the decision she felt she had to make, because at least her way, they had somewhere to live.

The conflict over Colin put a lot of extra pressure on Angry and Rosemay's relationship. Angry says, "As I got older Mum and I developed a real survival bonding, but there was distance between us, the more confused I became, and the more angry I became about the situation, the distance got greater and greater."

Angry decided he'd have to push the point. He decided to take a risk to try to force his mother into some action. Although he was easily old enough to leave home, it was something he thought he wouldn't do until years later. More than leaving home, he was leaving his mother. It was like splitting up the team, or breaking up the partnership. Rodney was still only very young, and Angry acted as a kind of stand-in father to him, so it made things even more difficult. He felt like he was letting Rodney down, just as Colin had.

When he weighed it all up, Angry thought he had to make a move. He says it was the most painful thing he's ever done, but he knew he was right. "I thought about it long and hard. I had nothing to keep me there and everything to make me leave." Things hadn't been great between them at home for some time, but still, Rosemay was devastated when he left. "I was doing a course in cake decorating," says Rosemay, "and one day I came home, and there was a note on the kitchen table. He'd left home. He'd gone. He said he couldn't stay. There was a friend with me and I was so upset, she had to go and get me some brandy. His note said he just couldn't stand it."

Rosemay tried to speak to him on the phone, and talk him into coming back. She hoped it was just another of his short trips away. She thought maybe he just needed to get his head together, but it soon became clear that, this time, Angry meant business. He was determined to see things through. "I left home because I had to. I was prepared to be the catalyst to make Mum leave Dad, and it worked. I knew I was doing the right thing because if Mum left Dad that was great...if she didn't, I knew I couldn't live in that house any more. I couldn't live like that any more."

After he left home, there was a period where he and Rosemay barely spoke. They kept in touch because the bond between them was so strong, but they only spoke in short, polite conversations. They were both confused, and they were both desperately trying to find some comfort.

As it turns out, Angry and Ron only survived away from home for about three months. Between them they had very little money and virtually no experience in housekeeping, so in that short time, their living conditions were reduced to squalor, and they were both sick and exhausted.

From Angry's point of view though, three months was long enough. He achieved exactly what he set out to achieve. He stuck to his guns, and although he desperately wanted to, he refused to return home until he had a total commitment from his mother to begin the long process of getting out of her marriage. He insisted that he would only return home on the proviso that Rosemay file for divorce and begin looking for somewhere else to live.

Angry moved back into the house, and true to her word, Rosemay put separation and divorce proceedings in action. The next time the family split up it was by mutual agreement. Only a couple of months passed before they all moved out of the original family house, and away from Colin. Rosemay moved into a little flat with Angry's younger brother Rodney. She was paying the rent with her pension, and she was much happier. She'd given in, not just to pressure from Angry, but also to pressure from her doctor. He said the strain was too much for her, and she had to take some positive, official action to get Colin out of her life. Angry moved in with another mate and his mother while things settled down.

IT WAS SOME YEARS BEFORE THE DIVORCE FINALLY CAME THROUGH, BUT FOR ANGRY IT WAS WELL WORTH THE WAIT. JUST BEFORE HIS 24TH BIRTHDAY, HE WAS THERE TO LEAD HIS MOTHER THROUGH THE FINAL CHAPTER.

It was some years before the divorce finally came through, but for Angry it was well worth the wait. Just before his 24th birthday, he was there to lead his mother through the final chapter with Colin.

Rosemay planned to go to court alone to finalise the papers, but her solicitor requested that Angry attend. He was needed just in case he had to take the witness stand. Rosemay protested, saying it would have been too hard for Angry to give testimony against his father, no matter how bad the relationship, but the solicitor insisted it was necessary.

Angry picked up Rosemay the morning of the hearing, and they went to the courtroom together. She was nervous, and he was

IMI HENDRIX - 'I STARTED A LOT OF DRAWING AND PAINTING. I DID LOTS OF WORK IN CHARCOALS AND THICK BLACK PENCILS. I WAS REALLY INTO BLACK AND WHITE. LOTS OF SMUDGES

anxious to get things finalised. Through all the proceedings they sat together, and listened and watched as the judge granted the divorce. As it turned out, Angry wasn't called to the stand, which was a huge relief for his mother.

For Rosemay the divorce was an enormous step. She kept turning to Angry saying "It's all over now. He's gone. That's it. It's over." But for Angry, it didn't mean so much. He'd declared his father "over" many years earlier. In fact, as he realised that day, he couldn't even recognise him in the courtroom. He spent the entire proceedings completely unaware that the man sitting just a few rows in front was his father. He'd blocked things out to such an extent that, although he'd only seen his father five or six years earlier, he was completely unable to recognise him.

Angry says, "As we left the court I remember talking to Mum. I made some reference to the old man not turning up as usual, but that's when Mum told me that he was there...he'd been sitting in front of us. From that time on, and for years and years after, if someone had come up to me in the street and said 'That's your old man,' I wouldn't have known. I didn't remember what he looked like. It didn't come back to me until I was looking through some pictures years later with Mum, and we suddenly came across this photo of him. She said 'Oh look, here's one I haven't ripped up yet'. Before then, I didn't remember how he looked. I didn't want to. Why should I?"

"WHENEVER I REALLY HURT MUM, WHENEVER I UPSET HER, I USED TO DESPISE MYSELF FOR IT, BECAUSE YOU KNOW, I USED TO THINK I WAS JUST LIKE THE OLD MAN. THAT'S WHAT HE DID. I USED TO SEE THE SAME EXPRESSIONS ON HER FACE."

'IT SUITED ME. I WAS AN ANGRY LITTLE ANT...PEOPLE JUST DIDN'T
BOTHER CALLING ME ANYTHING ELSE... ALL OF A SUDDEN,
BOOM, OVERNIGHT, I WAS ANGRY.'

4

HANGING OUT

By the time Angry hit his twenties, he was out of control, careering along. Through his late teens he'd been desperate for some security and some stability, but he couldn't slow down for long enough to get anything decent in his sights. He'd just been floundering from one thing to the next. For the first time in his life he'd been trying to do everything his own way. As he says, "It was like I was in limbo land, because my whole life had changed. I'd changed it."

He kept trying to do something constructive, but he was too busy with partying and pubs to follow anything through. He'd made his grab for freedom just in time to witness the revolution of the late 1960s and early 1970s. From music, to morals, to fashion, to feminism...everything was changing. Angry himself was like a man on a mission. All he lacked was direction.

FOR SUE

He'd quit the traineeship, so he was unemployed for a while. He just hung around doing nothing. He didn't really care about his future. He was too busy trying to block out his past. At one stage his grandfather came up with a plan he thought was foolproof. He decided the best thing to do with Angry would be to send him to the navy for twelve years. As Angry says, "Grandpa came around one day, and he said 'I've got him a job. It's the answer to all our prayers'. It was like this will cure him, this will fix him up. He brought round indentures for a twelve-year apprenticeship in the Navy. That was his idea of solving the problem, but Mum wouldn't sign."

While he was hanging around, he did start a relationship with another girl, Rebecca, who happened to be the sister of a mate. The relationship only went on for about a year, and it was all pretty convenient. Angry didn't try very hard to make things work, and he took her for granted most of the time, which is why he got such a huge shock when she suddenly turned around and dumped him to marry someone else. At the time, he couldn't understand it. He thought he had everything a girl could ask for. As he says, "She married an accountant. It's classic, isn't it? There I was with long hair, you know, being a wild child, and she went for stability. I was devastated."

ROSEMAY WORRIED CONSTANTLY ABOUT THE THINGS ANGRY WAS DOING, AND THE DIRECTION HE WAS HEADED. HIS WILD LIFESTYLE DIDN'T ALLAY HER FEARS.

By this time, Rosemay and Rodney had moved into a great little semidetached house. For Rosemay, life in Australia had never been better. She was getting on with things without Colin, and enjoying her freedom. The icing on the cake came for her when Angry moved back in with them. He told her he wanted them all to live together again so they could finally be a proper family.

It wasn't quite as easy as it sounded though, because too much water had gone under the bridge, and Angry was too wild. As he says, it was around this time that he hurt his mother most. Almost everything he did upset her. He was just out of control, and she couldn't understand why he didn't settle down and find some level ground. She knew he was unhappy and hurt about his father, but she thought he should be able to put it behind him. She wanted him to get a good steady job, marry a nice girl, and do all the usual things...but he just kept drifting further and further away from the norm.

Rosemay worried constantly about the things Angry was doing, and the direction he was headed. His wild lifestyle didn't allay her fears. "There were these caves opposite the jail in Coburg. There was a big park, and a spillway. We all used to go down and hang at weekends and have parties. There were caves back up in the reserve, and we used to go and sleep there. We'd light fires, smoke and drink. Mum used to get upset about that sort of stuff. I can remember me coming home drunk at night, and her crying herself to sleep, and her waking me up in the morning and finding me with a black eye or a split lip. You know, I was young, and in a mess."

"Whenever I really hurt Mum, whenever I upset her, I used to despise myself for it, because you know, I used to think I was just like the old man. That's what he did. I used to see the same expressions on her face. There's an expression my mother gets on her face, in her eyes, when she's completely shattered. I've done and said things to her that I've spent the rest of my life regretting. But you know, once you've done it, or said it, you can't take it back. You can spend the rest of your life trying to make up for it, but you can't take it back. It's done."

It took almost a completely non-productive year before Angry decided he needed a true vocation. He realised he'd been drifting too long. He knew he had to find something solid. He felt guilty about being such a financial burden on his mother, and he found there just wasn't enough in his life to keep him happy. There was no security. He wanted to work, and he wanted to do something steady. One morning he was looking at the employment pages and he saw an advertisement for a clothes cutter. He'd been for plenty of job interviews before, but his attitude was all wrong. His hair was down past his shoulders, and his clothes were all over the place, so he never got past the first interview. This time it was different, because he was determined. This time he turned on the charm. "I picked the job out of the paper, and just showed up for the interview. I endeared myself to the foreman, and he gave me a chance."

THERE'S AN EXPRESSION MY MOTHER GETS ON HER FACE, IN HER EYES, WHEN SHE'S COMPLETELY SHATTERED. I'VE DONE AND SAID THINGS TO HER THAT I'VE SPENT THE REST OF MY LIFE REGRETTING. BUT YOU KNOW, ONCE YOU'VE DONE IT, OR SAID IT, YOU CAN'T TAKE IT BACK.

Clothes cutting wasn't exactly the job he'd always dreamed of, but at the time, it suited him perfectly. "It gave me something to do, and it gave me regimentation. I liked the job because it didn't threaten me. I didn't mind going to work to do it. I enjoyed the work, and I enjoyed the company. I worked for a bulk manufacturer. It was mass production so it wasn't all scissors and pins. I used to lay up a table with material a foot high, and cut thousands of pairs of pyjamas and shirts. It allowed me to put back some of the stability in my life that I lacked."

The job also allowed Angry one major luxury. It gave him a chance to purchase the only thing he'd ever really wanted...a motorbike.

Owning a bike was a childhood dream. It was a must. A motorbike fitted into the image he had of himself as an outlaw. "It was my one ambition in life, because Marlon Brando was my hero, and I couldn't think of anything better than owning a bike and being just like Marlon Brando in *The Wild One*."

Angry and another bike-loving mate, Bob, spent every spare minute riding. As Angry says, it was one of his great passions, his great loves. They weren't revheads, they were real riders. They'd go out for hours every weekend, touring the countryside, taking in the scenery.

THE FIRST BIKE

They had some regular weekend routes which became favourites. One just happened to run straight through the territory of a fledgling bike club, the Vigilantes. After a few months, the local riders invited them to join the club. It was a sort of compulsory invitation. "If you want to ride through our territory, then maybe you want to ride with our club...and if not, why not?" It was that sort of thing. Angry and Bob jumped at the chance to join an official bike club. It was just what they were looking for.

The Vigilantes were a proud mob. They were good blokes who liked bikes and babes and drinking and tattoos, but they weren't thugs. They didn't like to be associated with the stereotyped image of the biker, and they were quick to let people know exactly what type of organisation they had going. Even years later, as he talks about the Vigilantes, Angry is keen to defend their reputation. "We weren't a gang. We prided ourselves in not being called a gang. We were a club. I remember the guys that ran it. They were great. We had a clubhouse. We were only allowed to wear our colours when we rode our bikes and we only wore them when we rode together. We had regular meetings, we payed monthly fees, we took minutes. It was a real club. We were fiercely proud to be Vigilantes."

When he wasn't with the club, Angry was just hanging out. He spent hours in the pub with his mates, and at around this time, made a discovery. He was introduced to his first illegal drug, the drug that he went on to use and abuse more than any other — marijuana. At the time he'd never even heard of it, so when a girl at a friend's house offered him some "pot", he wasn't exactly sure of what she was offering.

It was an older group of friends. They were university people, and some had even graduated into the professions. As soon as the marijuana came out, and the joints were lit, Angry recognised the smell. He'd often noticed it in the house before.

Willing to try anything once, Angry agreed to take a drag. As he says, "It just knocked me for a loop. I sat back in my seat trying to work things out, and I can remember that, after a few smokes, this girl took out a box of toys and started handing them out to people. You know, she had like kaleidoscopes and prisms and homemade stained glass. It was all that sort of psychedelia. She also handed out colouring books and pencils. I found that part of it really amusing. I mean, I thought it was hysterical. They were all giggling and looking at what one another was drawing and analysing it. They were having a huge laugh. Apparently, that's what people did in those days. They didn't just sit around and get stoned and watch TV or listen to music. They did much more childlike stuff. You know, it was real 'out there', hippy dippy stuff."

Angry didn't smoke pot again until a couple of years later, and when he was reintroduced to it, he took it on seriously. He became a real dope smoker. As he says though, his first experience was the best. He's never been to a place since where people have handed out kaleidoscopes and coloured crayons when they handed out the smokes.

The clothes cutting and the motorbike were distractions, they gave him something to do, but he knew they weren't permanent things. They weren't life decisions or life paths, they were just little diversions. He was grappling with himself. Although he appeared to have no real future, he was actually very determined. He wanted to be someone. He was ambitious, so

OWNING A BIKE WAS A CHILDHOOD DREAM. IT WAS A MUST. A MOTORBIKE FITTED INTO THE IMAGE HE HAD OF HIMSELF AS AN OUTLAW. "IT WAS MY ONE AMBITION IN LIFE, BECAUSE MARLON BRANDO WAS MY HERO, AND I COULDN'T THINK OF ANYTHING BETTER THAN OWNING A BIKE AND BEING JUST LIKE MARLON BRANDO IN *THE WILD ONE*."

even in his most desperate moments, he hadn't completely given in. As he says, "I wasn't a loser, but I wouldn't call myself a winner either. I was a survivor, which is probably more important. I think it's more important to survive so you give yourself another chance. If I'd just given in to it when I was a kid, and ended up doing stupid things like robberies or whatever, and ended up going to jail, then I'd have been a loser. If I'd ended up just accepting that as life...you know, that's all life has to offer and that's all I should want...I think that's a loser's attitude. I probably wasn't doing as well as I should or could have been, but there were elements of my life that were okay...I hadn't succumbed totally."

ONE BIG PROBLEM STILL REMAINED THOUGH...HIS HORRIFIC TEMPER. IT WAS LIKE HE WAS SITTING ON A TIME BOMB, DESPERATELY TRYING TO STAY ON SOME LEVEL GROUND. HE SAYS HE WAS LIKE A BOILING POT.

One big problem still remained though...his horrific temper. It was like he was holding a loaded gun, but still desperately trying to stay on some level, calm ground. He says he was like a boiling pot. He drank himself into a stupor whenever he could, and spent most of his time in the pub. He sat almost nightly with his face in a beer. Most times he was just a larrikin drunk, but every now and then, something would spark off the rage from his childhood, and he'd become dangerous.

ANGRY WITH HIS BELOVED CATS,
JOHN AND YOKO

"What happens is you get angrier and angrier and angrier as you go through life. It just builds up. You keep contributing to this unconscious pool which is all negative. It's all anger. It's all frustration. It's all sadness."

He says the biggest problem was that he had no access to advice on how to deal with himself, or how to cope with his feelings. There was just no education at the time. He didn't even know that it was counselling he needed, let alone understand where to find it. Whenever he talks now about abused children and the pent-up emotions they carry, he becomes passionate. He believes society needs to be more diligent when it comes to helping damaged children. As he says, "There should be a process where people are allowed to deal with their problems, and then just get on with their lives, instead of being told to put them in a bag. The bag just keeps on getting bigger and bigger, and the bigger it gets, the harder it is to carry around. In the end your frustrations and your anger get to the point where you think 'Shit, I've got to carry this thing around with me forever'."

He says he felt like hitting out at other people. He wanted everyone else to hurt more than him. "Instead of reaching out to give someone else a hand, I wanted to smack them under the ear...because if I've got to suffer, so has everybody else. Why should I be the only one dragging all this shit around? Shrinks will tell you that to avoid punishing the right people, you just punish all the people around you."

It's taken years and years, but Angry has managed to control his dark side. He says he knows it's there, but it doesn't frighten him so much any more. "I have an outrageous temper, and every now and then there's a crack and, wham, it just leaps through. It's like sitting back and watching. It's just a horrifying experience because when I lose it, I really lose it. My wife says there's only one thing to do, and that's get out of my way. Not that it's ever got to the point where she's been in danger, but she can see it in there. She's seen it flare up in me, and she can see it's just dying to get out. She says it's like 'If this thing ever got out, you'd throttle me'. It's like that.

"I have to constantly find the strength to suppress my anger because I'm potentially about to explode anywhere from ten times to one hundred times in just about any given day. In fact, I'm as potentially dangerous as I ever was. I really revel in it though, because it's a great personal victory. You see, I control it now. I'm no longer its slave. I keep it in check."

He describes his anger as a beast inside him, and in those early years he gave the beast great confidence, boosting its power with every drink. He started to lose control of things. Nothing fazed him. He was careless and defiant. He was a hot-shot loudmouth who was constantly testing the limits. He was into whatever came along, whatever drugs were around. No high was enough for him, no rush would do.

> **"THERE SHOULD BE A PROCESS WHERE PEOPLE ARE ALLOWED TO DEAL WITH THEIR PROBLEMS, AND THEN JUST GET ON WITH THEIR LIVES, INSTEAD OF BEING TOLD TO PUT THEM IN A BAG. THE BAG JUST KEEPS ON GETTING BIGGER AND BIGGER, AND THE BIGGER IT GETS, THE HARDER IT IS TO CARRY AROUND."**

He was still obsessed with fears about his own sanity. Girlfriends at the time would relate to him the incidents of the night before, and he'd have no recollection. He'd wander back into the house some mornings with no idea where he'd been or what he'd done. All he'd know was that he'd woken up in a telephone box, and that he was cut and bruised.

He was a loud drunk, but he was usually fairly amiable. Every now and then though he'd get himself into a situation where he'd be forced to back up the bluff with his fists. He didn't deliberately pick many fights, but he'd often tempt other drinkers with his big talk. "I was just a mouthy little guy with problems. I'd get myself into situations, but nine times out of ten I was okay...mainly because I hung around with fairly formidable friends who were quite willing and able to look after me."

IN THE HIPPY DAYS, WITH SUE

As he says, he didn't ever get involved in a fight if he thought he was going to lose, but there were many, many times when he miscalculated. The losing fights didn't deter him though, and being beaten up didn't bother him much either. He says, after you've taken a beating once in a fight, you learn it's not that bad. You never learn to like it, but it's not the end of the world."

While Angry was living with Rosemay and Rodney in the semidetached, he met his next girlfriend. Her name was Sue and she lived up the road. She was the girl-almost-next-door, and everything about her was perfect, except one small thing. She had promised to be married to another man, a friend of her family. He was a guy she'd been involved with since she was a kid, and both families were keeping the pressure on them to marry.

Sue went ahead with the marriage but it was short-lived, and when she went home, looking for a shoulder to cry on, Angry was right there for her. After a few months the friendship developed into a romance, and they decided to move out together. They rented a little unit, and set up Angry's first real home.

In many ways, Sue was more mature than Angry, and as he says, she played a very important role in his development. "Sue is really significant because I feel I really grew up with Sue. She came along and presented to me an opportunity to be more responsible. Here was a woman who was easily my equal in every way, shape, and form. Here was a woman I really respected. She was such a woman that I couldn't just be carefree with. I had to be more responsible and stable. This was a period of my life where I feel I made my first inroads to adulthood."

Sue was tolerant and understanding. She didn't complain about Angry's binges. She also liked to think of him as a muso, so she didn't complain about the jam sessions or the late night lifestyle. As Angry says, "For a while I was blissfully happy. I had a wonderful woman. I had a job I liked, music was starting to make sense, and life couldn't have been better."

By this time Angry had almost given up on motorbikes. While he was a Vigilante, he had embraced the whole lifestyle, but it had just become too much. He was passionate about motorcycles and he loved to ride, but he knew he could never devote his life to a bike club. It just wasn't in him.

The other problem was there was hardly any time left for motorbikes because Angry's great love, music, was now taking up every spare minute.

Angry had spent years playing around with music till this time. He wanted to be a blues guitarist because he'd always loved the blues. He imagined himself as some aloof, moody, soul performer, sitting on a stool in front of a huge audience with just his guitar. It's how he'd always seen it. His ambition changed regularly though...he wanted to be all things. "First of all I wanted to be like all the great blues guitar players, then I wanted to be like Bob Dylan, then of course I wanted to be like John Lennon."

There wasn't much call for a short, tattooed blues guitarist on the Melbourne music scene, so it was with rock and roll bands that Angry

PEACE, POWER AND PURITY IN REHEARSAL

slowly started to make his name. He moved from band to band. Guys just fell together for a couple of months, then fell apart. It was pretty fickle, but it was all experimental. Most of the bands were small outfits that played cheap gigs in pubs and clubs, but Angry loved the whole scene.

In those early music years, Angry was involved with bands mostly for the fun of it. He wasn't really serious. He was just dabbling. There were many more short term line-ups. "There was one band called the Urge. And there was another band I formed with my best mate Vernon. Vern called the band Le Primitive, because he was a bit of a romantic, but before too long we just called ourselves Primitive."

One band that evolved was called Peace, Power and Purity. It was an electric folk group of sorts, heavily into antinuclear causes, and with an emphasis on volume. Angry says he's never been allowed to live it down. As he says, he was in his hippy phase. He'd just read *War and Peace*, and he really believed that peace was the strongest force. He thought it was the only force that could overpower aggression. Angry had long hair, down past his shoulders and almost to his bum, and the band played songs from Joan Baez, Odetta, Bob Dylan. They did all the hippy anthems. They even did a ten-minute version of "Four Dead in Ohio".

As Angry says now, he was proud of what he stood for. "I was a real flag waver. I went to the protests and marched down the street yelling things like 'Ban the bomb', and 'Frogs out of the Pacific'. We were really optimistic. In the 1970s I really believed that by the 1990s the world would be a wonderful place, do you know what I mean? I believed in all that getting back to nature and people power. But, I never called myself a hippy at the time. I didn't realise that's what I was."

When Angry first got involved with bands, he didn't plan on being a singer. He wanted to be a guitarist. The singing came by accident. "At the time, with the particular line-up we had, we had three guitar players. The other two were much better than me, so the only other thing we needed was a singer. I remember how it happened. We went into the kitchen one at a time and then we had to sing "Twist and Shout" without accompaniment. I just happened to be the best one at it."

Although he was disappointed he didn't get to play his guitar, he found the advantages of being lead singer more than compensated. The best thing was that he was out in front, because it just seemed the natural place for him to be. He wasn't shy or nervous...he took to the job without a second thought.

In a way, through these years Angry was just hanging around getting ready for the real gig. He always knew he was going to do something with music. He was going to make it his life. He'd told his mother he was going to be famous. He'd even bumped into Shirley once at the shops and told her he was going to be the world's greatest blues singer. He just knew he wasn't going to find fame and fortune with a band like Peace, Power and Purity or Primitive. It was going to be something different.

ANGRY WAS JUST HANGING AROUND GETTING READY FOR THE REAL GIG. HE ALWAYS KNEW HE WAS GOING TO DO SOMETHING WITH MUSIC. HE WAS GOING TO MAKE IT HIS LIFE. HE'D TOLD HIS MOTHER HE WAS GOING TO BE FAMOUS.

Angry stayed with Sue for about three years, and they had a really good relationship, but when it came to the crunch, he was afraid of commitment. It would have been so easy for him to take the opportunity, and "go straight" with Sue. They could have married, had kids, etc. etc., and all lived happily ever after, but something always stopped him. "I didn't really know how to settle down. I had no role model to bring about any sort of belief in a man/woman monogamous wedded-bliss situation. I drove all my girlfriends away, or I created a situation that meant I didn't have to go ahead with it."

In the last few months with Sue, Angry became nasty, and belligerent. He neglected her, and ignored every chance she gave him to apologise. He says it became a terrible battle in his own head, because he knew what he was doing. "It was like the two little people on your shoulder. One's saying 'You can make this. You can do this. This is what you want. You've got a great girl...she's gorgeous, you love her, you're compatible.' The other little bloke's going 'You're kidding. You don't need this. There's plenty more where she came from. You meet them every weekend. You don't need to settle down and have children.'" It wasn't until many years later that the first little bloke won the battle.

Two of the most distinguishable things about Angry are his name and his bald head. A Melbourne bloke, known as Mangy Mick, takes credit for both.

The head shaving didn't happen until years later, but the nickname came when Angry was about twenty-four. He used to drink in the same pub as Mangy Mick. It was the musos' pub, the Station Hotel in Prahran. Angry barely knew Mick...they were just on a nodding basis.

As Angry says, there's a certain amount of myth attached to the nickname story. No one is exactly sure of some of the details because the story has been told and retold over the years. By now, it could have been coloured and distorted with a Chinese whisper effect, but as Angry says, that's not important. To him, this is how the story goes, and as he says, "If it's not the truth, it should be."

"Mangy" was a shadowy character, with loads of heavy mates with names like "Guts Gallagher". He had one super-serious mate whose name was just Nick, and they were all blokes to be reckoned with. In a way, they sort of ran the

RELAXING WITH THE BOYS AFTER REHEARSAL

pub. It was their territory. They drank there every day, and they fell into the category of regulars. Angry hung out there often as well, but he and his mates weren't quite as tough as Mangy's boys. They were younger, and a little bit greener.

One day, while Angry was at the pub, Mangy got into a fight with a group of other heavies. "He got into a stink," says Angry, "and there weren't too many people around to back him up. I was full of rum, and had a mouth as big as the doorway, so me and a couple of other blokes jumped in to help him." It was a big fight, with lots of people involved. Most of it took place outside on the street. It came to a natural end when the other guys backed off, but Mangy Mick wasn't really interested in who'd won or lost. He was suddenly intrigued with the little guy who'd come from the far corner of the pub to help him out.

"The story goes like this," says Angry. "After the fight we came back into the pub to have a wash and a drink, and the way it was told to me, Mangy kept on saying 'Hey, what about the ant? The angry ant.' He was like that. He was the sort of bloke who gave people nicknames. At the time people sort of knew me as Mouse, but Mangy kept talking about the Ant. Everyone in the pub had a big laugh about it. The nickname started that night. First Mick was always calling me the Angry Ant, then he dropped the ant and started saying 'Hey, Angry.'

"It suited me. I was an angry little ant. People just didn't bother calling me anything else, even people who up until that stage, had called me nothing but Gary. All of a sudden, boom, that was it. Just overnight, I was Angry."

'BUSTER ENCOMPASSED ALL THE THINGS IT SHOULD.
IT WAS REBELLIOUS AGAINST THE CONSERVATION OF
LOUNGE MUSIC, AND IT WAS MUSIC BEING PLAYED BY
BRASH YOUNG MEN, SO IT WAS VERY, VERY APPEALING.'

BUSTER BROWN

Buster Brown was Angry Anderson's first step up to fame. It was a band that took to the stage like it was taking to a battle zone. Buster was unpredictable, volatile, and spontaneous...everything Angry needed in a band.

There were six members...Geordie, the bass player who was only seventeen and still in school. Phil Rudd, the drummer, who later went on to AC/DC, two guitar players Paul Grant and John Moon, and the keyboard player Chris Wilson. Chris, Geordie and Phil grew up in the same area so they all knew each well. They'd basically pulled Buster together before Angry even came on the scene, but they were having trouble finding a singer and keeping a line-up. They'd tried plenty of frontmen, but no one really stood out as the right person for the job. When Angry got involved with the band, everything just fell into place.

THE BLEEDING HEART FOR VIVIENNE

It was like Angry's dream come true. He'd always imagined his perfect band, the ideal line-up. Bands like Buster had not actually been around for long when Buster formed. They were strange company, doing a cross-section of music from heavy rock to melodic ballads. But, to Angry, who'd always been tantalised by the whole concept of bands, it was hugely romantic. It was something he'd thought about for years, ever since he was a child. As Angry says, "I remember the first time I saw Bill Haley on the screens. It was like being hit over the head with a hammer, because here was this bunch of guys, not an orchestra, all sitting down with music. But they were a bunch of guys with all the latest, the drape coats and the baggy pants, and the shiny shoes. You know, all the latest...no ties, open-necked shirts, rockers' haircuts, sideburns, playing instruments. Sax and trumpet players took on a whole new meaning. They weren't backing players anymore. They stood out in front, and let it rip. It encompassed all the things it should. It was rebellion against the conservatism of lounge music, and it was music being played by brash young men, so it was very, very appealing. I remember that was the first time I ever perceived that this is a group...this is a band."

Buster gave Angry the opportunity to be everything he wanted to be. It became a sharpie band, a sort of Melbourne adaptation of the mod and skinhead trends from London. Buster's sharpie fans didn't wear boots and braces like the later sharpies. At that time, in Melbourne, it was a cleaner look. Most of the guys had square-back college haircuts with a part down one side. They wore baggy trousers with cream twin sets and Italian made chisel toe shoes. Most of the Buster boys were sort of lightweight gangsters, working class lads who'd been in plenty of trouble but weren't quite hardened criminals.

As Angry says, "The beauty of Buster was it was a real tiger on the end of a rope. It was a real happening band. The music was like high-level intensity, the way it was played, the characters were really phosphorus, easily-ignitable people, and it made for great chemistry."

Buster was an introduction to the joys of being a frontman. Angry loved every minute of it. It was like he'd finally found his calling. Standing on stage in front of a big crowd gave him a new outlet for his anger and his energy. He loved the attention and the applause. Every Friday and Saturday night Angry would become the Buster ringmaster. He'd be the leader, the boss. He'd take on the crowd, feed off them, yell at them, scream about them. He tested it out, and pushed the limits to see how far he could go. He'd get totally smashed and throw himself at the audience, or at the speakers, or on to the floor. He could say anything and do anything. In the context of a gig, it was all acceptable. He loved the performance. He loved the drama of rock and roll. On stage, he was out of control, just as he was in real life.

For years Angry had been told to pull himself into line, to get it together, but with Buster, suddenly everything changed. Nobody wanted him to calm down, on stage or off. They wanted him to be the maniacal rock and roller. They'd take anything from him. If he was wild and outrageous, he was encouraged. If he did something that shocked people, he was congratulated. "I was into everything. I was doing loads of dope, loads of booze, and I was finally living the lifestyle where it was not only accepted, it was encouraged. People within the industry wanted people like me to be like I was."

It was a new world for him. He could take the image as far as he wanted. Just as long as he was the loudest, or the drunkest, or the angriest, or the most outrageous, everyone was happy.

He was feeling great about himself too. "I'd come into my own. I'd gotten as physically strong as I could. I'd gone from being the potentially dangerous loony, to being probably more dangerous in a way. I'd spent years getting over being small, years getting over being a person who was used to being a victim. As I got older and more confident, people started to look at me and say 'He's a good rock singer, and he's a good bloke'. I became more self-assured. All of a sudden I realised I was quite formidable physically. I realised that I could handle myself pretty well."

BUSTER BROWN, THE LAST LINE-UP.
'DIGGER' DALLAS ROYAL (CENTRE FRONT)
LATER DRUMMED FOR ROSE TATTOO

Buster had a strange following. They played pubs and cheap gigs, and they developed an almost cult status. The typical Buster crowd was young, rowdy and streetwise. Most people came just to see the spectacle of the stage show. Buster had a reputation as one of Melbourne's most over-the-top bands. They were rabid and extreme, and they made a name for themselves as the kind of band that loses its head on stage.

People flocked to see Buster, just to make sure they didn't miss out on the one gig where something huge happened. Fans were loyal.

They turned up week after week to play it safe. Nobody wanted to miss a performance in case they happened to choose the one night where someone in the band went completely crazy and set themselves on fire or something. It was like that. Nobody ever knew what to expect.

Phil, Geordie and Angry were birds of a feather. When they weren't playing, they were testing the boundaries off stage. "We were just mug lairs basically," says Angry. "It was Phil, Geordie, and I that really played up the most. It was always us that got into trouble. It was always us that drank the most, and got into fights the most, and did the most dope. We just went at it."

Most days the boys were stoned and drunk before 6 pm. They weren't quite a gang, but they often travelled in a large, menacing group. They liked to intimidate people, and fights broke out whenever anyone was brave enough to take them on.

Many people who know Angry now say it's hard to come to terms with the man he was in those early years. They say they find themselves looking at him thinking "Were you really so terrible?". Even his greatest fans know he has rough edges, but they're reluctant to think of him as a real thug. But as Angry sees it, it's impossible to understand him without understanding what he really was. He says people have to know that he was an animal, that he was obscene, that he was irresponsible, that he did break furniture, and that occasionally he did break heads. It's not the side of him that he's proud of, but it's an integral part of the man he is. It's like you can't take the good, without taking the bad. He couldn't have related to street life if he'd never lived it. He couldn't have controlled and redirected anger if he'd never felt it.

By the time Buster Brown formed, Angry had already spent a year or so with his "child love". When he met Vivienne he was 24 years old, she was only seventeen. She was in school when they were first introduced. When Angry was still hanging around with small-time backyard musical outfits, Vivienne was brought into the group by one of her girlfriends. She was beautiful. She came from a wealthy family and lived in a wealthy suburb, and she was the kind of girl who seemed beyond the reach of a wild man like Angry.

In many ways, having Vivienne fall in love with him was one of the most significant events of Angry's life. Her attraction to him came like a bolt out of the blue, and it made him consider himself in a new light. She made him feel fantastic. Everyone wanted to date her, and for some reason she wanted to date him. He couldn't believe his luck. She was so young and so beautiful, and for a while he was walking around with his head in the clouds. It was like he kept saying "Me? She picked me? She could have had anyone and she picked me?"

When they got together as a steady couple they had everything going for them, except her parents. Her mother and father hated the idea of their daughter dating Angry. He was everything they didn't want in a prospective son-in-law. They were also worried because she was so young. But, as a twosome, Angry and Vivienne were completely compatible. Viv was around all through the Buster years. She was the one Angry came home to. She was the one he adored.

Buster was a huge success on the road. They went on major cross country tours, hitting every small town pub. In Sydney, they played regularly at Chequers, which, at the time, was a place with a fairly heavy reputation. They'd get loads of other would-be musos at gigs, checking them out. That's how Angry first met some of the other big names of 1980s rock and roll: Ted Mulry, Darryl Braithwaite, Jimmy Barnes. They were all just blokes trying to make a place for themselves, watching the competition, feeling their way.

Angry loved the rock and roll life. With Buster he was really happy. He had his music, and he had Vivienne. She was tolerant and understanding. Angry would rock home in the early hours of the morning, wired, and she'd put up with it. She even caught him out a few times when he tried the old trick of telling her he was staying on a mate's couch. She'd find out he wasn't there, and give him hell, but she tolerated it anyway.

Vivienne had a job too, which helped, because although Angry worked long and hard on the road with Buster, the pay wasn't great. In fact, it wasn't even nearly enough to live on. To supplement it, Angry took whatever unskilled work the CES offered him. "I worked as a

IN MANY WAYS, HAVING VIVIENNE FALL IN LOVE WITH HIM WAS ONE OF THE MOST SIGNIFICANT EVENTS OF ANGRY'S LIFE. HER ATTRACTION TO HIM CAME LIKE A BOLT OUT OF THE BLUE, AND IT MADE HIM CONSIDER HIMSELF IN A NEW LIGHT.

builder's labourer, as a brickie's labourer, and I worked on the rail loading trains. Sometimes, I didn't work at all. In between labouring jobs you could actually get on the dole for a couple of weeks, and then another job would come up. They sent me to seasonal jobs too, like sorting mail. Once I was sent to the Fitzroy Gardens in Melbourne as a labourer. I was just sweeping and turning dirt. I only did it for a week, but it was a great gig."

Everything was going right for Angry. Even his family life had suddenly taken a huge upswing, because by this time Rosemay had found a new man. Bert Roach had been a neighbour to the Andersons since they'd moved into their first family house in Australia. Bert and his family lived only two doors up. His kids had gone to the high school, when Angry had gone to the Tech, but they all lived in the same street so they knew each other well.

As Angry describes it, Rosemay and Bert's courtship was shy, but it led to a long, happy marriage. "Mum rang me up one day and she told me that Bert Roach had asked her out on a date. I don't know what she expected me to say, but I said 'Good, when are you going?'. She kept protesting saying he was married, and she couldn't go out with him, but I said, 'No Mum, he's not married, he's divorced and so are you. Give it a go'. Anyway, about a year later she rang me and said Bert had asked her to marry him, so that's how it all started."

EVERYTHING WAS GOING RIGHT FOR ANGRY. EVEN HIS FAMILY LIFE HAD SUDDENLY TAKEN A HUGE UPSWING, BECAUSE BY THIS TIME ROSEMAY HAD FOUND A NEW MAN.

Every would-be rock and roll star dreams of the moment they're offered their first recording deal. When the moment came for Angry and Buster, they didn't believe life could get any better. It was more than a dream come true...it was perfect in every way. Buster was one of the first bands signed on the Mushroom label with Michael Gudinski. At the time Mushroom was handling four acts: there was a band called Sid Rumpo, a band called Madder Lake, Skyhooks, and then there was Buster Brown.

Even more than the record deal, Angry was excited about the record producer. Mushroom had assigned Lobby Lloyde, the rock guitarist Angry had idolised for years. "We didn't think it could get any better," says Angry. "We had a record deal, and we were being produced by Lobby Lloyde."

The album was called "Something to Say". It was all original, bar one cover of "Roll Over Beethoven", which was just meant to be a jam version at the end of the recording session. Angry wrote all the lyrics, and the boys were confident the album would be the start of something big. "We were very much a naive band. We were all young, and excited by our own music."

They recorded at Channel 9 in Melbourne. "I remember we walked in and it was a new experience to walk around and look at the microphones and everything. In those days, recording was still a novelty." Over a twelve-hour session they put down all their songs, but it wasn't easy. The boys felt they couldn't quite translate their act to tape. There was no crowd, no stage, no yelling. They weren't used to the clean silence of the studio, and they had nobody to feed off. Angry himself was almost lost...he couldn't get into the music, and wasn't quite sure what to do with himself.

BERT AND ROSEMAY

Angry was disappointed in almost every aspect of his first taste of the recording industry. He felt Mushroom deserted them to some extent. Gudinski was having great success at the time with Madder Lake and Skyhooks, and Angry has always felt Buster were cast adrift to fend for themselves. There was no focus on Mushroom's part, and no major push to get the act together. Buster was a raw, live act, so the boys needed guidance to record successfully.

"They slashed our budget in half," says Angry. "Lobby was looking forward to making a great rock and roll album, like blood and guts, but he ended up having to work with an extremely limited budget and an extremely limited time frame. He had to produce an album that had all the elements of Buster the band, which was like maniacal rock and roll, and package it comfortably. You know sanitise it to the point where it would be accepted."

As it turned out, the album was a big failure. Buster was too much of a cult band, and the audience just didn't take to their sound on vinyl. As Angry says, "Buster just couldn't capture what they did on album. It was too unpredictable and spontaneous, too out of control." The chemistry just couldn't be packaged.

When Angry was about 29, Buster Brown came to an end. As

EARLIEST DAYS AS THE FRONT MAN

Angry says, "It was actually sad about Buster because it started out being a fantastic band. I don't even know why it ended really. Like with most bands, you have personality problems. That was one thing. But another thing too, I sort of think Buster was a bit like Rosy Tats. The band was so extreme...and this is the very nature of extreme bands...they operate on such a high energy level and everything's so intense. Everything's so absolutely 100 per cent. It's like straining, you know, this effort. It's like this thing that pushes the whole time. It's almost like there's a burnout factor, and to maintain the rage as it were, and to maintain the passion, there's a price to pay."

Buster wasn't just disbanded suddenly one day...it fell apart slowly. One by one the other guys lost interest and were replaced. Booking gigs wasn't a problem, even with the line-up changing, because Buster Brown had such a good reputation they could always work and make money. But with each change, the band was gradually losing its identity. "The band just ran out of use. It ran out of steam. I kept thinking about how Buster Brown had started, and what it became, and I thought this is two totally different bands with the same name."

They kept on going for months with different members until Angry says he suddenly realised it was like he was standing on stage with a bunch of strangers. They hardly even knew each other's names. "In the end, I was standing there one day. I was on stage, and I looked around, and I was seriously thinking to myself 'Who are these people?'

"We ended up with a bunch of people who were good musicians, but it wasn't Buster Brown. Buster was a street stance, but we ended up being a musicians' band, and that's why I stuck out, because I had a group of musicians around me who were real musos, and I was the heavy metal kid. I was meant to be in a band like Buster Brown or Rose Tattoo, not so much a band that was trying to play serious music."

Angry felt like he'd lost everything with the end of Buster. He'd lost his place, his little piece of the world, and he was back as just another brick in the wall. He'd even lost his only respectable means of expressing his anger. He had no stage, and no audience. His outrage lost its outlet.

Viv tried to nurse him through. She offered him all her support, but once again, Angry deliberately closed her out. By the time Buster ended, Angry and Viv had been together five years. The natural step was for them to get married, but Angry shied away from the commitment.

Vivienne was ready to push the issue. As Angry says, "She became really demanding. She needed stability. It must have been fun to be living with a maniac when she was younger, but as she became older, she really wanted me to calm down, settle down and be what she wanted me to be. I wanted that too. I just couldn't"

It's one of those things. Angry's mother says he's been obsessed with family all his life. He was the one who, even as a little boy, was desperate to see his mother and father in love. He was the one who tried, when Colin was away, to pull what was left together and make it a family. Now, Angry says his family is the one thing that keeps him stable. It's the best thing in his life. It's the thing he always wanted. Back in those early years, he saw the opportunities and a huge part of him wanted to take them, but in the end, he turned his back.

Vivienne offered him ultimatum after ultimatum, and eventually just packed her bags. Angry didn't even try to stop her. He was too busy wallowing in self-pity. He was too busy drowning the sorrows of Buster.

Mangy Mick was still on the scene, and was one of Angry's closest mates. They loved getting pissed together, and they loved

ANGRY FELT LIKE HE'D LOST EVERYTHING WITH THE END OF BUSTER. HE'D LOST HIS PLACE, HIS LITTLE PIECE OF THE WORLD, AND HE WAS BACK AS JUST ANOTHER BRICK IN THE WALL. HE'D EVEN LOST HIS ONLY RESPECTABLE MEANS OF EXPRESSING HIS ANGER.

getting stoned. They had an old reel-to-reel audio recorder, and one of their favourite hobbies was to invite people around to drop acid or smoke dope, and record their conversations. They'd hide the recorder behind the couch, then spend hours listening to the tapes. Some they thought were really funny, and others they thought were boring. It was like their own little bugging device. Their own ASIO set up.

NOW, ANGRY SAYS HIS FAMILY IS THE ONE THING THAT KEEPS HIM STABLE. IT'S THE BEST THING IN HIS LIFE. IT'S THE THING HE ALWAYS WANTED. BACK IN THOSE EARLY YEARS, HE SAW THE OPPORTUNITIES AND A HUGE PART OF HIM WANTED TO TAKE THEM, BUT IN THE END, HE TURNED HIS BACK.

It was at this time that Mangy encouraged another of Angry's most identifiable characteristics...the shaved head. By then, Angry's hair had begun to recede severely, so he was wearing it very short, almost crew cut. The bald patch had finally extended across the crown so Angry decided he had to address the problem. He just wasn't sure what to do about it.

Over the years, he'd heard just about every old wives' tale about balding men. He'd been told it was a sure sign of impotence and some people had suggested it was a mark of insanity. In the time when he was wearing it long, in the hippy style of the 1970s, he'd even had people telling him that his balding was caused by the length of his hair. They said the weight at the bottom was pulling it all out at the roots.

He started weighing up his options. Wigs and hairpieces at the time were horrendous things that balanced on top of the head, and blew off when the wind came up, so he decided they were a dead loss. He knew tonics didn't work and hats didn't suit him, so there seemed to be no hope until, one day, Mangy Mick came up with the answer.

Mangy was also thinning on top, and he'd decided on a radical solution. He shaved his head. The first time Angry saw Mick bald, he was blown away. He just loved the look. He was green with envy. "Mick walked in the door one day, and he was bald. I just thought there was nobody else on earth who could carry that off. It was the coolest thing. It was great. I kept saying 'Look at you. Man, it's fantastic!'." Soon after, Angry did it himself.

One day, he just decided he'd had enough of hair. He was fed up with it, so he went to the barbers and asked for the shortest cut possible, a number one razor cut. The barber did as he was told, but even after he'd finished, Angry wanted his hair shorter. He kept telling the barber to go over it again and again with the razor until finally the barber said he couldn't do it anymore without just shaving off the lot.

Angry went home with his new super-short haircut, and that afternoon he took the final step. "I had a few rums, and I was feeling just good with the world, and I kept walking into the bathroom and looking in the mirror at my head and saying 'Yeah, that's fantastic'. But then, I'd turn around, and I'd hold the mirror up and you could still see the pink patch where I was balding. It was the only thing that annoyed me.

"Anyway, I got in the bath with the flask of rum, and I was feeling frivolous enough. I just laid back in the bath. It was one of those beautiful big, oldfashioned deep baths. You know, those cast-iron type baths on legs? And I was just lying back there, sipping the rum. I stood up, I got this mirror from the sill, I put it down on the taps, and I just got the shaver and I laid back in the bath and soaked my head. Then I just sat up, picked up the razor, and shaved it off. When I was doing it, I felt like I'd been waiting to do it forever. I thought to myself 'Why haven't I done this before? Why have I gone through all this agony about losing my hair at a young age?' The sense of freedom, liberation...it was the most delicious feeling. I mean it was just the best.

"From that moment on, I knew I'd never have hair again. And when I stood up in the bath and looked in the mirror holding the little mirror up so I could see the back, there it was. No bald spots. There's wasn't hair, then a thin bit, then a bald part. It was just complete, 100 per cent. It was fantastic. That's why I walk past people in the street, and it's like I'm a born-again Christian, I have this compulsion to say to every balding guy 'Hey, set yourself free!'"

"ANYWAY, I GOT IN THE BATH WITH THE FLASK OF RUM, AND I WAS FEELING FRIVOLOUS ENOUGH. I JUST LAID BACK IN THE BATH... THEN I JUST SAT UP, PICKED UP THE RAZOR, AND SHAVED IT OFF. WHEN I WAS DOING IT, I FELT LIKE I'D BEEN WAITING TO DO IT FOREVER."

Angry was delighted about every aspect of his new "chrome dome", until it came time to break the news to his mother. Rosemay says she was horrified when he finally came to see her. "I remember he rang me and he said 'I've done something, Mum, that's going to upset you.' I remember saying 'What is it now?' because I was getting to the

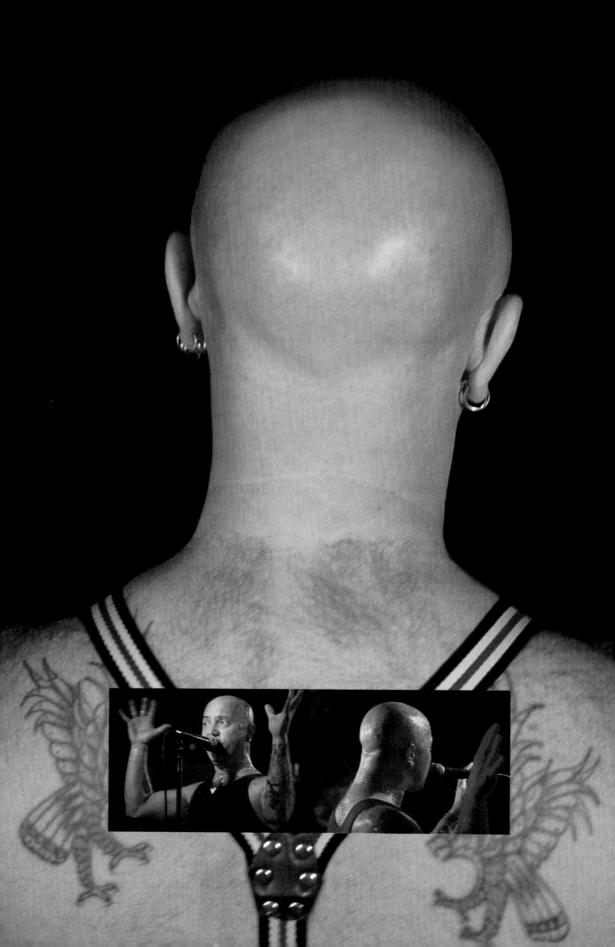

stage where I was used to being upset about different things. He said, 'I've shaved all my hair off.' For a minute I was stunned. I just couldn't think. I thought he must have cut it off short, but he came round to dinner the next night I thought 'Oh, my stars!' After he went home I sat and I cried and I cried. I thought he would let his hair grow back, but he never did."

The bald head has just become part of Angry's image. He says he loves the feel of it, and he loves the strength it gives him. It used to create a stir when he walked into bars, particularly if he was with Mangy and the other boys. They looked like trouble, and Angry says he was often aware of people looking at them suspiciously. For a little bloke though, Angry believes it does no harm to look intimidating.

THE BALD HEAD HAS JUST BECOME PART OF ANGRY'S IMAGE. HE SAYS HE LOVES THE FEEL OF IT, AND HE LOVES THE STRENGTH IT GIVES HIM.

Angry's never considered growing his hair again, and the bald head has almost stopped shocking people. "Every morning when I get up and go to the shower, I shave my head, and it's just a great, great feeling. I look in the mirror, and there's me!"

Over the years, even Rosemay says she's become used to it.

After the breakup of Buster, Angry just hung around for six months or so. He did get a band together with Lobby Lloyde. Lobby's band the Coloured Balls had just split up too, so it was natural for them to come together. They had pretty much the same idea about rock and roll, and pretty much the same fan club. They worked together under the name of the Angry Anderson and Lobby Lloyde Band. It didn't last long because they were just too much to handle. As Angry says "The band was monstrous...it was just a big heavy rock band. We weren't getting a lot of work because we were too loud, and they didn't like the kind of crowd we attracted."

When that line-up folded, Angry was truly at a loose end. He hung around in Melbourne until the end of 1974 and most of 1975. He was doing very little, but he had big dreams "I was a huge fan of Rod Stewart and the Faces, and I wanted to form a concept band like that with lots of Rod Stewart covers."

Whenever he'd sit around drinking and smoking with his mates, he'd start talking about all his big ideas. He wasn't prepared to give up.

He was sure there was something out there for him. One day some friends started talking about Sydney saying it was the place to be because the music scene was really moving. Angry had a new mate at this stage called Mick Cocks, and when he suggested they move to Sydney together, Angry jumped at the offer. More than anything else he wanted to escape Melbourne. As he says "As soon as Mick suggested we move to Sydney, I was there. Someone gave me the opportunity and I just said 'Yes!'"

"Don't worry, Mrs Clark
— most babies look like
Angry Anderson."

WITH ROSE TATTOO, THERE WAS
MONTHS OF REARRANGEMENT -
DIFFERENT DRUMMERS, DIFFERENT
GUITARISTS, DIFFERENT SINGERS.
BUT THE MISSION WAS ALWAYS THE
SAME. IN THE BEGINNING IT WAS
JUST THREE GUYS, PETE WELLS, IAN
RILEN, AND ANGRY ANDERSON,
TRYING TO PULL TOGETHER THEIR
VISION OF ROCK AND ROLL.

'ROSE TATTOO WAS A WAY OF GETTING RID OF
ALL THAT BOTTLED-UP ANGER AND VIOLENCE AND SADNESS
AND FRUSTRATION THAT I'D BEEN SUBDUING FOR SO MANY YEARS.'

THE BOYS CLUB

These days, when people talk about Angry Anderson, the camps are split. Some people think of the maniacal rock and roll bad boy from Rose Tattoo. Others think of the rough diamond, champion of causes from the "Midday Show". It's hard to reconcile the two different sides to his character. As he sees it, it's all just part of his make-up. It's not that he's reformed over the years, or that he somehow turned over a new leaf and became a nice guy after Rose Tattoo. From his point of view, he's still both things, the bad boy and the do-gooder rolled into one.

When you hear some of the stories though, it's hard to imagine that one man can be capable of such extremes...that the madman who screamed his way to fame with Rose Tattoo, is the same guy who gently comforted a little girl dying of cancer. That the loud-mouth with the head-butting habit is the same guy with a dedication to making parents buckle their children safely into cars. It just doesn't seem possible.

ROSE TATTOO THE YIN AND YANG

In fact, when Angry first made his move to stardom with Rose Tattoo, there was only one thing the reviewers could agree upon - that he was a surprising person. That he was more intelligent than he made out, that he was deeper than he cared to let people know, and that he was much more than just a moronic brawler.

Moving to Sydney took Angry into a different music scene, and a different lifestyle. Eventually it led him to Rose Tattoo, international stardom, and one of the most extraordinary chapters of his life.

No rock band in history has just come together without some juggling or some compromise. The perfect line up has never just clicked immediately into place. With Rose Tattoo, there was months of rearrangement - different drummers, different guitarists, different

singers. But the mission was always the same. In the beginning it was just three guys, Pete Wells, Ian Rilen, and Angry Anderson, trying to pull together their vision of rock and roll.

Pete and Angry were nothing more than acquaintances when Rose Tattoo was first conceived, but as it turned out, they had loads in common. By fate or coincidence, they had actually been doing rounds of the same pubs and gigs for years. Without knowing it, they were members of a mutual admiration society. Whenever Angry had been in Sydney he'd gone out to see Pete's band Buffalo. Whenever Buster was in town, Pete had done the same.

They didn't hit it off immediately as partners. Although Pete had always admired Angry's antics on stage, he wasn't sure he wanted to get so involved with such a lunatic. Angry's reputation was already travelling fast, and Pete had heard he was nothing but trouble...a bald-headed nut from Melbourne who wreaked havoc wherever he went. But, eventually, friends persuaded them to put their heads together. After that, it was just a matter of time. Pete and Angry had almost exactly the same idea of what they wanted to do in rock and roll, so after some negotiating and some changes...wham...bam! Rose Tattoo was born.

As Angry says, the first few months of uncertainty were essential to get the mix right. "The band was so unique and so much larger than life. It's a process of experimentation, attracting different people. All the ingredients were there...we just had to go through some minor adjustments to find the right band chemically. When we'd got it all together, and we'd consolidated the line-up, then we knew it was going to work."

Pete and Angry set one early rule for the band. They agreed upon it in an instant. Even if nothing else was certain, all the members of the band would be tattooed. For Angry and Pete, both covered extensively, there was just no case for anything else.

The band's name was Pete's idea, but people have often thought it was Angry's. They've assumed that the Rose was for his mother, and the Tattoo was for obvious reasons. In fact, the name has more romantic origins. Pete took it from the Tennessee Williams novel *The Rose Tattoo*. He liked the notion of the yin and the yang, the feminine Rose and the masculine Tattoo. Angry wanted to call the band "Assault and Battery", the name eventually given to their second album, but when Pete suggested Rose Tattoo, Angry agreed it was perfect.

The official birthday gig was on 1 January 1976 at Chequers in Sydney. There was Angry as lead singer, Peter Wells on slide guitar, Ian Rilen on bass guitar, Michael Cocks, and a bloke named Stork, on drums. Digger and Geordie, who are both considered to be part of the "original" Rose Tattoo joined slightly later.

Rose Tattoo was Buster Brown grown up. They performed like no other band. They were as wild and as outrageous as a band could be. They lived the bad life, but they knew they had all they needed to make a huge mark on the Australian music scene. As Angry says "The great thing about the band was that it was just so arrogantly, so bombastically self assured. There was no stopping it."

The music was loud. Seriously loud. Some reviewers described it as mind-bending. And the boys were rough. They looked about as dangerous as any group of guys could look. They were punks, tattooed, with wild aggressive hairstyles and rings through their ears. When an English writer first saw them he was amazed. He said in his review the next day, "This band are so *tough*. They could knock your head off just by strumming a guitar chord."

They looked like something from out of this world. If they walked through the door of a pub together they silenced the crowd. They were rough heads. Their clothes were always filthy, but more than that, their clothes were always tight.

ROSE TATTOO WAS BUSTER BROWN GROWN UP. THEY PERFORMED LIKE NO OTHER BAND. THEY WERE AS WILD AND AS OUTRAGEOUS AS A BAND COULD BE … AS ANGRY SAYS "THE GREAT THING ABOUT THE BAND WAS THAT IT WAS JUST SO ARROGANTLY, SO BOMBASTICALLY SELF ASSURED. THERE WAS NO STOPPING IT."

Super, super tight. They made it a practice to wear clothes that stuck to them, and they loved to shock people with the size of the holes in their jeans. Often members of the band wore jeans that opened and gaped so badly around the crutch that they may just as well have not worn anything at all.

The clothes and the haircuts weren't the result of any lack of care or thought. In fact, they were all meticulously designed to suit. It was all part of a look, part of the total image of the band. As Angry says, "Pete Wells was responsible for the artistic inspiration of the band, but Ian Rilen was in charge of the look. He'd go out to the shops and buy a whole bunch of black T-shirts. Then he'd wash them, like, a couple of dozen times, and then throw them out in the backyard so we'd all jump on them and drag them around, to give them that rough, worn-out look. Then we'd put them on and he'd walk around us with razor blades and put nicks and cuts in them, so that they were suitably slashed and hacked. He'd take the sleeves off, because sleeves were out, and he'd rip off the neckband. It was even worse with our jeans.

ROSE TATTOO 1980 - MICK COCKS, PETER WELLS, GEORDIE LEACH, 'DIGGER' DALLAS ROYAL & ANGRY

"We still laugh about it now, because it must have been so funny, but there's visions of us...this group of grown men standing around in their underpants, while one stands on the table or on a chair, with his jeans on inside out, while the other guys pin them as tightly as they can to the body shape, right? Then you'd take them off, without getting stuck with the pins, and sew them up with the sewing machine. Turn them inside out, and of course, they fit your body perfectly because they're the same shape as your legs. When you actually sewed them and turned them the right way, you actually realised they weren't straight-legged jeans anymore, they actually had thighs and knees and calves to them, so they were completely skin tight."

The image was only one aspect of the band. Everything about them was different. They didn't talk like anyone else, they didn't act like anyone else, and they didn't play music like anyone else. They were like five buccaneers taking on the country. As Angry says, "Rose Tattoo was the ultimate boys club. We created it. We wrote the rules. It was like belonging to the most exclusive bastion of blokedom in the country. There wasn't, and hasn't been anything quite like it. It was a real exclusive club to belong to."

The band's impact was immediate, but its success was not. They certainly didn't hit the big time overnight. In fact, in the beginning, they were better at emptying a room than they were at filling one. "I can remember at some of our earliest performances we used to play gigs where there was a big audience, and like two or three songs into the set, they'd all leave. I mean there just wouldn't be anyone left in the room. The four or five or six people who were sort of pressed up against the bar ordering drink after drink, who wanted to stay there, who were sort of obsessed with it...they were the people we were playing for."

At first Chequers was the only venue that would have them, but slowly, some of the other clubs and pubs became more willing to take the risk. For many months, as a fledgling band, they just performed three or four times a week, doing four to six brackets a night. "I think we used to make 20 or 30 bucks out of it each week. But we'd get all the grog we could drink, and they'd feed us too."

Like Buster, they developed a cult following. "They were all radicals, people from the services, army, navy...every sort of misfit from Darlo to Paddo to the Cross to Bondi...we used to play at the Astor Hotel in Bondi. It was the lunatic fringe, it was the desperado territory. You know, it was all the misplaced, unwanted desperates."

Their first photo shoot wasn't even connected with music, or with the band as such. It was a fashion shoot. Peter Courette was working at the time as a photographer with *Mode* magazine. He'd seen Rose Tattoo perform and he just couldn't get over the way they looked. He took a chance and asked the guys to pose for him with some of the models. As Angry says, it was a strange assignment for a bunch of hard rockers. "There we are, blind drunk, with all these models and we were just there as props. We were incidentals."

It didn't take long though, before Rose Tattoo started making real news. Their major selling point was that they had street credibility. It was almost like they had the stamp of approval from the fashion makers and fashion followers of the day. They were just arty enough, in a blood and guts sort of way. They spent their whole time, either in rehearsal, or in pubs in Darlinghurst or Paddington, hanging out with unemployed actors and other musos. People like Jack Thompson and Bryan Brown.

They were down and dirty, and although they hated the description, they were being hailed as Australia's first real punk rock band.

The punk movement was already starting to emerge across Europe. Some of the first punk rockers had already made an impact on the major music charts with their safety pins and snarls. Rose Tattoo didn't quite fit into the category. They weren't true punks, but they were the closest thing on the Australian scene so it was a label they had to wear. In fact, they didn't really fit into any recognised music group. They were almost unclassifiable, somewhere near the ugly edge of rock, a loud mix between heavy metal and blues, but for that first year they were happy just to be getting the attention.

When Mick and Angry first arrived in Sydney they were forced to rough it on other people's lounge-room floors or spare bedrooms. But, as soon as they were able to, they established a house in Barcom Avenue, Darlinghurst. It was a band house. There were about twelve residents, the members of three different bands. The front room was lined with mattresses and egg cartons, homemade soundproofing. As Angry says, "We lived there for two reasons. Economically it was okay because those of us who could get on the dole could support and sustain the others. Also, it was such a trashy area that we fitted in. We

IT DIDN'T TAKE LONG THOUGH, BEFORE ROSE TATTOO STARTED MAKING REAL NEWS. THEIR MAJOR SELLING POINT WAS THAT THEY HAD STREET CREDIBILITY. IT WAS ALMOST LIKE THEY HAD THE STAMP OF APPROVAL FROM THE FASHION MAKERS AND FASHION FOLLOWERS OF THE DAY. THEY WERE JUST ARTY ENOUGH, IN A BLOOD AND GUTS SORT OF WAY.

were part of the Darlo crowd so we could walk around looking like freaks, and it didn't really piss anyone off."

Each band had a bedroom, and Rose Tattoo's bedroom was upstairs. Pete and Ian didn't live there. It was just Digger, Mick, Angry and occasionally Geordie. They had three mattresses on the floor in the one room. It was textbook stuff for a rock and roll band. "We're talking squalor," says Angry. "We're talking like mattresses where you wake up during the night and you literally have to brush the cockroaches off you. We're talking about mattresses that we've pulled off rubbish heaps. We're talking about sheets that were disgusting. I mean, what can I tell you? It was squalor."

The boys from Rose Tattoo revelled in it. They had no possessions...maybe one or two pairs of jeans each, two pair of socks, and nothing else. They were always broke, always out of work, but that was just the way they liked it. As Angry says, "It was just our lifestyle. We went at it. We had no money. You know our clothes...we wore on stage what we wore on the street. We'd go for a job interview, and we'd turn up looking like a member of Rose Tattoo, so of course we'd never get the job, which was fantastic because we didn't want it anyway."

The sleeping arrangements were unusual. There were always girls coming over to stay, and with twelve blokes and only three bedrooms, there was very little privacy. Angry says somehow it wasn't as debauched as it sounds, but it wasn't unusual for three couples to share the same room every night. "Sometimes we'd try to drift upstairs one couple at a time. You know, we'd give them forty minutes, and then go upstairs. I can remember us talking to one another in the dark while we were having sex...not just talking to your partner, but your partner talking to the girl in the bed next door, and her talking to the girl in the next bed. Do you know what I mean?"

The parties at Barcom Avenue were legendary. There were outrageous drinking and drug festivals, and wild wild nights. "We did everything on a really base level. Everything was reduced to its base...we drank cheap grog and we took almost anything anyone ever gave us."

THE PARTIES AT BARCOM AVENUE WERE LEGENDARY. THERE WERE OUTRAGEOUS DRINKING AND DRUG FESTIVALS, AND WILD WILD NIGHTS. "WE DID EVERYTHING ON A REALLY BASE LEVEL. EVERYTHING WAS REDUCED TO ITS BASE...WE DRANK CHEAP GROG AND WE TOOK ALMOST ANYTHING ANYONE EVER GAVE US."

Drugs were just part of the household requirements. For Angry, he was mostly into hashish and cannabis, but the regular drugs of the day were acid trips and Mandrax, and they were always in abundance. Someone always had a bag of something in their pocket.

It was like they were living in the world's longest rock and roll party. Many nights just degenerated into orgies of sex, drugs and alcohol. The typical scenes were extraordinary. As Angry says, "Changing partners in one night, that was just what you did. You know, the object of the game was to sleep with as many people as you could. That's what they were all about. It wasn't unusual to swap partners from week to week. You're in bed with a girl one night, and then she's in the next bed with someone else."

Talking about it now, Angry says it all seems wild and outlandish, but at the time, it was just the way things were. They accepted the lifestyle. It was part of being in a rock band. It was part of being in Rose Tattoo.

It was in Barcom Avenue that Angry had one of his closest calls with the police. It was virtually a "Hawaii 5-0" scene, and it got way out of hand. Angry and the boys looked so serious and so mean, they sent police into a frenzy of suspicion. As Angry says, it's funny looking back now, but it wasn't funny at the time.

One of the girls who stayed in the house was arrested for shoplifting, so when she told the police where she lived, they turned up at Barcom Avenue to check things out. They got much more than they bargained for. "We were rehearsing in this small room at the front of the house, five guys with amps and mattresses, and about twelve police just kicked the front door down. They couldn't get in to the bandroom because it was all padlocked for the equipment and stuff."

The guys were rehearsing so loudly, they couldn't hear anything, so the police were banging on the door for a good few minutes before

IT WAS IN BARCOM AVENUE THAT ANGRY HAD ONE OF HIS CLOSEST CALLS WITH THE POLICE. IT WAS VIRTUALLY A "HAWAII 5-0" SCENE, AND IT GOT WAY OUT OF HAND. ANGRY AND THE BOYS LOOKED SO SERIOUS AND SO MEAN, THEY SENT POLICE INTO A FRENZY OF SUSPICION.

they got any response. "We came to the end of a song, and we could hear this dull thump thump thump on the door. So, we've opened it, and the house is full of coppers. There were a couple of older blokes, senior detectives, and they had all these young coppers with them. Most of them were pissed. The uniformed guys weren't, but some of the others were. They saw us, and they just freaked. There we all were, stripped, because this place had no air-conditioning...like not even a window. It was like an oven in there. There we are...one of us is short, bald, tattooed, another one is big, tattooed, with cropped hair. In those days, I think the guys were going through their flame red phase, halfway through fluorescent pink and henna red, and they all had real crew cuts. When we opened the door the cops all pulled guns and stuff. It was like they freaked. They probably thought they were going to come across some long-haired hippy band. They backed off, they did the whole thing...stuck guns in our mouths, in our ears. You know 'One move and we'll blow your heads off'. It was that kind of thing.

"They just went berserk. I remember we were in the kitchen and one copper pulls this packet of sugar out of the cupboard. 'Aha', he says and he holds it up. So he puts it on the table, rips the top off, and he just tips it out on the table, looking at us in the eye the whole time. You know, he'd watched too much TV. He poured it all on the table, and he said 'Before I go through this stuff, you're going to tell me what's in it'. I was a bit cocky, and I said 'Sugar'. I got a crack in the side of the head for that. So, he spreads it all out, and there's nothing in there but sugar and he said, 'This might look like sugar now, but it mightn't be sugar when it gets down to the station'. In other words, he was saying we're going to drop on you. We thought 'Oh, now this is serious'. We sobered up basically, and from then on, we just said yes sir, no sir, three bags full sir. An older bloke, a senior detective, arrived just after the circus got under way. But there was ten or fifteen minutes of just absolute lunacy before he arrived. I mean these blokes were cowboys, they were idiots.

"This senior, senior bloke arrived smoking a pipe. He said 'What's happening?' We told him, and of course it contradicted what the

IN THOSE DAYS, I THINK THE GUYS WERE GOING THROUGH THEIR FLAME RED PHASE, HALFWAY THROUGH FLUORESCENT PINK AND HENNA RED, AND THEY ALL HAD REAL CREW CUTS. WHEN WE OPENED THE DOOR THE COPS ALL PULLED GUNS AND STUFF. IT WAS LIKE THEY FREAKED.

younger cops were saying. He basically looked at a couple of these guys who were in charge of the pack, and he said 'I think this is just a colossal waste of time. I think the best thing we can do is just take names and addresses and get about our business.' He was speaking very quietly. So they just lined us up, and did the name and address and they just left."

The raid was a one-off event, and most of the time Barcom Avenue was just a band hang-out. It was a messy, noisy rehearsal space, an over-crowded boarding house.

On stage, Angry was pushing the limits even further than he'd pushed them with Buster. His performances were always physical and out of control. He came home from every gig covered in blood and bruises. Newspapers and magazines were incredulous at his level of self-abuse. It was like, if Angry didn't knock himself out for the audience, his heart wasn't in it.

As he says, he found everything in Rose Tattoo that he'd found in Buster, and more. He used the band as an outlet. He figured if he could express some of his rage on stage, then perhaps he'd find it easier to tone down his behaviour off stage. To some degree, it worked. As he says, "Rose Tattoo was a way of getting rid of all that bottled up anger and violence and sadness and frustration that I'd been subduing the wrong way for the right reasons for so many years to fit in. To be like anybody else. Not to be the person that nobody wants to invite to a party because he throws up in the dip and wants to fight the host. There was a constant struggle just going on with me the whole time. Not to just give in to that. Not to be that."

Buster Brown had given AC/DC their drummer, Phil Rudd, a few years earlier, so the relationship between Rose Tattoo and AC/DC was very affectionate. The AC/DC boys used to regularly turn up at Rose Tattoo gigs, and often Angus and Bonn would end up on stage with Angry and the boys. For the fans, they were great nights - spontaneous and raw. Sometimes, there would be so many guys on stage at once, there would barely be enough room for them all to move. The venues would shake and thunder, with the whole crowd thumping and yelling as one.

At the time, AC/DC were huge in Australia, and were just beginning to take off overseas. They were being handled by Alberts of

IN ALL THE EARLY PHOTOGRAPHS, IT'S HARD TO SPOT A FEMALE FACE IN THE FIRST FEW ROWS OF THE AUDIENCE. THERE'S JUST ROWS OF MEN, REACHING OUT TO ANGRY, FACES TWISTED WITH THE NOISE, AND THE HEAT AND THE PUSH FROM THE CROWD BEHIND.

Sydney, so with all the common gigs, it didn't take long for the Alberts producers to take an interest in Rose Tattoo. They came along to a gig one night, and within a week, Rose Tattoo had an offer to join the Alberts stable.

Angry was totally committed. He loved the lifestyle. He loved Rose Tattoo. He loved the boys club. As he says, it was a special time in the music industry. "In those days there was a real brothers in arms mentality. There was a real camaraderie. You know, members of Sherbert used to come and watch the Tatts. So did members of Ted Mulray Gang, John Paul Young's band at the time, and other bands who seemingly had nothing in common with us. And vice versa. I've always loved Sherbert, but the reason I so publicly put shit on them in those days was because Angry Anderson, the frontman for Rose Tattoo, would not be expected to love Sherbert, where in truth, I loved pop music. Also, I liked Sherbert because I thought they were better than a lot of the other bands around at the time."

Rose Tattoo cut their first single with "Bad Boy (for love)" on the A side, and "Snow Queen" on the B side. Almost as soon as the single was finished, Ian Rilen decided to quit the band. That made an opening for Geordie, who'd been hanging around on and off since the band had first started. With Geordie, the boys recorded their first album...it was released under the name of "Rose Tattoo" in Australia, but overseas it had a more punchy title. The importers called it "Rock n' Roll Outlaws".

As soon as the album was out, Rose Tattoo hit the road. They spent the next year living literally out of a suitcase, touring the length and breadth of Australia. They played at just about every pub and club in every small town. They were a small-time band, so they still had to rough it with most things. "First we travelled in a kombi, then in a series of cars...later on when the band got more of a profile we hired cars and vans. I can remember, like so many other people in this country, doing trips to Melbourne where you'd pack the van or the truck so that there was three feet between the top of the stack and the roof where you could put mattresses and the band could sleep. In the early days we only had one roadie, and Geordie and I used to do the rest. We enjoyed it because it was such physical work."

They were very much a boys' drinking band. They were seen as brute macho, so they were recognised as blokes' territory. In all the early photographs, it's hard to spot a female face in the first few rows of the audience. There's just rows of men, reaching out to Angry, faces twisted with the noise, and the heat and the push from the crowd behind.

They started making big news. Towns geared up for their arrival weeks in advance. In many places having Rose Tattoo arrive in the main street was something like playing host to a freak show. Angry and the boys looked out of place enough in the city, but in some of the country towns, they stood out so severely they looked more like they came from another planet. Loyal fans turned up everywhere, and word travelled quickly about the sensation they were causing at live gigs.

The band went through good times and bad times. "We broke up and reformed all the time...we were irrational, taking lots of drugs, doing lots of booze, living on the road. We shuffled members, and we'd have a disagreement and walk out saying 'That's it', but two weeks later we'd be crying on each other's shoulder and looking forward to the next tour."

ALTHOUGH HE WAS LIVING THE WILDEST LIFESTYLE, ANGRY HAD A SOCIAL CONSCIENCE EVEN THEN. WHEN ROCK WRITERS CAME TO TALK TO HIM, THEY'D ASK HIM ABOUT THE BAND, AND HE'D START TALKING TO THEM ABOUT HOMELESSNESS OR STREET KIDS.

When it came to the press, Rose Tattoo always made good copy, so writers were never short of fodder. Although he was living the wildest lifestyle, Angry had a social conscience even then. When rock writers came to talk to him, they'd ask him about the band, and he'd start talking to them about homelessness or street kids. Writers weren't interested, and it was a hard lesson for him to learn.

"After a few months of being newsworthy, magazines wanted to talk to us and photograph us, and you know, I was doing endless interviews," says Angry. "There's only so much you can say about the band, and then you've got to talk about other things. But basically, rock journos just want you to tell them that over the last month you were with so many women, took so many drugs, drank so much alcohol etc. In other words, they want you to be what they think you are. When I first started doing interviews, you know I loved the attention, but some of the best interviews I've ever done were cut down to about two paragraphs, and none of the issues were ever raised."

For writers, Rose Tattoo was the copy. Angry Anderson was the news. No one was interested in what he had to say about it.

In the Rose Tattoo years, stories about Angry grew and grew. As he says, if he'd done only half the things of which he was accused, he'd

"ANGRY" ANDERSON — IN FULL CRY

TATTOOED TERRORS!

"Angry" Anderson, Australia's original punk rocker, loves shocking little old ladies in buses.

by BRYAN PATTERSON

"You see them staring out of the windows when you walk down the street. They're horrified," says the lead singer of Rose Tattoo.

"We all love being outrageous."

The band's effect on elderly females is hardly surprising.

Angry — he answers to no other name — is bald, short and stocky.

His tall, gaunt partners sport flaming red hair short-cropped at the front with tails at the back.

And they all wear the band's trademark ... anti-social tattoos.

This motley crew never wanted fame.

They originally formed a year ago as an underground punk band: Australia's answer to the likes of Johnny Rotten and The Sex Pistols.

"We thought it was highly unlikely that we'd get anywhere but it was possible that we might," said Angry.

"We just wanted to sing punk songs and have a nasty image.

For the first six months the band achieved its aim. People hated them.

"We were spat at, punched and abused. It didn't worry us at all."

But something went wrong.

Bad Boy, a single the band recorded, suddenly sprung up the charts.

Rose Tattoo became something it neither wanted nor expected — a well-known band.

But Angry and the boys have learned to live with this fact of life and to continue "freaking people out".

Their personalities have remained intact and they all live together in a room in Sydney "where we breed cockroaches."

"We've managed to remain anonymous," says Angry.

"People can't tell the band members apart, except for me of course.

"And we dig dropping clangers on stage and getting kicked out for playing too loud."

Angry is glad that Rose Tattoo was the first punk rock band to make it big in Australia but doesn't think the musicians look all that unusual.

"You see more extravagant punks on the streets. There are a lot of sharp-looking guys around.

"Our stage act is really theatre but it's not contrived.

"We all had tattoos long before the band and we're playing ourselves.

"When I was young I was a larrikin. You don't grow out of something like that.

"Some people stay with us at concerts but others come once and never return. They're freaked out."

When he's not freaking out people, Angry travels incognito — he wears a hat to cover the bald pate.

"It's nice not to be recognised sometimes.

"I'm not a lair all the time."

have been a monster. At one time, a newspaper reported that he'd been charged with carnal knowledge, which simply wasn't true. The newspaper did print a retraction many months later, but it was hidden toward the back pages. It hardly made up for the headline which basically screamed that Angry Anderson had taken sexual advantage of a fourteen-year-old girl.

Many articles also talked about Angry as a person who'd spent long periods of time in prison, when in fact Angry's only experiences in prison cells were for eight or twelve hour spells, usually for being drunk and disorderly. There was one night in Perth where Angry was arrested for using offensive language on stage, and another time in

Kempsey where he was arrested for assault, but he was never the longtime ex-crim that people talked about. As Angry says, "The things I'm supposed to have done are unbelievable. I could have been locked up for most of them. You know, people come up and still say 'I heard this about you', or 'I heard that about you', and you say 'No, that didn't happen'. They just look at you. They want to believe it, but they look at you and they're saying, 'I know you did you bastard.' Even though you're saying no, they're saying they know you did. It's damned if you do, and damned if you don't."

Angry copped most of the flak without too much complaint, but he did get frustrated with the stereotypes. He didn't mind so much if someone met him, talked to him, and then decided he was a jerk, but he hated the articles that summed him up unfairly. Some writers would analyse him without ever meeting him, and others would arrive at the interview with such a definite preconceived idea of who Angry was, and of what he was about, that they may just as well have not turned up at all.

It was all part of being a rock and roller. There were just so many critics who weren't comfortable with Angry because he broke the mould.

"THERE IS NO SUBJECT ON WHICH HE WILL NOT OFFER A MOUTHFUL, AND THE WORK OF THE INTERVIEWER WAS ESSENTIALLY TO KEEP HIM TO ONE SUBJECT AT A TIME. ALTHOUGH HE LOOKS LIKE A MIDGET WRESTLER, ANGRY IS IN FACT A SENSITIVE PERFORMER, A DEEP THINKER, AND A PHILOSOPHER."

At one stage, a *Juke* magazine article basically admitted the press was selling Angry short. The writer made what almost amounted to an apology: "The fifteen minutes allocated for the interview extended to a three hour yap session about everything from science and philosophy to the latest in porno movies. I left impressed with his courtesy and general knowledge, and somewhat sheepish that I'd dismissed him as a moronic jerk, simply for the way he looked."

Years later, when Angry's profile was big enough to earn him a complete feature article in *Playboy* magazine, the senior contributing editor Phil Jarratt made a similar observation. "There is no subject on which he will not offer a mouthful, and the work of the interviewer was essentially to keep him to one subject at a time. Although he looks like a midget wrestler, Angry is in fact a sensitive performer, a deep thinker, and a philosopher. One could disagree with some of what he said, but the force and intelligence with which he presented his argument could never be faulted. Above all else, what came through in the taping sessions was his genuine love for people and life, and his almost frightening ambition to make this a better world."

Even comedy writers and cartoon artists had their turn when it came to Rose Tattoo. Angry says he realised the band had made its mark in Australia the day they were the subject of a skit on "The Paul Hogan Show". For him, that was the big time. That was real media coverage, real fame. He wasn't in the least bit upset about the send-up. Paul Hogan was the best-known, most loved comedian of the time, so it was flattering enough just to earn a mention on the show, let alone an entire skit.

Angry took it as a real indication of the success the band had achieved. "I turned on 'The Paul Hogan Show' and saw him wearing a skull cap, with tattoos, pretending he was so awfully, awfully camp, singing 'I'm a rock 'n roll outlaw'. They were all mimicking the band, ripping off Rose Tattoo, and they'd made me camp. Paul Hogan was skipping from one side of the stage to the other, swinging a chain. When I saw that...that's when I knew we'd arrived. Pete Wells rang me the next day and he said 'We've made it'."

In many ways a band is a bit like a biker club, and like a biker club, Rose Tattoo had some unspoken club laws. To outsiders, the rules would have seemed bizarre, completely hypocritical. Drugs were part of everyday life...loads of them, but heroin and the other "hard drugs" were just no go. Angry had tried heroin, along with just about every other drug, but by the time he reached Rose Tattoo he was radically opposed to it. It was a habit drug, not a party drug, and the only habit any of the Rose Tattoo members had was alcohol. Heroin did come to play a part in the lives of some members of the band in later years, but it wasn't until the band had basically broken up.

Even some of Rose Tattoo's earliest songs pushed the antidrug message. On the first album, there's a song called "Astra Wally", written by Ian Rilen. The lyrics make the message clear: Astra Wally/He's a real mean cat/He gets around with caps in his hat/He drives around in a Jag Mark 10/Go do a deal Wally, Kill another friend.

When Angry talks to kids now about drink driving, he says they sometimes question him on his own history and reputation. They want to know how he can tell them what to do when his own behaviour was obviously so reckless. As he says, "I'm not like I was any more, but even in the old days, when I was drinking I used to worry. I never got a licence because I drank. At gigs I would always say 'If you've been drinking don't drive home'. That was when I was at my worst. So even though I was a chronic drunk, I hated and despised people who drank and then drove cars and killed other people. The good thing was that I always had enough self-respect and enough compassion not to do it myself either. Even when I was at my worst."

"AT THE END OF 'SUICIDE CITY' IT GETS INTO A REALLY CRAZY THING. IT'S SUPPOSED TO BE INSANITY, AND I'D STRANGLE MYSELF WITH THE MICROPHONE CORD UNTIL I PASSED OUT." THIS WAS THE DARK SIDE, THE MADMAN. IT WAS THE SIDE THAT FRIGHTENED EVERYONE, EVEN ANGRY HIMSELF.

Just as the first album was climbing slowly up the charts, Rose Tattoo got a new manager. His name was Robbie Williams. He was a committed rock promoter, who had tremendous faith in the band. He believed wholeheartedly they could make it to number one worldwide. He had absolute confidence in Angry as a dynamic frontman, and he believed he had the talent and charisma to be the next big name in rock.

Once with the band, Robbie decided he was there for the long haul. Rose Tattoo weren't an easy band to manage. They were unreliable, irrational, and usually drunk, but he believed in the band, so he ended up staying until the very last gig years later.

The band's profile grew, and as they got bigger, Angry's stage antics got wilder. He became as extravagant and as outrageous as the crowd wanted him to be. They'd yell for blood, sweat and tears, and Angry would deliver. He was the tragic, drunken outlaw, the bad boy of rock and roll at his worst. No one knew what to make of him. He was dangerous, radical, and stupid. He had one trick on stage that shocked even the hardest fans. "When we wrote the album there's this song on it called 'Suicide City'. It's about Canberra because Mick told me that there was this article talking about how Canberra has the highest suicide rate of any Australian city. So we wrote a song about it. We used to do this as the last song in the set. So what I used to

ROSE TATTOO AT THE MARQUEE.
'THE SAME STAGE AS JIMI HENDRIX,
PINK FLOYD AND LED ZEPPELIN'

do...I'd sometimes put a plastic bag over my head till I passed out. All the audience can see is the eye sockets, and the plastic bag pumping in and out over the mouth. The crew would all rush over after I'd passed out, and thump my chest."

He had another trick too, which was just as obscene. "At the end of 'Suicide City' it gets into a really crazy thing. It's supposed to be insanity, and I'd strangle myself with the microphone cord until I passed out."

This was the dark side, the madman. It was the side that frightened everyone, even Angry himself. Pete used to talk about it, saying there was something magic in the drama of rock and roll. He used to say, "You know you've made it as a rock performer when the crowd comes just to see whether or not you die." As Angry says now, there's no doubt that's why some of the fans were there. If it ever happened, they wanted to play their ghoulish part in history. And, the fact was, if there was an Australian rock star likely to go to those extremes on stage, Angry Anderson would surely have taken honours on top of the list.

IN THE EARLY YEARS, ANGRY'S STAGE ANTICS EVEN EARNED ROSE TATTOO THE DISTINCTION OF BEING THE ONLY ACT BANNED FOR LIFE FROM THE ABC'S "COUNTDOWN" SHOW.

As manager of the band, the 'Suicide City' finale was the one thing Robbie couldn't tolerate. He witnessed Angry taking a thousand risks in their years together, but he never got used to watching him go through the suicide motions. He always though he'd go too far. Every time Angry tied the cord around his neck and passed out, Robbie would argue the prank should be cut from the act. It was something he and Angry locked horns over many times. As Robbie says, "When I first saw him do it, I really freaked out. We had a lot of heated arguments. I was really worried about it, but in the end I had to take his word for it that he was very much in control of things. He'd say 'I'm not going to die, because once I pass out, I can't keep any pressure on the rope around my neck because I lose my strength, so I'm not going to die'. You see, it was one of those things. It was so honest. To him, it wasn't theatrics or anything like that. You know, it was part of the song. It was like he couldn't deliver the vocal without strangling himself."

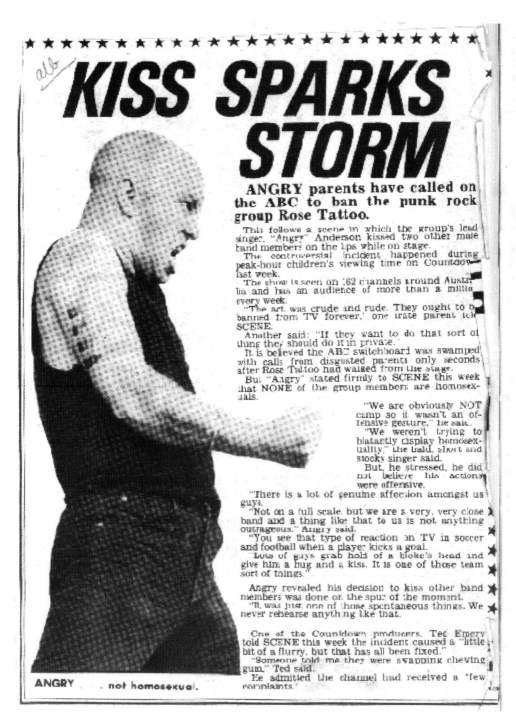

★ ★

KISS SPARKS STORM

ANGRY parents have called on the ABC to ban the punk rock group Rose Tattoo.

This follows a scene in which the group's lead singer, "Angry" Anderson kissed two other male band members on the lips while on stage.

The controversial incident happened during peak-hour children's viewing time on Countdown last week.

The show is seen on 162 channels around Australia and has an audience of more than a million every week.

"The act was crude and rude. They ought to be banned from TV forever," one irate parent told SCENE.

Another said: "If they want to do that sort of thing they should do it in private."

It is believed the ABC switchboard was swamped with calls from disgusted parents only seconds after Rose Tattoo had walked from the stage.

But "Angry" stated firmly to SCENE this week that NONE of the group members are homosexuals.

"We are obviously NOT camp so it wasn't an offensive gesture," he said.

"We weren't trying to blatantly display homosexuality," the bald, short and stocky singer said.

But, he stressed, he did not believe his actions were offensive.

"There is a lot of genuine affection amongst us guys.

"Not on a full scale, but we are a very, very close band and a thing like that to us is not anything outrageous," Angry said.

"You see that type of reaction on TV in soccer and football when a player kicks a goal.

"Lots of guys grab hold of a bloke's head and give him a hug and a kiss. It is one of those team sort of things."

Angry revealed his decision to kiss other band members was done on the spur of the moment.

"It was just one of those spontaneous things. We never rehearse anything like that.

One of the Countdown producers, Ted Emery told SCENE this week the incident caused a "little bit of a flurry, but that has all been fixed."

"Someone told me they were swapping chewing gum," Ted said.

He admitted the channel had received a "few complaints."

ANGRY . . . not homosexual.

THE STORM ERUPTS OVER ANGRY'S CONTROVERSIAL KISS

In the early years, Angry's stage antics even earned Rose Tattoo the distinction of being the only act banned for life from the ABC's "Countdown" show. As Angry says now, it was one of those freak events that snowballed. The band were slammed in the press from one end of the country to the other. Angry is full of contradictions. On one hand he horrifies an audience by suffocating himself on stage, on the other he's full of concern that people understand that he never really meant to offend anyone the way he did that day at the ABC.

It was just a kiss, tame in comparison to his other antics, but it developed myth-like proportions. Angry's adamant that people understand exactly what happened, how innocent it really was.

It was the day of the AFL grand final, and "Countdown" was going to air live in the Sydney studios of the ABC. Rose Tattoo was not the kind of band that usually appeared on "Countdown", because the show was designed for a very young audience. Most of the ratings points came from real teeny boppers so the producers usually stayed safe with the more clean-cut pop acts. But when it came to Rose Tattoo, Ian "Molly" Meldrum convinced them to take a risk.

As far as Angry's concerned, Molly Meldrum is one of the exceptional people of the Australian music industry. As he says, "Molly put us on television against all better advice. I know he took a big personal risk and so did the producers of the show. 'Countdown' was probably the most innovative rock music program in the world at the time. Ian had an uncanny knack of being able to recognise the two aspects that make up this industry...the show and the biz. He can recognise things that are artistically inspirational, and he can also recognise things that are going to be bankable. So he put Rose Tattoo on his show. Now the band was always appreciative of this...we recognised the benefits of this kind of exposure so we played the game. We really wanted to. If we were going to be on 'Countdown' we were going to be true to ourselves, but we weren't going to swear, and we weren't going to punch anyone or anything...you know, we were going to play the game."

By the day of the famous kiss, Rose Tattoo had already performed on 'Countdown' a couple of times, and they'd behaved themselves, so there was no reason for anyone to worry that this occasion would be any different. Rehearsals started at 10 am so the boys had a lot of hanging around to do. They put a television set in their dressing room so they could watch the big game, and they just drank beer and Scotch until the show went to air at 5.00 in the afternoon. As Angry says, "During the course of the day we got progressively more and more drunk. We'd go out and rehearse, then run back to the room and suck down as many cans as we could to make up for lost time watching the grand final. By the time we got to do the show we were not only in a highly charged state, we were caught between the two poles...the adrenalin rush of going on stage, and the lethargy of the alcohol dragging us back. That is enough to create an atmosphere of volatility and unpredictability.

THE KISS WENT OUT TO EVERY SINGLE TV SWITCHED ON TO THE ABC, AND WITHIN SECONDS THE ABC SWITCHBOARD WAS SHUT DOWN WITH COMPLAINTS. ANGRY THOUGHT NOTHING OF IT UNTIL HE SAW THE PRESS THE NEXT DAY WITH HEADLINES ABOUT 'BLATANT HOMOSEXUAL BEHAVIOUR ON LIVE TELEVISION' ETC.

"We'd been through rehearsal four or five times, without a hitch...did it exactly the same way every time. So, there we are on stage, going out live to people's lounge rooms. There's a slide solo in the middle of the song, and while that was happening I would either just stand there, clap my hands or stand around and look sufficiently sour and moody or whatever, but not on camera. This is where the collision of events come together.

"I used to have this little trick with Mick on the stage. I'd say something on stage, and he'd say 'What?' Then I'd mouth the words, and as he came in to hear what I was saying I'd bite him on the ear or the nose. It was just a game, just a playful thing.

"Anyway, this day I've said something to Mick, and he's just walked towards me because he knew he wasn't on camera, and I knew I wasn't on camera. He's walked towards me, and I've said something again, and he's looked at me as if to say 'You're not going to get me this time.' I've said... 'No, no, no'. Well, he was only a step away, so in that one moment he stepped towards me, slightly off balance, I reached up and put my hand around the back of his neck and pulled him down towards me, and he was saying something, and I kissed him full on the mouth. I don't know why, but I tongue kissed him. I don't think anyone in the control room knew what was happening, but two male faces are seen on camera, coming together, with one's tongue disappearing into the other one's mouth. The kiss only lasted a brief second, then he recoiled in shock, and I turned away laughing because I'd caught him yet again."

The kiss went out to every single TV switched on to the ABC, and within seconds the ABC switchboard was shut down with complaints. Angry thought nothing of it until he saw the press the next day with headlines about 'blatant homosexual behaviour on live television' etc.

A few days later the band got a phone call saying the ABC board had decided Rose Tattoo were to be banned from "Countdown" for ever. It was unprecedented. The ABC board had never before acted so swiftly, nor so adamantly.

It was one of the events of television folklore, like the Normie Rowe and Ron Casey punch-up, or the "60 Minutes" admission by Jan Murray that she'd made love to her husband on his desk in Parliament House.

Angry has never quite lived it down, and he still gets furious about accusations that it was a deliberate stunt. As a father, he is passionate about monitoring his kids' television viewing habits, so he understands the rage that erupted. However he says it really was an accident. The camera was not meant to be on him at that moment.

Eventually, slowly, the publicity began to die down. Some radio stations backed the ABC ban and refused to play Rose Tattoo, but the initial hysterics calmed. At this time, the band was still touring. Their first album was out and selling, and they were just going from town to town, from party to party, from girl to girl, from gig to gig. The problem was though, they had no direction. The Rose Tattoo they'd launched with a bang was still making plenty of noise, it just wasn't getting anywhere. As Angry says, "We were sort of just hanging around, but you see the road in Australia is colourful enough and entertaining enough at that time of your life that it could go on for years, and sometimes it does. There are still some bands out there that are trying to relive the glory days of old, because they remember the early days as being an endless party, which is exactly what it was. You are on the road anything from between eight and ten months of the year. If you haven't got a deal, you're on the road as much as possible because it's the only way you can make your money. If you've got a deal, then you have lull periods where you write. The record company had been trying to get us to settle on a line-up and record another album. In the meantime, our first album was moving a lot of records."

LINDY (LOU)

Suddenly things started happening. Management got a call from Alberts, and they asked for a meeting with the band members to try to mount Rose Tattoo's first tour through Britain and Europe. They'd developed quite a cult following overseas, predominantly in England and Germany and France. At that stage, the band was going through one of its many brief break ups, so Geordie and Mick were both temporarily off the scene.

At an afternoon meeting Alberts made the band an offer too good to refuse...they told them to patch up their differences, get back together, write some songs, do another album, and then they could head over to Europe. It was just what the boys needed....a new focus. The prospect of popularity overseas was exciting, so it gave them all something to work towards.

JUST AS THE PLANS WERE BEING MADE TO GET THE BAND TO EUROPE, ANGRY GOT LUCKY...REALLY LUCKY. HE DIDN'T WIN LOTTO, OR STRIKE GOLD, BUT WITH THE BENEFIT OF HINDSIGHT, HE NOW THINKS HE FOUND SOMETHING JUST AS GOOD. HE WON THE HEART OF HIS FUTURE WIFE.

Just as the plans were being made to get the band to Europe, Angry got lucky...really lucky. He didn't win lotto, or strike gold, but with the benefit of hindsight, he now thinks he found something just as good. He won the heart of his future wife.

Her name is Lindy Michael, but Angry's never called her that. His nickname for her is Lou, as in Lindy-Lou, because her middle name is Louise. As he says, in the beginning he had no idea how much she would eventually come to mean to him. "When I first met Lou I didn't know that she was going to change and affect my life. I couldn't have known that. All I saw was a cute girl, but I really wanted to get to know her."

The pair had actually met when Angry first moved to Sydney. Lindy was at a nightclub one night, watching her boyfriend's band. When Angry first set eyes on her, she was not even out of school. They both remember that first night differently. Angry just remembers taking a fancy to her and spending the rest of the night trying to make improper suggestions, but Lindy has a more complete recollection.

She says she remembers meeting a monster. "We first met at Chequers, a nightclub in Chinatown. I was only seventeen. That's where I used to go. I used to sneak in when I wasn't allowed. I was going out with the guy called Bob Spencer, and he introduced me to Angry. At the time, Angry was totally wild and outrageous. My first impression was 'Oh yuk, what a horrible person'. I can hardly repeat the things he was saying to me. He wanted to take me home. He wanted to sweep me off my feet. He bought me bottles of champagne to get me full. This is all with my other boyfriend there. At the time I didn't like him much at all."

They bumped into each other at many other gigs after that, and Angry would inevitably offer to take Lindy home, or take her out some time. Lindy would always have some good excuse. She'd either say she was busy, or she just wanted to be friends, or she just didn't like one night stands or whatever. In fact, she'd heard so many terrible stories about Angry over the years, she didn't want to get involved.

Angry's reputation was fierce. The stories that went around about him were so ridiculous they were almost comical. If only half of them had been true, he'd still have been dangerous. Lindy was young and naive, so she believed all the gossip. During their first few meetings she was so terrified, she didn't know what to do. She didn't want to insult Angry because she was so sure he'd turn nasty, so she just kept trying to ignore him and be polite. As she says, "I'd heard terrible things, like, you know his broken front teeth? Well, a friend of mine used to tell me that he filed them down every day....you know with a great big file. Someone else told me he'd been up on dozens of assault charges, and that was what scared me. I thought this guy is a wild animal. But they were all stories. It was the first thing I asked him when we got together. I said 'Do you really file your teeth?', and he just laughed and told me how they'd broken in a fight. "

At the beginning, it was very much a one way relationship. Angry had more than just a passing interest in Lindy. He couldn't forget about her, and every time they met, he pursued her for a date. As he says, the attraction was something he couldn't quite describe. "There was just something about her. I just liked something about her."

Despite the fact he was always making sexual suggestions to Lindy, Angry was actually most impressed by her personality. He found her incredibly easy to talk to. He hadn't had a serious relationship since Vivienne, and he'd missed being able to chat openly with a girlfriend.

By chance, she was the first girl Angry had ever taken an interest in who was actually shorter than him. All his other girlfriends had either been around the same height, or had towered over him. "I've never purposefully gone out to win tall girls to compensate for the fact that I'm short, but I certainly didn't narrow down my field of selection by height. I actually went out with a girl who was five foot ten at one stage. Size has never really worried me as far as girls go...I mean girls are girls. If someone is going to take an interest in you who is five foot seven, you're not going to say, 'Well, I'm sorry. We can't have anything pass between us, because you're above the right height'."

Through their many meetings Angry made some degree of progress with Lindy, but he couldn't quite manage to move the relationship on to any other level, until, by chance, he asked her if she'd like to become his new flatmate.

By that time, Lindy had already started to question the validity of some of the rumours. She was having trouble believing he was such a villain, because she hadn't seen any evidence, and as she says, he seemed too nice.

Angry was living in a house in Surry Hills, and because he was going overseas he was looking for a flatmate to take care of things while he was gone. Lindy just happened to be looking for somewhere to live, so she and a friend decided to take the risk and move in. There were plenty of bedrooms, so that wasn't a problem,

> SHE GOT TO SEE THE REAL HIM...TO WITNESS THE FACT THAT HE GETS UP AND EATS BREAKFAST NORMALLY, THAT HE WASHES, THAT HE WATERS PLANTS, EVEN THAT HE SLEEPS IN A BED. SOME OF THE EARLY GOSSIP HAD HIM SLEEPING ON NAILS. THAT'S WHEN SHE FELL IN LOVE WITH HIM.

but living in the same house gave Lindy a chance to get to know Angry better.

She got to see the real him...to witness the fact that he gets up and eats breakfast normally, that he washes, that he waters plants, even that he sleeps in a bed. Some of the early gossip had him sleeping on nails. That's when she fell in love with him. As Angry says, "When she got to see me up close, she found out what she'd suspected all along. You know, that the bark was worse than the bite. I mean, no one could have been that bad."

The whole experience had been a struggle for Angry. It had never been an issue before, but in the early days with Lindy, he felt frustrated and stereotyped. It was as if he'd painted himself into a corner. He'd spent years trying to look formidable with the tattoos and the earrings, only to find that he'd disguised himself too well. He became very aware of how people perceived him, and realised that there were occasions when he was scaring even those people he was trying to attract.

It was really the first time in his life that his reputation stood in his way. It was the first time he felt desperate to have someone look underneath the image, and underneath the rough exterior. As he says, "The truth was, as with most hardened people, most of us still have that sensitive, vulnerable side that needs to be listened to. Even with the interviews I was doing at the time, I used to talk about certain songs and their meaning and about the album, but that's not what people wanted to hear. They didn't want to know that we could write a sensitive album. It was the same with me. The sensitivity, the love, the compassion was all hidden by this grotesque exterior."

It's something that's come up time and time again. Over the years, whenever he's been disregarded and judged unfairly, Angry's come out vehemently to argue that people can't be judged just by the way they look. As he say, "People used to perceive me as super resilient...you know, nothing can hurt me, and watch out anyone who tries. It was that sort of thing. But, people weren't seeing the real me. They were just judging me by the way I looked. You know...yes, I

> "THE TRUTH WAS, AS WITH MOST HARDENED PEOPLE, MOST OF US STILL HAVE THAT SENSITIVE, VULNERABLE SIDE THAT NEEDS TO BE LISTENED TO ... IT WAS THE SAME WITH ME. THE SENSITIVITY, THE LOVE, THE COMPASSION WAS ALL HIDDEN BY THIS GROTESQUE EXTERIOR."

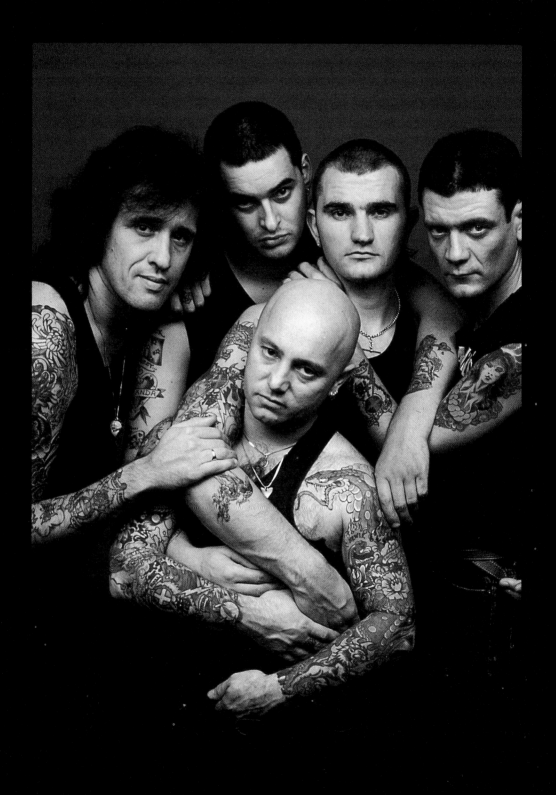

look like this, but that's not all there is to it. That's not all there is to any kid. If a kid walks into a shop and he's got sixteen earrings, and he's covered in tattoos and he's got a Mohawk haircut, that's what he looks like. It's not who he is. They have to be like that. Sometimes they have to be like that, just to get by. They look tough, they look belligerent, but it's what they have to look like."

The timing of Lindy and Angry's romance wasn't great. Through those first few months of getting to know each other, and enjoying the new relationship, the European tour was always hanging over their heads. Angry wasn't just going overseas for a month, or even two months. Basically Rose Tattoo had committed themselves to at least three years on the road. On a personal level, Angry had not only committed himself to the band, but he'd committed himself to making his name as an international rock singer. He couldn't have given that up then for anybody. Not even Lindy. He wouldn't have just been letting himself down, he'd have been letting the band down too.

When they said their goodbyes, Angry and Lindy promised only to write. They didn't promise to stay together, or to be faithful. They just promised to keep in touch. And they did. They spoke on the phone almost every day, sometimes for hours, and the first letter Angry received in England was addressed to Mr Angry Anderson, Queen Street, Mayfair, London. It was on the back of an Alberts Production Rose Tattoo postcard. All it said was "I love you, I love you, I love you". The words were written 24 times, and at the end it just said "Guess who?"

7

'HE LOOKS AND SINGS LIKE A MARVELLOUSLY
MINDLESS, MAN-EATING BOILED EGG.'

ROSE TATTOO

O ver the years hundreds of rock writers and reviewers have tried to describe Rose Tattoo. They were, in many ways, the band the media loved to hate. In England, the descriptions were as colourful as the members themselves. When it came to Angry, critics relished the challenge of summing him up in words, trying to find the exact analogy. As one writer said, "He looks and sings like a marvellously mindless, man-eating boiled egg". In the words of another, Angry was nothing more than a "midget misogynist with skin problems".

When it came to the actual band, the British press had a field day:

THE ROSE TATTOO

"This bunch of bone-headed, black-hearted braggadocios."

"...and once you've got over their appearance, the next daunting challenge is the music. Being a safe distance away from the band, this reviewer would have to say it was painful rubbish."

"For a start their music is, to say the least, lethargic and over-loud if not just plain dull. As for their stage show, all I could hear was a very unpleasant one chord rhythm guitar and a slimmed down Buster Bloodvessel lookalike with a voice not dissimilar to a wounded mouse."

"These Australians seemed determined to avenge the dramatic Test defeat of their cricket team by pulverising the ears of any Pom within 20 miles."

"They're even less delightful than AC/DC, Rolf Harris, the Chopper Squad, and Ian Chappell all rolled in to one, and are led by a bald headed midget called Angry Anderson."

It didn't matter what the press said, though. When Rose Tattoo got started with the British crowds, when they actually hit the stage and took their shows out to the audience, they were big news. It just took a little while for word to get around.

When they first arrived at London airport, they were hardly treated like visiting rock stars. There was just a road crew to meet them. They travelled in to town in a fifteen year old Cortina and a transit van. They were given a lecture along the way. Graeme Swinerton, "Swin", was tour manager for the band. He already handled other acts with reputations comparable to that of Rose Tattoo. His biggest act at the time was Slade. When Swin got the boys in the car he read them the riot act. As Angry says, "He had this great accent, and he just said 'Listen guys, we're going to stay at a f...ing musos' hotel, and they're f...ing expecting you. I've shown them an f...ing photo, so they know what to expect. Now, don't f... up. You can f... up in your own country. But, just don't f... up in mine. It's me who'll f...ing suffer. So, just don't f... up.'"

THE BAND'S FIRST GIG IN ENGLAND WAS AT THE MARQUEE. AS ANGRY SAYS, "IT'S THE MOST FAMOUS VENUE IN THE WORLD. WE WERE REALLY NERVOUS AND THE PLACE WAS PACKED. I MEAN SO PACKED THEY HAD TO OPEN UP THE SIDE DOORS SO PEOPLE COULD WATCH FROM THE LANE. "

When they arrived at the hotel in Paddington they got a surprising reception. They bowled in, excitable and loud, ready to take on the world, but the staff on the desk wouldn't even give them a smile. They were greeted with frosty silence. Angry couldn't work it out. The band hadn't even had a chance to disgrace themselves yet, and according to Swin, the hotel staff had all seen a photograph of the boys, so they knew what to expect. What was the problem? In fact, the problem was not their appearance, or the premature judgement of their behaviour. It was their list of demands. The hotel staff were annoyed that all the members of the band had insisted, in advance, on a private shower in each room. Only the fanciest rooms, the rooms meant for real tourists, had showers. The rest had shared bathroom facilities on each landing. The hotel management couldn't justify why such a dirty rock and roll band would insist on showers. It didn't seem possible that they washed at all, let alone that they needed to do it in private luxury.

Angry says that even after they'd gone off on tour, and come back to the hotel numerous times, the girls were still sarcastic. "Showers?" they'd ask with a sneer as the guys checked in their bags. "Of course," Angry would reply, "Of course."

It was Angry's first trip overseas with the band. He'd travelled all over Australia, but England was a different story. The English fans were a different story too. Rose Tattoo had a small group of loyal followers who'd loved the "Rock 'n Roll Outlaws" album. They were all the same kind of heavy rockers who followed the band at home...lots of bikers, lots of desperates. Again, the majority of the fans were male but they were different. The British fans were more vocal, and more obsessed. Rose Tattoo were just like no band they'd ever seen before.

ON THE ROAD IN THE U.K.

The band's first gig in England was at the Marquee. As Angry says, "It's the most famous venue in the world. We were really nervous and the place was packed. I mean so packed they had to open up the side doors so people could watch from the lane. There we were, playing on the same stage as the likes of Cream, Hendrix, Led Zeppelin, Pink Floyd. People had travelled miles to see us. There were people there from Norway, Italy. There were bikers who'd ridden across Europe and got on a ferry. There were lots who had ridden down from Scotland just that day. And they were wild. They bombed the stage, diving from each other's shoulders."

Word travelled quickly that there was an outrageous live act in town, and the crowds grew and grew. Everyone wanted to see the head thumping bad boys from down under. "We didn't do it as tough as AC/DC in England and Europe. We kind of walked in on that middle shelf. We were already halfway up the ladder. Basically what consolidated it was, that once we went out and did some stuff, we really took off."

In Australia, Angry was accustomed to being recognised in the street. Most people knew his face and knew that he was a rock singer. But the English experience exposed him to something he wasn't accustomed to - being admired and adored. He wasn't actually used to being popular.

"It was incredible. I mean it was like we just couldn't do anything wrong, and it was like that the whole time we were there. I remember in the first few days, once we got sort of used to venturing outside the hotel we went down the street to buy some jeans and leather jackets and boots, you know. It only cost about 50 quid. We walked into one shop and there was a photo of us on the wall. The people in the shop couldn't believe it was us, and we couldn't believe that they couldn't believe it, if you know what I mean. We never got treated like that. We were sort of infamous in Australia, not famous.

"There was another day too. We were walking down the street, and these metal heads from across the road bolted over, and they were just aghast that we were there. We were looking at one another saying 'You've got to be kidding, this is great'. I mean, after all the shit canning we'd had at home!"

The routine in Europe was strenuous. After the first few Marquee gigs, they did a headlining tour of France and Germany, then came back to England again to do a tour with Rainbow, Richie Blackmore's band. Because Richie Blackmore had achieved so much success with Deep Purple, the Rainbow tour was huge. Some nights the bands played to more than ten thousand people.

The other big tour was the ZZ Top tour through Europe. The gigs were almost seven days a week, and they moved through seven different countries in a month, so the travelling was a major strain. As Robbie says, the band would get sort of lost on tour. They'd never know from one day to the next where they were, or what time it was. The itinerary was more than demanding.

Rose Tattoo European Tour

ZZ TOP   AUTUMN 1981

OCTOBER

SATURDAY 3	MARQUEE	LONDON, ENGLAND
SUNDAY 4	TRUCK DEPART LONDON	
MONDAY 5	SLEEPER DEPART LONDON	
TUESDAY 6	HAMMERLEINHALL	NUREMBURG, GERMANY
WEDNESDAY 7	DAY OFF	
THURSDAY 8	STADTHALLE	OFFENBACH, GERMANY
FRIDAY 9	RHEIN NECKORHALLE	HEIDELBERG, GERMANY
SUNDAY 11	NEUE WELT	BERLIN, GERMANY
TUESDAY 13	WESTFALENHALLE	DORTMUND, GERMANY
WEDNESDAY 14	CIRCUIS KRONE	MUNICH, GERMANY
THURSDAY 15	VOLKHAUS	ZURICH, SWITZERLAND
FRIDAY 16	DAY OFF	
SATURDAY 17	HALL POLYUALENT	ARLON, LUXEMBORG
SUNDAY 18	RODAHAL	KERKADIE, HOLLAND
MONDAY 19	PHILIPSHALLE	DUSSELDORF, GERMANY
TUESDAY 20	MUZIEKEENTRUM	UTRECHT, HOLLAND
WEDNESDAY 21	DAY OFF	
THURSDAY 22	RHENUS HALL	STRASIBOURG, FRANCE
FRIDAY 23	PALAIS DE SPORT	DIJON, FRANCE
SATURDAY 24	PALAIS DE SPORT	GRENOBLE, FRANCE
SUNDAY 25	PAVILLION BALTARD	PARIS, FRANCE
MONDAY 26		MADRID, SPAIN
TUESDAY 27		MADRID, SPAIN
WEDNESDAY 28		MADRID, SPAIN
THURSDAY 29		MADRID, SPAIN
FRIDAY 30		MADRID, SPAIN
SATURDAY 31		MADRID, SPAIN

RETURN TO UK 2 NOVEMBER

No matter how hard the guys worked on the road though, they always put in their hardest hours behind the bar. As Robbie says, "They were a big drinking band. It's funny, because a lot of the stories you hear about these bands, you know the Guns N' Roses stories, they tend to be the promoters' and publicists' ideas of what it should be like

on a rock and roll tour. Rose Tattoo were actually like that. They just drank all the time. Whatever the next level is after alcoholic, they were that. They didn't need food. They just just needed alcohol."

The boys club was in full swing, and there was nothing to stop them. As Angry says, "It was like being an outlaw biker...it allowed us to do all the things we wanted to do publicly, and because we were a rock and roll band, we were allowed to do it."

Every now and then management would try to tame the boys a bit, quieten things down. Robbie put out this memo before the ZZ Top Autumn tour of Europe. It was addressed to all Rose Tattoo tour personnel. It read:

AS AN EXPERIMENT IT HAS BEEN DECIDED THAT THE OVERALL APPROACH TO THIS TOUR WILL BE SLIGHTLY DIFFERENT TO OUR USUAL APPROACH, I.E. RATHER THAN HAVING A 25-DAY PARTY WITH A FEW GIGS THROWN IN TO BREAK THE BOREDOM WE SHALL HAVE 25 DAYS OF WORK WITH A PARTY AT THE END.

As an experiment it has been decided that the overall approach to this tour will be slightly different to our usual approach, i.e. rather than having a 25-day party with a few gigs thrown in to break the boredom we shall have 25 days of work with a party at the end. To achieve this unfortunately we will have to leave the party ingredients alone. There will be no alcohol allowed to be consumed on the bus or at any time on the day, or prior to the performance. On days off alcohol may be consumed on the bus in reasonable amounts. This tour is vital to the band's progression in Europe therefore everyone must maintain a sober nature and do what you are paid for; WORK. Anyone not giving his 100% will be putting his wages on the line. It goes without saying that if you go on this tour you accept these conditions.

The supposed booze-free tour didn't last long. Basically Angry and the band ruined the plans on the first day. As band manager, Robbie was trying to set an example by drinking coffee and tea all the way over to Europe on the ferry, but little did he know, his drinks were all spiked with vodka. By the time the ferry arrived in France, Robbie was so drunk he had to be carried off the ferry and on to the bus waiting to take them to the hotel. He fell off his seat when they went around a corner, and ended up sliding all the way to the front, landing with his head on the clutch. It wasn't the kind of start to the tour he'd hoped for.

He did manage to keep the band sober for the first three days, but as soon as they drove through the corridor into Berlin and saw how cheap the alcohol was, there wasn't much Robbie could do to stop them. That was Robbie's first and last attempt at setting drinking restrictions.

At one stage, during a welcome reception in France, the band showed just exactly what they were capable of when given free rein. In Angry's words, they just went mad. They became the animals the French distributors feared. "We'd been upstairs doing interviews. They told us to come down, and wait for the people for the reception. They said the reception would start in about an hour. But, an hour? Within an hour, the five of us, plus two of our roadies had drunk half the booze that was meant for thirty people. We were just pissed...we were pigs. We were just animals. That's what people expected of us, and that's what we were going to deliver."

AS THE BAND'S PROFILE GREW, ROCK WRITERS HAD MORE AND MORE FUN REPORTING ON THEIR ANTICS. IN BRITAIN, ANGRY WAS THE ORIGINAL LIZARD OF OZ. IT WAS ANGRY'S CROWN. IT WAS THE HEADLINE THE POPULAR PRESS LOVED TO USE WHENEVER ROSE TATTOO HIT THE NEWS. THEY'D ALWAYS FIND A SHOT OF HIM, WITH HIS TONGUE OUT AND HIS TATTOOS BULGING.

As the band's profile grew, rock writers had more and more fun reporting on their antics. In Britain, Angry was the original Lizard of Oz. Paul Keating may have snatched the title when he put his arm around the Queen in 1992, but in the early 1980s, there was no competition. It was Angry's crown. It was the headline the popular press loved to use whenever Rose Tattoo hit the news. They'd always find a shot of him, with his tongue out and his tattoos bulging, to illustrate exactly what they meant. Angry Anderson, the Lizard of Oz.

Rose Tattoo made perfect copy. Whether writers loved them or

hated them, they always found plenty to write about. As Angry says now, "In England we got front covers and fold-out pages of the most prestigious rock magazines. Even though certain writers for those magazines just hated us dogmatically, and just canned us, you know, no matter what we did, the magazines themselves supported us. I actually saw it in print once which made me shrivel, because we hated seeing stuff like this, but I saw stuff like 'I've just been to see Rose Tattoo, and this is the future of rock and roll'. It's things like that you don't need because it's sort of like the kiss of death. But, we got so many accolades that we truly enjoyed from the right people about the right things.

"The mags that were pro Rose Tattoo were almost embarrassing. You see, when you're in a band that's not up itself, when you read something that makes you think 'Wow, this woman  is gushing', you always say, 'Well, thank you very much, but it wasn't that good', you know. We were always realistic enough to say, 'Well, actually no, the sea wasn't about to open up. There was no divine intervention in that performance. You know? Thanks very much for the accolades...but!' Then, there were other writers who'd say, 'I've just been to see Rose Tattoo, and you had to be there. It was one of those special nights of rock and roll', and you'd think 'Yeah, well I was there. I was part of it.' Those kind of experiences were quite special."

The band got coverage from straight, traditional press too. They knew they'd really made it when one English magazine with a huge readership actually based their daily cartoon on Angry. There's a picture in a little frame, and there's an obstetrician saying to a desperate looking new mother "Don't worry, Mrs Clark - most babies look like Angry Anderson."

Halfway through the European tour Mick Cocks left the band, so another Australian guitarist "Rockin" Rob Riley was flown over to replace him. There was a certain amount of concern from management about Mick leaving, but Angry didn't want to be fazed by it. It was just politics, internal band problems...just the way things were. And anyway, Rob Riley fitted into the outfit perfectly. As Angry says, "He had all the requirements. I mean he was a boozing, belligerent, boorish, ugly Australian. I mean he fitted in beautifully with the rest of us. He was heavily tattooed, he was a big, bulky bloke, and he had a wicked sense of humour which was one of the things you needed to survive."

Rose Tattoo played all venues, from small town pubs to the major stadiums. Their approach to the bigger venues was laid back. They didn't set off rockets, or use huge special effects. They just played like they were playing in a pub...a small group making a loud noise. There were always a few theatrics, but for the most part, the band just went out there and played.

READING IS LIKE THE MARQUEE. I MEAN THERE'S HISTORY ATTACHED TO IT. I REMEMBER WALKING ON THE STAGE. IT WAS AMAZING. IT WAS HUGE, THE BIGGEST CROWD WE'D EVER PLAYED TO. YOU COULD JUST SEE PEOPLE GOING ON FOREVER.

The biggest gig the band ever did was the Reading Festival, in front of a huge crowd. Reading is part of a tradition in Britain, the biggest outdoor rock festival of the year. Rose Tattoo was about the middle of the line-up, but there was no doubt that, on the day, they made the biggest impact. It was one of those days where Angry walked on to the stage, but was carried off.

As he says, "It was a great day. Reading is like The Marquee. I mean there's history attached to it. I remember walking on the stage. It was amazing. It was huge, the biggest crowd we'd ever played to. You could just see people going on forever. I mean the band were fantastic that day. We played really well...really well."

In England, Angry had a thing going with the crowds that he could drink a bottle of vodka every performance. He couldn't, but he always gave it his best shot. It just became part of the show, a sort of sight gag. Angry would begin each gig with a full bottle on stage for himself, plus all the beers for the rest of the band. During the show he'd pour drinks for the boys, and toast the crowd with his vodka. After a while the British crowds turned it into a regular challenge. Toward the end of the band's set, they'd start calling for Angry to drink

up and finish whatever was left in the bottle. "Skol, skol, skol" they'd yell. As the band was only on stage for just over an hour at most gigs, it was a big call. They'd want the bottle finished every time.

At the Reading gig, Angry had been drinking even more than usual, and he was way past his limits before the challenge even began. The combination of the alcohol and the adrenalin was potent. In the latter half of the band's set on stage, Angry was obviously feeling really extravagant, and in one passionate moment, head butted Pete's guitar amplifier stack. Although Angry did a lot of head butting in those days, this time, he hit his head even harder than usual. He dropped to the floor, virtually unconscious, covered in blood, and had to be carried off stage by roadies.

He was mindless and reckless, too drunk and too high. But even now, you can see as he talks about it, that although it may not have been one of his proudest moments, it certainly was one of his most memorable. The image is unforgettable, Angry in the arms of the roadies, bloody, sweaty, tragic, in front of a sea of screaming fans. It's the kind of image that makes you realise he's serious when he says, "You feed off the crowd. The commitment is so great that sometimes you just want to die for them. Not in the true sense, but you know what I mean. You just want to give that much."

The next day Angry was infuriated when some rock writers reported that he'd been "bottled off stage". It was the suggestion that there were some fans there unhappy enough to do that which bothered him most. He tracked down the journos involved, and found out that they'd never even left the media tent, where they were too busy drinking the free booze to figure out what happened.

But, at the end of the day, it was Rose Tattoo's Reading. They stole the whole show. Angry can't help smiling when he thinks of it. "It was huge. I mean we could have walked on their hands. It was our gig. The crowd were ours. Even kids years later would say, 'I was there at Reading. I saw you.' We walked out on stage and the place went just nuts...I mean really nuts. It was goose bump territory. No, bigger than that. It was goosebump on goosebump on goosebump territory."

But not all Rose Tattoo gigs went over so well. There was one performance on a really hot day in France where the audience experienced the real Angry rage. They saw the side of Angry that earned him his nickname, and his reputation. As Robbie says, it was one of those small scuffles that somehow escalated into a full-scale riot. "There was a wire fence on the oval, between the band and the audience, and the audience were all sitting in the grandstand. They'd been waiting in the hot sun for hours because the gig started late, so they were all pretty restless. Someone had thrown a can onto the stage, and Angry had picked it up and thrown it back. It hit someone else in the crowd, and people started to get pissed off. So then a couple of people started throwing more cans, and Angry started throwing them all back. Suddenly 10,000 people started throwing cans, oranges, apples, anything they could get their hands on. This was all within the first minutes of them being on stage. All the other guys were playing behind their amplifiers, and Angry was just out in the middle of the stage, fighting on his own. Geordie actually got hit in the middle of the chest with an orange while he was singing, and he got winded. Angry jumped off stage, got a piece of pipe and tried to climb the wire fence. He was mad, really mad. I don't think I ever saw him that angry. If he'd got across to the crowd he would have done a lot of damage. I think he probably would have been killed in the process, but he was just crazy. I mean the veins were popping in his head."

That night Angry went home covered in cuts and bruises, but he didn't care. He was just outraged. The bruises were nothing out of the usual. As Robbie says, seeing Angry with a new bruise is a bit like seeing Angry with a new tattoo. He wears them well, and it's just part and parcel of the show. You almost don't notice.

More than the everyday knocks and scrapes of the stage though, during the European tour, Robbie feared the drunken stupors. He says he thought if he didn't lose Angry to a botched 'Suicide City' strangulation, the next most likely thing was that he'd lose him to alcohol. "I couldn't tell you how many times I sat up all night watching him, making sure he didn't drown in his own vomit. This was just after Bon Scott had died, so I was very conscious of the fact that I couldn't let Angry go like that. That used to worry me more than anything else. Many nights I slept beside his bed with him propped up like a Buddha."

After a nine-month tour, Rose Tattoo went home to Australia. They arrived heroes. Their songs had charted really well in the independent and heavy metal charts, both internationally and at home, and they were tipped to be the next big rock band to take over where AC/DC had left off. Many critics tipped them to be the biggest rock band in the world.

As soon as he got home, Angry moved back into the Surry Hills house with Lindy and one of her girlfriends. Lindy had been dedicated with the letter-writing vigil, and Angry had made plenty of phone calls, so they'd kept up their long distance romance. At first they were a bit clumsy with each other. They'd been apart so long, and so much had happened and changed, that for the first few months the relationship was strained. But, after a while, things settled down and they got to know each other again.

Angry was in love. There was no doubt about that. As he says, he can't remember many details about those months at home. He doesn't remember romantic strolls in the park, or candlelight dinners. He doesn't remember any particular wonderful day. All he remembers is that he was happy. He had found a girl who saw beneath the facade, who loved the real him.

The band were desperate to come home to do a number of things. They needed a holiday, but they also wanted to spend time re-establishing their relationship with the Australian audiences. The other thing they wanted to do was to take some time off to come up with the crucial third album. They were riding on a wave, and it was essential that they consolidate their success in Britain and Europe with a great third album. "We'd done the first very bluesy album, 'Rock 'n Roll Outlaws', then we'd done a very very heavy rock, almost metal album, 'Assault and Battery', then we came up with 'Scarred for Life'. It was a very philosophical album. The business purpose behind it was to capitalise...to really tie up what had happened in Britain and Europe. Going by the Alberts plan or strategy, to then move on, using Britain and Europe as the launching place. As they'd done with AC/DC, and were in the process of doing with the Angels, they wanted to push us into America."

But things didn't happen quite according to plan. First, guitarist Rob Riley broke his arm, so the band was forced to lie low for a while. As Robbie says, "I see that as one of the vital points of the band's problems...when you've got a roll happening like they did, you've got to keep on going. The plan was, they'd come back from England, go straight into the studio, record the album, and then get back out there. You know, we wanted to turn it around in three or four months. But when Rob broke his arm, we had to wait around, so we just lost the momentum."

The other big problem was that, although the record company had always been interested in recording the album overseas to give it an international sound, at the last minute they pulled the money so it had to be recorded in Australia. As Angry says, it was a huge let down for the band. "There were some producers, both English and American, who thought we were going to be huge. They'd talked to management about doing the album in either England of America under the guidance of a really happening producer. One of the guys who was interested was the guy who produced the last AC/DC album, the one that really had them recognised. But it didn't happen. We recorded the album here."

THEN, THE NEXT BIG DISAPPOINTMENT CAME WHEN THE RECORD COMPANY TOLD US THEY WOULDN'T GIVE US THE MONEY TO GO BACK TO EUROPE. THEY WANTED US TO GO STRAIGHT TO AMERICA INSTEAD. THEY WERE TRYING TO LEAP AHEAD A YEAR OR TWO.

"Then, the next big disappointment came when the record company told us they wouldn't give us the money to go back to Europe. They wanted us to go straight to America instead. They were trying to leap ahead a year or two. Instead of touring the album in Britain we'd cut that year out and go directly to America. Now when we questioned this, it was sort of touted to us that we were ready, we were good enough. But, I didn't believe any of

HE IMAGE IS UNFORGETTABLE, ANGRY IN THE ARMS OF THE ROADIES, BLOODY, SWEATY, TRAGIC, IN FRONT OF A SEA OF SCREAMING FANS. IT'S THE KIND OF IMAGE THAT MAKES YOU REALISE HE'S SERIOUS WHEN HE SAYS, "YOU FEED OFF THE CROWD. THE COMMITMENT IS SO GREAT THAT SOMETIMES YOU JUST WANT TO DIE FOR THEM"

it for a second, because I knew we weren't."

Management started organising the American tour, when suddenly Angry was confronted with the biggest event in his life.

He was 36 years old...a recognised star, frontman for one of the most outrageous rock bands in the world, yet one night, at home in their flat in Surry Hills, Lindy turned him to jelly. She announced she was going to have a baby, and asked what Angry thought about it. They weren't married, and they'd never talked about children, but Angry's always been certain the pregnancy was no accident. As far as he was concerned, Lindy was like a woman on a mission. She said, "I'd like to have my first child with you, so regardless of how you handle this from now on, this is my baby, but it can be ours. What do you think?"

As Angry says, at the time, parenthood was the last thing on his mind. "If destiny hadn't dealt me the hand, I never would have sat down at the table and looked for it. I was at an age where I was almost

thinking, 'Well, you're just about at the stage where no one will want you, so you don't have to worry about that responsibility. I just thought I'd end up as an ageing rocker with a solo career or something."

Lindy was committed to becoming a mother, and she'd have been a single mother if she had to. She told Angry he could do whatever he wanted. He could have nothing to do with the baby, or he could have everything to do with it. It was his choice.

Angry says now, it was a huge decision, but one that really only took a moment to make. "I told her that if I commit myself to something, I try my hardest. I said 'It will be rocky, and up and down. It won't be easy for me to do it but,' I said, 'I'll tell you one thing. I'll give it my best shot.' I told her there are some promises I cannot and will not make, but I will promise to try my best. And, here I am eleven years later, and four kids later, still trying my best. I'm not the perfect husband, and I'm not the perfect father, but I'm trying."

Someone once asked Angry if he thought he was ever the kind of

person who could have been classified as a loser, in those early years before Buster Brown, when he was just hanging around getting drunk and picking fights. Was he a loser? He thought about it for ages, and eventually he said, "No, I wasn't a loser in those days. But, if I'd walked away from Lindy and the baby when they came along, then I would have been a loser in a big, big way. Definitely a loser. I'd have lost out...big time!"

Once again the timing was terrible. Angry only had a couple of months or so at home before heading off to America, and if things went as planned he wouldn't even be back in time for the baby's birth. He was definite about a few things though. Parenthood for Angry meant a change in lifestyle. He wasn't happy with the communal living, so he and Lindy rented a house in Coogee together. He needed to feel that Lindy was comfortably set up in a "family home" before he went to the States.

In the last month leading up to the tour, Angry started to play music to the baby in the womb, because he'd read that it was soothing. He'd play Simon and Garfunkel and he'd talk to Lindy's belly saying things like "This is your Daddy talking. I may not be here when you come, but I just want you to know that this voice is mine."

In the latter part of 1982, Angry and Rose Tattoo set off to take on the United States. America was nothing like England. The crowds were different, the music was different. Rose Tattoo arrived with their Australian-produced album, and their Australian-produced sound, and basically no one knew what to make of them.

For a start, the Americans couldn't get over their appearance. One of the first record company executives spent ages on the phone with Robbie trying to get a handle on what was required to prepare the band for a performance. They'd seen photographs, so they thought the band members needed to spend hours in the dressing room having their tattoos painted on before walking on stage. They'd already experienced the make up and costumes of Kiss, so they assumed Rose Tattoo was just an extension on the theme. They thought the tattoos were just a gimmick. As Angry says, "Basically they just didn't believe that five guys in a band could all have tattoos. It didn't make sense to them. They started asking questions like 'How long is it going to take to airbrush all those tattoos? How much will it cost?' They just couldn't come to grips with the fact they were real and wouldn't wash off."

Even when they understood the tattoos weren't fakes, they couldn't believe the band had come together like that. They thought they'd all sat down one day, and said "Gee, Rose Tattoo is a good name for a band", then spent months with the tattoo artist getting ready to look the part.

They couldn't really cope with any part of the band's image. "Robbie had to say to people in the record company 'Look, you've got to be prepared. Don't expect them to walk in, and be like me. Don't expect them to look like me. Look at the album cover, that's what they're really like.' In other words, it was like they thought the whole image was part of a costume...like we might actually clean up to be really nice guys underneath it all. We were nice guys of course, but not to their standards. It was like, you know, having your daughter bring home twelve Hell's Angels and you're a church minister. It really freaked them out."

After a while though, people did cope, and as Angry says, "Once they got used to the fact that we didn't beat people up, and we didn't molest small dogs and children, we had a really good relationship with the record company."

"ONCE THEY GOT USED TO THE FACT THAT WE DIDN'T BEAT PEOPLE UP, AND WE DIDN'T MOLEST SMALL DOGS AND CHILDREN, WE HAD A REALLY GOOD RELATIONSHIP WITH THE RECORD COMPANY."

Work was tough in the States. Rose Tattoo played every night of the week, sometimes twice a night. The picked up part of the ZZ Top tour, which was great for them because they'd worked so well together in the tour across Europe. They also did a tour with a guitar player called Pat Travers, and then did a full tour with Aerosmith. They couldn't afford to take a single day off. They'd open for Aerosmith early, then go on to a pub on the other side of town and do a later gig.

They were being pushed to their limits with work, but they were still partying as heavily as ever. As Robbie says, it's all part of road life. It's a strange existence. "When you go touring, you get lost. The daily routine was incredible. You know, we'd roll into town at about 10.00 in the morning, sleep until about 4.00 in the afternoon, get up and do some press. Then we'd go to the venue, do a sound check, do the show, then hang around for a few hours while the bus driver got his full sleep, and then be on the bus by about 11.00 or 11.30 at night. Obviously everyone would start drinking at about 6.00, so it was pretty well on to the bus, and then drink all the way through to the next stop which was usually about six or ten hours away."

Rose Tattoo had two major problems in the States. The band just wasn't gelling the way it had in the past. There were some bitter internal conflicts between the members and management. A couple of the guys were really unsettled and unhappy about the way things were turning out. They were still convinced they should have consolidated their success by touring England and Europe for a second time, because they felt like they'd sort of hit America half-baked.

They weren't properly prepared for the US audiences, and their music wasn't packaged properly for the American promoters. Although they were getting rave reviews from their live gigs, the album wasn't getting any airplay. "It wasn't recorded in America, so it didn't sound like it was recorded in America," Angry says, "We were told that to get radio airplay we had to re-record the whole album. There just wasn't the time or money to do that. We were led to believe that if the record had an American sound, it would have got a lot more play, which would have meant a lot more sales and a lot more promotion for our spots on the tours. But, that didn't happen."

On stage, the band was having problems relating to the American style. The band was so rebellious and defiant, their reception on stage was always somewhat guarded. As Robbie says, "Obviously when they used to go on stage they got a reaction. You could always hear this expression of 'oh'. It was this sort of group sigh, because most of the time they looked like they'd just been dragged out of graves. They were constantly pale and grey."

Angry's style as a front man also caused some problems with the American audience. He was too brash, and he wanted to say too much. Instead of just standing on stage saying, "Let's party", Angry always wanted to rant and rave between songs about the evils of the world. His approach suited the English audiences, but the American audiences found it too confronting. They didn't want to hear what he had to say, they just wanted to have a good time.

There were even quite a few gigs where the band was booed off stage. Angry would hear the wisecracks of a heckler near the front of the audience, and in taking on one individual, would end up taking on the entire crowd. As the booing got louder and louder, he'd get angrier and angrier.

After gigs like that, the whole band would have to go somewhere quiet to try to settle down. Angry would have to sit alone trying to calm his rage before he could speak to anyone.

In many respects the American tour was a disappointment, but it wasn't a complete disaster. Despite the problems, the boys kept up the appearance that things were terrific, so outsiders would never have known what was really going on. As Angry says, "To anyone else the band would have seemed supremely confident. Their perception of us was that we compared to the early Rolling Stones because we had the same stance. We were very brash, very arrogant...it was like 'You don't like this? Well, piss off' you know."

Some great things also came out of the tour. While the death knell might have been sounding for Rose Tattoo, another rock band was only just getting things together....Guns N' Roses, the band that later became the biggest rock act in the world. If it hadn't been for Angry and the boys touring the States, Guns N' Roses may never have formed. In 1982, they were just a backyard band, performing under another name. They were nobody's, but they happened to be fans of Aerosmith, so one day they went along to one of the concerts. That's when they first saw Rose Tattoo, and in their own words, they were never the same again. Later, when Guns N' Roses had achieved worldwide recognition, they freely admitted that Rose Tattoo was their inspiration. They even, to some extent, followed in the same tradition with their names...they matched the feminine rose with the masculine gun.

"They openly, gushingly credited us with their beginning, to the point where it's almost embarrassing," Angry says. "It took them a year

SOME GREAT THINGS ALSO CAME OUT OF THE TOUR. WHILE THE DEATH KNELL MIGHT HAVE BEEN SOUNDING FOR ROSE TATTOO, ANOTHER ROCK BAND WAS ONLY JUST GETTING THINGS TOGETHER....GUNS N' ROSES, THE BAND THAT LATER BECAME THE BIGGEST ROCK ACT IN THE WORLD.

'FAT AND FORTY', AS SUPPORT
FOR GUNS N' ROSES

or two to actually adopt our look and go out and get tattooed. Then they started to play like we played. I met them all when I was living in LA in 1989. They'd got word I was in town and they called and suggested we hang together for a while. They say that we were the spark that lit the fire that became Guns N' Roses. We were very flattered, and mightily pleased that we'd left our mark on the US."

Since finding fame, Guns N' Roses have twice toured Australia. Both times, they requested that Rose Tattoo support them. The first time, it was years since the band had played, so they didn't feel they could pull things together quickly enough. In 1992 though, it was a different story. Angry and the boys took the gamble and decided it was possible to re-form, so they did end up doing a full Australian tour with Guns N' Roses. It was a nerve-racking reunion, because in Angry's own words, they were all 'fat and forty' by then. Angry was nervous about letting down the image of Rose Tattoo, of being guilty of not knowing when to quit.

Even as they were accepting the Gunners' offer, and signing the tour papers, in the back of all their minds was the fear that they were past it. That they'd be a terrible failure. But, in the end, even the critics agreed, age did not weary them. The tour went off without a hitch. They may have had the beer bellies and the double chins of older men, but they still had the never-say-die, bad boy rock and roll attitudes.

EVEN AS THEY WERE ACCEPTING THE GUNNERS' OFFER, AND SIGNING THE TOUR PAPERS, IN THE BACK OF ALL THEIR MINDS WAS THE FEAR THAT THEY WERE PAST IT. THAT THEY'D BE A TERRIBLE FAILURE. BUT, IN THE END, EVEN THE CRITICS AGREED, AGE DID NOT WEARY THEM. THE TOUR WENT OFF WITHOUT A HITCH.

Rose Tattoo spent less than six months in the United States. Angry was very anxious to get home to Lindy because the baby's birth was getting closer. At first there was talk of him coming home alone, just for the birth, and then returning to continue the tour, but in the end it was just decided that basically the whole band would call it quits and go home together.

For Angry, they made it home just too late. He missed the birth of his daughter by two weeks. She was born on the 2 January 1982. Lindy went through the whole birth on her own. It's something Angry says he will always regret, and if he was ever given a chance to change one thing in his life, that would be it. "I harboured a really deep resentment that I missed the birth, for the fact that I had to be with the band. I had to hold up my end of the bargain, because I couldn't jeopardise all these other people's incomes, even for something as important as a baby's birth. But now, I wish I had. It was one of those situations where you feel you should do something, but you reason against your instinct, and it was wrong. I should have been there."

On the way home from the States on the plane, he was in tears with excitement at the prospect of meeting his baby daughter. The flight gave him some time to think. He was already assessing his

THE FIRST MEETING - ANGRY AND ROXANNE

situation, and his future. He knew life would change with a child, but he didn't realise on what level. He'd always imagined he'd be affected in a purely practical sense, in that he wouldn't be able to live the kind of carefree existence he'd always lived. But, he had no idea how overwhelming his emotions would be the day he first saw his daughter. He had no idea that, on that day, any practical consideration would simply fade into insignificance.

As he says, "There's a terrific change that takes place in a man while you realise that this woman is pregnant with your baby. That's a big enough thing in itself, but the first time you actually see...when I looked at that little face...it was one of the few moments that actually - snap! It changed my life. It's the moment I remember the most."

When Angry walked into the house on that first day it was full of people. Lindy was there with both sets of grandparents, Lindy's parents and Rosemay and Bert, but they weren't the people he was interested in. He just marched straight past them. He barely even stopped to kiss Lindy. He was just on a mission. Suddenly there was someone new he was desperate to see, someone even more important. She was the little person asleep in the nursery.

Roxanne didn't get her name until Angry came home. In Lindy's

T HERE'S A TERRIFIC CHANGE THAT TAKES PLACE IN A MAN WHILE YOU REALISE THAT THIS WOMAN IS PREGNANT WITH YOUR BABY. THAT'S A BIG ENOUGH THING IN ITSELF, BUT THE FIRST TIME YOU ACTUALLY SEE...WHEN I LOOKED AT THAT LITTLE FACE...IT WAS ONE OF THE FEW MOMENTS THAT ACTUALLY — SNAP! IT CHANGED MY LIFE. IT'S THE MOMENT I REMEMBER THE MOST.

words she was a no-frills baby. "That's what we called her. You know, like the brands in the supermarket...no-name. We waited till Angry got back, then we picked the name Roxanne. It was a name we both liked. Then Hannah, her middle name, was picked after Hana Mandlikova, because she was our favourite tennis star at the time."

So that was it. That was her name...Roxanne Hannah Anderson.

In many ways, meeting Roxanne was the event that tamed Angry. Most people who knew him before Roxy's birth say that if they had to pick the one event that completely altered Angry's attitudes and lifestyle, it was the birth of Roxanne. It mellowed him. He'd had so many opportunities in his life to settle down, but it wasn't until that moment with Roxanne that he was completely knocked off his feet. It was like the moment of instant realisation, instant love, instant commitment. And he couldn't have walked away, even if he'd wanted to.

"YOU KNOW FROM THAT MINUTE ON THAT YOU WILL NEVER BE THE SAME AGAIN. IT'S THAT PROFOUND. THE FIRST TIME YOU ACTUALLY LOOK INTO THE EYES OF THIS HUMAN BEING YOU'RE RESPONSIBLE FOR CREATING..."

It was like, within a moment, this tiny baby was bigger than any other thing in his life. As he says, "You know from that minute on that you will never be the same again. It's that profound. The first time you actually look into the eyes of this human being you're responsible for creating..."

"I walked in, just come off tour, and you know, I was the rock and roll animal. Like I said, being in a rock band gives you a licence to kill in a sense. It gives you a licence to be as gross and as self-indulgent as you want to be. I swaggered in there...but I just crept out. I have never been so humbled in all my life. I have never been so affected. This little being, who was only days old, didn't do anything. She just laid there, and just BANG, it changed me."

8

'ONE OF THE THINGS THAT GEORGE REALLY LIKES IS
THAT YOU BECOME THE CHARACTER. YOU GET FROCKED
UP THREE HOURS EARLY AND YOU CAN'T PUT ON ALL
THAT SHIT WITHOUT GETTING AN ATTITUDE.'

HIGH NOON

There's a chronic burnout rate for rock performers, and by the time they came home from the United States, all the members of Rose Tattoo were on the verge. After the months on the road, with the disappointments and the drinking, they were tired and unsettled. They'd lost their drive. They'd hit America hard, and come home to a grinding halt.

One of the first things Angry did when he got back to Sydney was go to see a doctor. He was exhausted. He'd been sick with virus after virus, and he'd never given himself a chance to completely recover. He was run down. There had been many nights on the US tour where he'd drunk himself into a stupor, and just as many where he'd pushed himself to be on stage, despite feeling drained and hung over. He was 37 years old, but starting to feel fifty.

THE SAMURAI - THE TRUE WARRIOR HOLDING THE SWORD AND THE QUILL, WITH BOTH THE ABILITY FOR WAR AND THE QUEST FOR KNOWLEDGE

The doctor did just as Angry expected. He told him all the things he feared. He told him he was killing himself. He said he was an alcoholic who was well on the way to drinking himself to death. He said he was wasting his life.

As Angry says, "He asked me 'What do you want to be? Do you want to be the Jim Morrison of Australia? Do you want to be the rock and roll outlaw, and go out in typical fashion...you know die in a motorcycle accident or drink yourself to death? What's it to be? Is that what you want out of your life?' And of course, that wasn't what I wanted out of my life. I didn't want it before Roxy and Lou came along, but I certainly didn't want it once they'd arrived."

Angry took the warning seriously. It was a confirmation of

everything he already knew. Slowly, methodically, he started to cut down his drinking, and over a period of months he made the first steps toward breaking ties with the band. It wasn't just a health issue. It was much more than that. It was as if a phase in his life was gradually coming to an end, and although he wasn't quite ready to turn his back completely on Rose Tattoo, his commitment was beginning to change.

He didn't have the same fire and ambition. Fatherhood had presented him with a new perspective, and he suddenly felt he needed more out of life. As Angry says, "It wasn't that rock and roll was less fun. It just didn't fill up the picture any more. You know, the picture had all of a sudden got bigger. When there's just rock 'n roll in your life, it is your whole world, but at the same time, it's a small world. Then, there's another human being, and a baby to accommodate. All of a sudden rock and roll wasn't all my universe. Basically it was as simple as that."

ANGRY HAD SPENT MORE THAN TEN YEARS ON THE ROAD, BETWEEN BUSTER BROWN AND ROSE TATTOO, BUT HE HAD ALMOST NOTHING TO SHOW FOR IT. HE HAD EARNED NOTHING MORE THAN A WEEKLY WAGE IN ALL THAT TIME.

The financial side of being in a rock and roll band had also started to lose some of its appeal. Angry had spent more than ten years on the road, between Buster Brown and Rose Tattoo, but he had almost nothing to show for it. He had earned nothing more than a weekly wage in all that time. The band itself had grossed millions of dollars, but only a very small proportion of that money had actually made it into the pockets of the musicians. The bulk of the band's income had been siphoned off to record companies, distributors, managers, publicity agents, and all the other people in a long, long list.

Angry and the band often laughed with each other about how far down they were in the queue when it came to handing out the money. They'd make jokes about having to pay for Joe Blogg's new boat and BMW before paying for their own dinners. As the years wore on though, the joke became less funny.

Although the desire was there, making the actual break from the band was not such an easy move. Angry needed to find something else to do. The prospect of spending the rest of his life as the unemployed ex-front man for Rose Tattoo loomed large. He was terrified of his alternatives. It was a matter of trying to find a suitable career direction.

He was already sailing down the path of new fatherhood, and all he needed to top things off was to sail down the path of some new job. Although he would have done anything to support Lindy and Roxy, as a retiring rock star, he didn't know what he was really capable of doing. He didn't think he had many options.

As with almost everything else in his life, when Angry finally made the move he made it a big one. He didn't just slip quietly into life as a painter or a builder. He found himself two new jobs...one in the movies, and one in television as the youth reporter for the "Midday Show". The move to film was almost understandable. There's some similarity between performing on stage and performing for the movies, but Angry could hardly have chosen a more radical career move than the one to "Midday". The irresponsible rock star becomes the moral crusader. The bad boy becomes the do-gooder.

It was a career move that paid off. Turning his attention to daytime television was one of the best things Angry ever did. But it wasn't something that happened overnight. The new job direction turned out to be a very rocky road that took quite some time in the making.

When Rose Tattoo first arrived home from the United States, they had a huge job in front of them. Half the guys had lost interest in the band altogether, but their contract with Alberts still required them to record one more album.

IT WAS A CAREER MOVE THAT PAID OFF. TURNING HIS ATTENTION TO DAYTIME TELEVISION WAS ONE OF THE BEST THINGS ANGRY EVER DID. BUT IT WASN'T SOMETHING THAT HAPPENED OVERNIGHT.

"There was just myself and Geordie, and we sort of battled on," says Angry. "We got a couple of guitarists who were unusual enough to fill the role, and we recorded another album. It basically didn't turn out quite the way we expected. Understandably the record company wanted another heavy rock album from us. It was an album based on heavy rock, but it had a bit of a ballad format. There was lots of melody. That was the fourth album."

The album was called "Southern Stars", and it was the first album that wasn't recorded by the original band. It was full of patriotic songs and feelings. Angry says when he came home from America he was flushed, not only with the pride of being a new parent, he was suddenly flushed with a new national pride. Like many homesick people, he'd spent the months in America remembering what a wonderful country he came from, so he was going through a really patriotic stage. As he says, "I wanted to write and record something that was painfully Australian."

Even the album cover was patriotic. It depicted Angry as some modern day buccaneer, proudly brandishing a flag that combined a skull and cross bones with the Southern Cross.

After the album was done, the band did an extensive Australian

tour. Angry wasn't really happy about any part of it. The tour took him away from Lindy and Roxy, and he felt like he was wasting his time. As he says, "I tried to wean myself off the band slowly. It was basically your typical rock and roll tour. We got a couple of hundred bucks each, and everyone else made thousands. I just thought, 'What's the point?' You know, this is bullshit. But I couldn't quite stop. It was like I was dead, but I wouldn't lie down...you know what I mean? The change had already taken place, I was just straining against it. Everything had changed. It was never going to be the same again."

Giving up alcohol also proved tougher than he expected. He couldn't just quit cold turkey, because he felt it was too dangerous. He'd go "ratty". So he tried to do with alcohol what he was doing with the band. He tried to wean himself off slowly. It wasn't easy. He found the addiction almost overpowering.

When he was at home with Lindy and Roxy, avoiding a drink was simple, but as soon as he was on the road again, the temptation would become too great. He'd control himself for a week or so, then let loose and fall back into his old habits. There were many, many nights where he willed himself to walk past a pub, or turn down a drink, but then ended up hating himself when he eventually gave in to the pressure.

It posed a problem for Lindy and Angry's relationship, because although Lindy had never hated rock and roll, she quickly began to hate the lifestyle. It was like Angry was taking two steps forward at home, and falling three steps back on tour.

In the beginning he lied to Lindy about his drinking. As he says, "She'd ask me if I'd had a drink, and I'd always say 'Oh yeah, but only a couple'. And, you know, I'm standing there and I've put on half a stone of fluid, my eyes are hanging out of my head and I look puffy, sick and jaundiced. I wasn't fooling anybody, certainly not Lou."

Touring was the major problem. It had lots of drawbacks. It didn't just make it hard for Angry to avoid alcohol. It also made it impossible for him to be the kind of father he was committed to being. He was just away from home too often, and Roxanne was growing up too quickly. As he says, he began to get impatient with himself. "It started to dawn on me that I should have been getting my act together more quickly. I kind of realised. I thought Roxy can't get too much older having me away all the time, because you know, once she got past swaddling so much was changing. I mean, I wasn't going to miss her walking for a start. But, I was missing things like new sounds. You know, you don't realise when you have your first child, but some changes take months to eventuate, and some just happen in seconds. One day they can't say something, and the next day they're saying it all the time. The first time Roxy got up and walked, we were there. The first time that she let go of a table and walked those first two or three steps. We were there when she turned around to say 'I'm walking', just as she fell over. When you actually see it in their eyes. It's like she says 'I walked' and you say 'I know.' Do you know what I mean? Everyone collapses in a heap and cries. It's beautiful. I wasn't going to miss moments like that."

One of Angry's first jobs outside Rose Tattoo was a role in an Australian film called *Bullamakanka*. He was chosen to play the ASIO agent, with the three piece suit and the dark sunglasses. His character was supposed to be protecting the Premier. The film was shot in Sydney, and starred many of the other big names in the Australian music industry at the time...Glenn Shorrock, Donnie Sutherland and Molly Meldrum. The trio of

ONE OF ANGRY'S FIRST JOBS OUTSIDE ROSE TATTOO WAS A ROLE IN AN AUSTRALIAN FILM CALLED BULLAMAKANKA. HE WAS CHOSEN TO PLAY THE ASIO AGENT, WITH THE THREE PIECE SUIT AND THE DARK SUNGLASSES.

gangsters were Derryn Hinch, Gordon Elliot and Peter Russell Clarke. Even swimmer Tracey Wickham had a role as a choir girl. It was quite a line-up.

There was a group of young actors who made up the core of the ensemble. They were NIDA would-bes, bright young hopefuls at the time. The film didn't ever make it to the big screen, it just went straight on to television.

As Angry says now, his introduction to the film industry was full of satisfaction and laughs. He got a big kick out of working in a new medium, and he really enjoyed his character role. "You know, I was the guy who always walked around with my hand inside my jacket, and always wore the dark shades, even at night. It was all that sort of hammy stuff, because it was a real slapstick comedy. The shooting took a few months, and was very good fun while it lasted I was still working with the band a bit, but we cut back on the touring. Of course, that meant that another dilemma presented itself in that I wanted to be a part-time rock star, with guys who wanted to be full-time rock stars so, inevitably we had to just sort of split the band."

It was like the official end of Rose Tattoo, the end of an era. The actual band had changed so much since the US tour anyway, that they'd effectively split up months earlier, but this was formal. It was the end of the adventure. Even Angry and Geordie were content to let it slip away quietly.

"ANGRY COULD DO ANYTHING. HE COULD BE A NEWSREADER. TO SEE HIM ON TV ...YOU KNOW, HE'S VERY BELIEVABLE. HE'S GOT A REALISTIC PERSONA, AND HE'S TOTALLY SINCERE. THAT COMES ACROSS."

Robbie Williams stayed with Angry after the break up, and by this time, was madly trying to help him carve out a new career path. He understood that Angry's priorities had changed, and that he needed a new profile. When Rose Tattoo ended, Mushroom records signed Angry as a solo artist, so he still had some commitments to music. He was writing and recording part time with some of the guys from the last Rose Tattoo line-up, so they were doing limited gigs as the Angry Anderson Band.

As a manager, Robbie had complete faith in Angry. He believed he was an enormous talent who could take on any challenge. As he says now, "Angry could do anything. He could be a newsreader. To see him on TV...you know, he's very believable. He's got a realistic persona, and he's totally sincere. That comes across."

Robbie was convinced that Angry should be a character actor in movies or on the stage. He'd witnessed first hand for many years the enormous Angry Anderson personality, the larger-than-life outlaw, and he thought it was exactly the kind of talent that could be channelled into drama.

Angry had made almost the same decision. He'd loved his role in *Bullamakanka*, and he'd impressed both the critics and the producers. He was determined to follow it up with another movie role. He wanted desperately to be part of the *Mad Max* movies. It was his dream. He was obsessed with the idea.

When Angry first saw the original *Mad Max* at the cinema, he was amazed and wildly impressed. He thought the movie was taking the Australian film industry in a new direction, and he was determined to be a part of it. As he says, "I remember going to see the first movie...and for anyone who's into combustion engines and petrol, you just can't help being affected by it. It might be about some lunatics in cars with society breaking down, but it was more than that. When we walked out of the movie, I said 'There'll be a follow-up', because I knew it just couldn't end there, and I said 'I'm going to be in it.'"

Angry was set on the idea, and as soon as he heard a sequel was being workshopped, he actually phoned Kennedy Miller and asked them to consider him. He even had a firm idea of where he saw himself fitting into the movie. He had the character all figured out. He was convinced that he should be brought in as the second fiddle in a comedy partnership with Mel Gibson. As Angry says, "If they couldn't see their way clear to make me Robin to his Batman, then I'd have to be the baddie. But I desperately wanted to be a Robin. I thought that it would have been terrific for him to pick up a Robin along the way. I just thought, well, what he needs is a comedy mate, you know, a Porky Pig to his Bugs Bunny. Someone who couldn't possibly rival him in the blue-eyed glam puss stakes...someone who was shorter. In other words, it couldn't possibly be like 'Starsky and Hutch', or 'Miami Vice', where they are two sort of 'good lookin' dudes'. That wouldn't do. It's like Tonto. All the girls say 'Hello Tonto', but then they turn around again and say 'Who is that guy again?' Do you know what I mean? I saw myself as that."

But, it wasn't until the third *Mad Max* movie that Angry got his chance. The Kennedy Miller producers decided to overlook him when they were casting for the second movie. He's always thought they weren't exactly sure what to make of him, or his phone call, so they probably didn't know whether to take him seriously. At the time he had a reputation for trouble, and hadn't proven himself as anything more than a bald rock singer. Besides, *Mad Max Two* was before the Rose Tattoo breakup, so the band was still heavily into tour mode at the time. Angry was forced to the let whole idea drop for a while.

Then came *Mad Max III: Beyond Thunderdome*, and this time Angry wasn't going to miss out. As soon as heard the first whispers on the grapevine that casting had begun, he started to nag Robbie to make another phone call. He saw the whole thing so clearly. It was just perfect. He hassled Robbie daily to phone the Kennedy Miller organisation to throw his name in the hat again.

George Miller knew nothing of Angry at the time, except that he sang in some loud rock band. He'd heard he was trouble, and no one in the main office seemed to have any different opinion. He wasn't sure if he was worth the risk but he was quite tantalised with the idea of using someone like Angry in the film. He thought the attitude fitted. He was someone who barely even needed a costume and make-up to look the part.

So, in consultation with the other producers and the casting agents, George Miller tried to find a way to use Angry. He was considering giving him a small part in a couple of scenes, so that he would only be on set for a few days. That way, if it was all a terrible disaster they could just drop Angry's character, and there'd be no major harm done.

Luck was on Angry's side though, because it emerged that he had one major fan in the *Beyond Thunderdome* production office. She was the girl who'd worked on continuity in *Bullamakanka*, and when she heard that the producers were concerned about bringing someone like Angry on to the film set, she jumped to defend him. She told George Miller that his work on *Bullamakanka* had been exceptional, he'd arrived on set on time every day, he'd worked dawn till dusk without

complaint, and he'd been a really nice guy. Basically she told him all the things directors and producers want to hear, so on the strength of her testimonial, George MIller decided to give Angry a go.

Angry was given the role of a guy called Fister Crunchman. Originally the character played a small part offside one of the other characters. It wasn't exactly the Mel Gibson - Angry Anderson duo that Angry had pictured, but he was still determined to make something of the opportunity.

Angry had learned a lot about the way a film set works with his part in *Bullamakanka*, so he felt supremely confident. He'd spent months on the set watching the directors and the producers and the cameras so that he'd know exactly what was required of him. It was his big chance. He grabbed it, and developed the character into something much more than an offsider. Fister Crunchman became larger than life.

Within the first few weeks workshopping the script and adapting the characters, Angry was so impressive the producers decided to extend his part. Angry loves telling this part of the story. As he says, "I remember George walking up to me one day, and he's got this way of walking up. He just looks at you, and he slowly nods his head, and he smiles. And he's got this wonderful face. I mean he's a wonderful looking bloke. He put his arm around me and said, 'The part's working out very well'. He said 'Do you think you could be available for the rest of the shoot?' And I just said 'You bet!' He told me they were going to enlarge my part and bring me into the cast. By that time, they'd changed my name to Ironbar Bassey, and I became Tina Turner's lieutenant...in charge of the home guard, the elite fan heads."

The scriptwriters and casting agents went to town with Angry's new character. They auditioned the actors to play the soldiers in Angry's army and came up with a group of huge men. Every one of them towered over Angry. "They specifically went out and got the biggest people they could get," says Angry, "I mean there were some very large people. The bloke who played Blaster...he and I became

"I REMEMBER GEORGE WALKING UP TO ME ONE DAY, AND HE'S GOT THIS WAY OF WALKING UP. HE JUST LOOKS AT YOU, AND HE SLOWLY NODS HIS HEAD, AND HE SMILES. AND HE'S GOT THIS WONDERFUL FACE. I MEAN HE'S A WONDERFUL LOOKING BLOKE. HE PUT HIS ARM AROUND ME AND SAID, 'THE PART'S WORKING OUT VERY WELL.'"

very close. I mean he's huge. He's over seven foot. He's just the biggest human being you've ever seen in your life. Paul Larson is his name. I mean he's extremely large. He's not just tall, he's big."

Beyond Thunderdome was one of Angry's greatest triumphs. Shooting took place over a period of about six months, with six weeks in Coober Pedy. Angry got a big kick out of working with all the cast...Mel Gibson, Tina Turner, and as he says, one of his favourite performers, Frank Thring. "One of my fondest memories about doing Thunderdome was Frank Thring. It was delightful because he was obviously the person out of the main cast that I spent the least amount of time with, but he had an indelible affect on me. He's a giant of a man, not only in physical size, but as an intellect and as a thinker. I mean he is just a wealth of fabulous knowledge about acting and about film and about performance."

More than anything else though, Angry loved the whole atmosphere of the film set. He just loved going to work, and he ended up hanging around for hours, even when he wasn't needed, just because he didn't want to miss any of the action.

As he says, "*Mad Max,* you know, it was the biggest budget movie ever produced in Australia. There was nothing spared, which was just fantastic. I mean there were hundreds of people working on it. Just the stuntmen alone...there was just a tribe of them, there was like dozens of the buggers. I mean they were everywhere.

"I'd go and hang around on set, and do whatever I could do. I'd go and work in the kitchen, or be the water boy. There's lots of odd jobs you can do. You'd rather go to the set than not go, you know, because you're part of the company. One of the things that George really likes is that you become the character. You get frocked up about three hours early and you can't put on all that shit, without getting an attitude. You know it looks and feels terrific. So you put your frock on, and you start thinking, 'Well, I am Ironbar Bassey'."

There were only two parts of the entire movie experience that caused Angry any discomfort. First, he found the screening of the rushes unbearable. As he says, "You can tour with a band and play in front of thousands of people, but it's just not like a movie. Once you see yourself! I went to the rushes and George is sitting behind me, and

GETTING THE ROLE
IN BEYOND THUNDERDOME
JUST STARTED THE WHOLE
BALL ROLLING FOR ANGRY.
IT WAS THE FIRST BREAK
HE'D BEEN LOOKING FOR.
HIS CONFIDENCE WAS
BOOMING. HE FELT LIKE HE
COULD DO ANYTHING. HE'D
TAKEN ON THE CHALLENGE,
AND MADE IT WORK FOR
HIM. HE WAS FLYING HIGH.

I'm sitting next to Mel, and Mel turns to me and says, 'This is really weird isn't it?' You know, you can hear George telling them which scenes to keep and which scenes to lose, and you see the same scene six or eight times, and it starts to dawn on you that you have no hold on it. They can do what they like. If they want to take it to Mars and show it to people, they can. In other words, there's going to be thousands, if not millions of people that are going to go and sit in the theatre and watch you. They're going to see you. It's different to performing live in a band. It's really spooky. Really eerie."

The only other down side to Angry's movie experience was the official premiere. Mel Gibson makes it a rule not to even attend premieres, because he can't bear to watch himself. Angry, after his first and only experience, says that Mel has the right idea. Next time, if there is a next time, he'll be sitting it out as well. "It was just awful," Angry says. "It's just embarrassing. There's nowhere to go. It's like there it is, you know, and it's like you can't get away from it. It's a really strange experience. I mean, I enjoyed the other facets of the movie because, having done it, I wanted to see what it looked like. I wanted to see it in big living colour. Once I could get past me. You see, the point is, you go and see yourself in a film and you watch yourself the whole time. You're not watching the film, do you know what I mean? You're watching what you're doing, and you've got your hands over your face saying 'Oh shit, oh gee, I wish I hadn't done that', and you're watching yourself, and it's like every time you're on screen it's like nothing else exists."

ON THE SET, 'BEYOND THUNDERDOME'

After the official screening, Angry has only ever managed to watch the movie again on video at home with the kids. He says he can handle it on the small screen, and he can handle it without the audience. Although, it hasn't always been so easy for the kids. At times, they've had trouble coming to terms with Dad's new role. The family have watched it together many times, and Angry says the kids have always reacted differently. "They got scared at first. All the kids did, even Roxy. She didn't like it at first because they hurt her Dad." Angry says, "You know, Galen, the first he saw it, he was just reduced to tears. He was hysterical. He said to me once, you know, he was sort of looking at me, and he said 'Gee Dad, you got really mad there', and I said 'It's only playing. It's only pretending', but he was quite concerned for a while. But, he was still on my side, because he turned around and he said to me 'You're the bad guy?', and I said 'Yeah, the other guy, Mel Gibson, he's the good guy. He's the hero'. And he smiled and he said 'Oh yeah, Dad, you're always the bad guy'."

Getting the role in *Beyond Thunderdome* just started the whole ball rolling for Angry. It was the first break he'd been looking for. His confidence was booming. He felt like he could do anything. He'd taken on the challenge, and made it work for him. He was flying high.

People suggested he look for parts in other movies, but for Angry, that wasn't really the point. He'd been desperate to be part of the *Mad Max* movies because he thought they suited him so perfectly. Just because things had turned out, he didn't want to suddenly be running from film set to film set looking for new roles. As he says, he was always hugely flattered with the attention and the praise he received for *Mad Max*, but he didn't want to get too carried away. "Even years after the movie came out, people would come up to me and say, 'You're Ironbar Bassey'. They'd always say 'You were great', you know, but they don't mean you're a great actor. They just mean that you were one of the pieces that actually fitted to make up the jigsaw puzzle. That's why I've never really had any inclination to go back to drama classes, and say ooh gee, I've just discovered I'm an actor. I mean, I've been an actor all my life. Being a rock and roll singer, unless you're really, really serious about yourself there's a huge amount of chicanery, and myth making and legend making and fantasy...even in a straight band, let alone in a band like Rose Tattoo."

Then came the next big offer. As Angry says now, it was

THEN CAME THE NEXT BIG OFFER. AS ANGRY SAYS NOW, IT WAS PROBABLY THE BIGGEST OFFER OF HIS LIFE. IT WASN'T IN MOVIES, AND IT WASN'T IN MUSIC. IT WAS THE CALL FROM THE "MIDDAY SHOW" OFFERING HIM A JOB.

probably the biggest offer of his life. It wasn't in movies, and it wasn't in music. It was the call from the "Midday Show" offering him a job. The producers wanted him to take on a new position as the regular youth commentator.

He'd done a couple of segments on the show before, as the lead singer of Rose Tattoo, and he'd been impressive. 1985 was Ray Martin's first year at "Midday". The programmers had just made the change from the "Mike Walsh Show" so they were looking to take the program in a new direction. They were trying to find something completely different. Angry Anderson was it.

When the first call came through from Paul Melville, then the executive producer of "Midday", Angry couldn't quite believe his luck. He says he thought at first they must have been kidding, but after going in for the meeting, and hearing what they had to offer, he became really excited. The producers were basically giving him free rein.

They wanted a reporter-presenter who could get out among the kids, and who could talk about the real issues of street life and youth problems. As Angry says, "My immediate reaction was 'You're kidding', but I talked to some friends in the industry, and after finding out what capacity I'd have, they all said it would be invaluable if someone got on TV and was able to talk about these issues...street things. It all appealed to my ego and my sense of worth. You know, it was like 'Does this mean I can really be a worthwhile citizen?' No matter where I looked, there wasn't a reason why I shouldn't do it."

When the news was announced that Angry Anderson - the meanest, roughest, craziest rock singer in the country - had been signed as a reporter on daytime television, the rock industry went mad. Angry's still bitter about the reaction. He says, "Let's face it. I mean the first couple of years I was with 'Midday', according to 'rockdom' I was a washout. I'd destroyed all of my credibility, whatever that's supposed to mean, and I'd sold out.

"The thing that annoyed me was that there were even a couple of rock critics who were trying to insinuate that I'd sold out on the kids, that I'd left them behind, abandoned them. They told me I'd never sell another record. People in the industry were saying things like, your

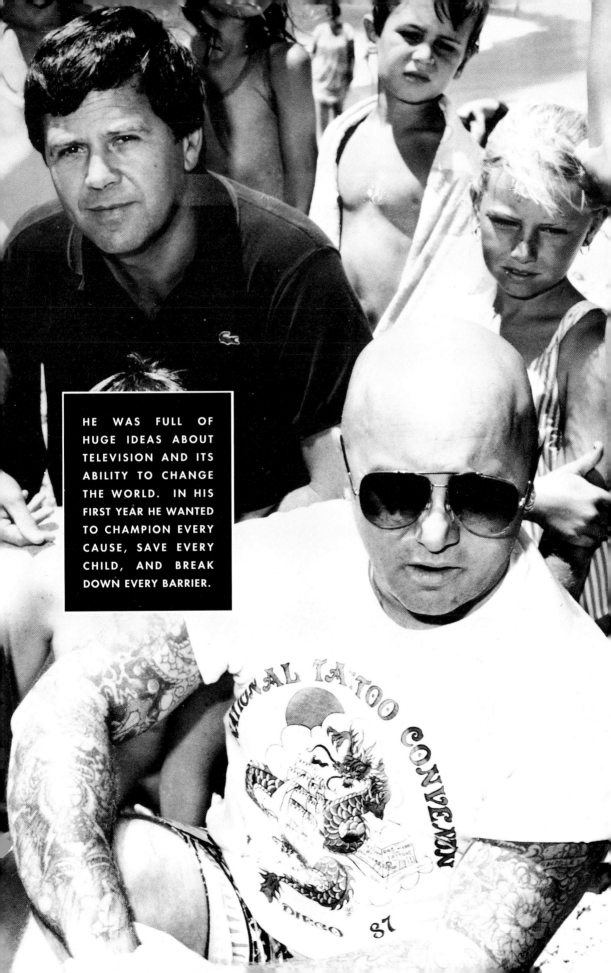

HE WAS FULL OF HUGE IDEAS ABOUT TELEVISION AND ITS ABILITY TO CHANGE THE WORLD. IN HIS FIRST YEAR HE WANTED TO CHAMPION EVERY CAUSE, SAVE EVERY CHILD, AND BREAK DOWN EVERY BARRIER.

next album should be called 'Fifty-Two Golden Oldies', or it should be a duet with Julie Anthony, you know?

"It was like all of a sudden I did an about-face. That's why they all said I was a phony and a fake, because I'd gone from being the man in the black hat to being the rhinestone cowboy, you know, the guy in the white hat. I was sitting on TV with Captain Smiles, being the do-goody. People's head were spinning because they just couldn't lock on to it. The whole rock industry canned me. They said I was only going on daytime television to suck up to daytime Ray."

As with everything else, Angry thumbed his nose at the critics. He was determined to prove them all wrong, but even more importantly, he was determined to make the most of the new opportunity.

HE WAS ONE OF THE FIRST REPORTERS TO GO INTO KINGS CROSS AND SPEAK TO TEENAGE PROSTITUTES ON CAMERA. HE TALKED TO YOUNG GIRLS ABOUT THEIR HEROIN ADDICTION, AND THEIR HOMELESSNESS. HE COVERED TEENAGE CANCER, CHILD SEXUAL ABUSE, PEER GROUP PRESSURE, FATHERS IN JAIL, ETC

He was full of huge ideas about television and its ability to change the world. In his first year he wanted to champion every cause, save every child, and break down every barrier. He was obsessed with the power of television, with the magnitude of the live audience. He'd go on air one day talking about prostitution or drug addiction, and then have viewer after viewer come up to him in the street saying things like, "Hey Angry, I saw you on 'Midday' and I think what you said was great."

It was like he'd tapped into something he'd never experienced before. He suddenly realised that TV matters, that it really does have an immense power, and after a while he became the unbearable fanatic. He wanted to leave no stone unturned. He wanted "Midday" to take on the world.

In his first year he covered many topics. He was one of the first reporters to go into Kings Cross and speak to teenage prostitutes on camera. He talked to young girls about their heroin addiction, and their homelessness. He covered teenage cancer, child sexual abuse, peer group pressure, fathers in jail, etc.

Although he admits now he was probably overzealous in his early years at "Midday", he's adamant that he was no phony. As he says, if he was, he'd eventually have been exposed, and wouldn't have had any chance to make the impact he's made. "I certainly don't get shit canned now by kids for trying to relate to older people on their behalf, or for trying to relate to them on behalf of older people. I've always been of the opinion, and Ray said this to me right from the start, he said 'If you try to fake this, if you try to turn yourself into something you're not, more than likely, they'll bury you.' And I reckon that's true."

For people who want to argue that a lunatic rock singer like Angry Anderson has no place as a daytime television reporter, he has an answer for that too. He says, "My commitment to youth was there from day one. I'd always given opinions to kids, I'd always said, be responsible for yourself. Look at the lyrics of Rose Tattoo songs and then tell me that I wasn't concerned or worried. Sure, the bad boy image is part of all the great rock legends, but I'd made a commitment by the time I got to Ray's set. By the time I'd sat down on the set for the very first time, I'd made a commitment not to be like that anymore."

Angry's "Midday" segment took off very quickly. Viewers warmed to him, and listened to him. Ray Martin describes his role as that of the "wayward grandson". Viewers recognised Angry's sincerity, and they gave him the licence to get away with far more than other television personalities. He could talk about almost anything. He was one of the few people who could get away with having an argument with Ray about a particular topic.

He was still a loose cannon though, and it was always hard to pick his reaction to certain topics. As one of his producers says, "We'd decide that Angry should talk about something controversial like the legalisation of marijuana, or condoms for teenagers, but until you spoke to him, you'd never have any idea which side he was going to be on. It was impossible to second-guess him."

As Ray used to say, "You couldn't read him with a radar".

But there was one thing you could always be sure of, his segments were never boring. He was spontaneous and reactive...a producer's nightmare. He'd change tack and topic at the drop of a hat. He was completely undisciplined. Nothing ever went as planned. If Angry felt the audience weren't attentive enough, he'd get up out of his seat and yell at them. If he didn't like a comment made by the guest before

ONE OF THE MOST REGULAR COMPLAINTS THE "MIDDAY SHOW" EVER RECEIVED WAS THE COMPLAINT THAT ANGRY WAS BEING CUT OFF. VIEWERS WERE ALWAYS SAYING THINGS LIKE, "WHY DIDN'T YOU LET ANGRY FINISH WHAT HE HAD TO SAY?"

him, he'd challenge it. If someone in the audience shook their head in disagreement, he'd rush over to tell them to speak up and let their opinion be heard.

Of course, television commentary tapped in on Angry's undeniable talent and strength - the ability to talk, anytime, anywhere, about anything, for ever. But, the audiences never tired of hearing what he had to say. One of the most regular complaints the "Midday Show" ever received was the complaint that Angry was being cut off. Viewers were always saying things like, "Why didn't you let Angry finish what he had to say?" The quick answer from the producers is that Angry never finishes what he has to say. If he wasn't cut off, he'd probably just go on forever. But, the viewers wouldn't have been satisfied with an answer like that. To them, no segment was ever long enough. It seemed that whether he was talking on a topic for 30 seconds, two minutes, ten minutes, or even twenty minutes, there was always at least one complaint to say the segment was too short.

By the end of 1985, Angry had everything going at once. Newspapers kept saying things like "Angry gets busy". He had the movie under his belt, and he'd solidified his position at "Midday". He'd also been invited to do a December tour of Australia as the guest singer with the Party Boys, so it was a perfect opportunity to get back up on stage as a singer for a while.

Although it was, once again, work that took him on the road and away from the family, the money being offered for the Party Boys tour was just too good to turn down. They had a great line-up, and Angry was amazed to suddenly find he could earn more money as a hired singer in a band, than he could ever have earned as the front man for Rose Tattoo.

It was like 1985 was Angry's year. He'd taken a new path, and it was all paying off. He was still hugely enthusiastic about the sort of issues he could tackle on "Midday". While the producers talked about their holidays at the Christmas party, Angry kept talking about the kind of stories they could do next year. It was as if he'd been given a platform, a perfect soapbox. He had an opportunity to do anything he wanted, always with the power and back up of a Channel 9 identification card and a Channel 9 camera crew.

Perhaps even more importantly, 1985 was the year where Angry finally managed to put the "ex" in front of the word drunkard. It was a struggle that caused him great heartache, but he won. Even now, when he performs on stage he only has two beers. That's all he needs, and he says there is no way he will ever fall back into his old ways.

As Angry says now, he's always been proud of the fact that he was able to move on to other things after Rose Tattoo. He says during his days on the road, before Lindy, he used to imagine how he was most likely to end up. He could easily see it all. Life as an ageing rocker...fat, drunk, and alone sitting on the front porch in some little house, reliving past glories.

He says instead, when he came home from America, he started to carve out a different scenario. It was a matter of closing one door, then desperately trying to find a handle with which to open another. As he says, "If I wasn't willing to free myself, to jump into the void...if I wasn't prepared to say 'Okay, that's the finish of that life. I can't be a rock singer full time for the rest of my life'. If I hadn't been brave enough to do that, then these other opportunities would not have been open to me. Because otherwise, I would have had to turn them all down saying 'No, sorry, that's not what I do. I'm a rock singer'."

In some circles though, he still had problems with credibility. People were just not willing to let him change. They weren't prepared to accept that he didn't want to be the bad boy of Rose Tattoo anymore, that there was more to him than just the loudmouth on stage. But, he doesn't actually regret who he was in the early years, or even what he did. It was all part of Angry Anderson. It was all part of the one complex character. As he says, "I'd tell you I wished I had never been like that, but if I hadn't gone through exactly what I went through, we wouldn't be sitting here today, and I wouldn't have missed

IT WAS A MATTER OF CLOSING ONE DOOR, THEN DESPERATELY TRYING TO FIND A HANDLE WITH WHICH TO OPEN ANOTHER. AS HE SAYS, "IF I WASN'T WILLING TO FREE MYSELF, TO JUMP INTO THE VOID...IF I HADN'T BEEN BRAVE ENOUGH TO DO THAT, THEN THESE OTHER OPPORTUNITIES WOULD NOT HAVE BEEN OPEN TO ME."

this for quids. Do you know what I mean? I would not have met Lou if I'd been different. We wouldn't have had those four wonderful kids. If I hadn't been the completely irresponsible person I was, I would never have had a go on 'Midday'."

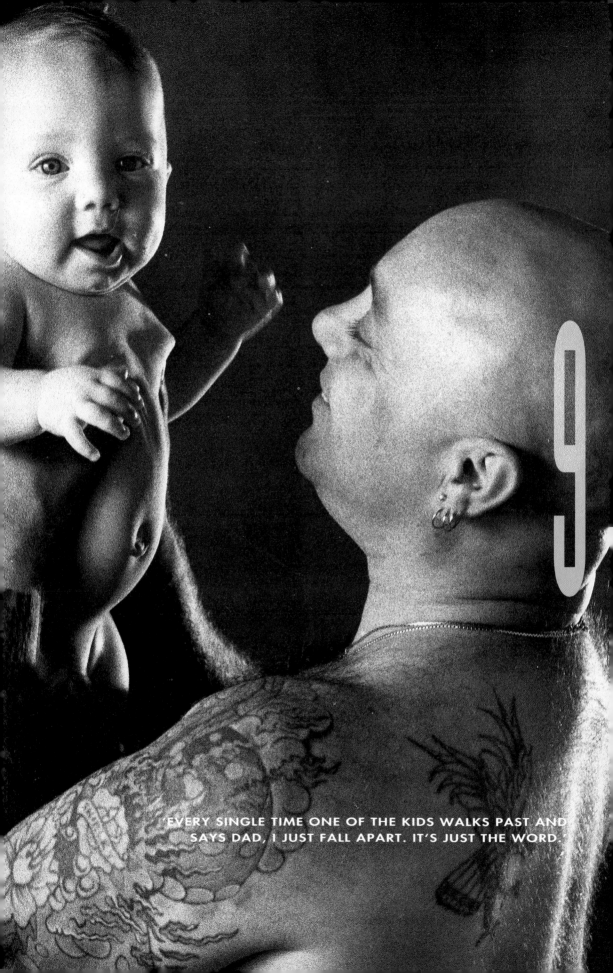

'EVERY SINGLE TIME ONE OF THE KIDS WALKS PAST AND
SAYS DAD, I JUST FALL APART. IT'S JUST THE WORD.'

THE FAMILY MAN

In 1986, Angry and Lindy finally decided to marry. They set the date for the first Saturday in January, one day after Roxy's third birthday.

Although Angry had committed himself to parenthood without too much effort, the giant leap to marriage hadn't come quite so easily. Whenever the topic came up in conversation, Angry would maintain that he and Lindy would not marry until the day he was certain he could keep his vows. He didn't want to make any commitments he couldn't keep. He knew what he was like, and he didn't want anyone to be disappointed. Unlike anything else in his life, this was an area he approached with great care and caution.

THE SNAKE FOR VIRILITY

It wasn't really an issue for Lindy. Marriage was not something she ever thought about. She felt she didn't need the traditional formal commitment. It wasn't that she was against the institution, she just wasn't fussed. She had a partner, and a great father for her daughter, and that was all she needed, so when marriage did eventually become a consideration, it was Angry who was doing the pushing.

He suddenly decided that he was ready, not just that he was prepared to make the commitment, but that he really wanted to. He became quite desperate to formalise the partnership. As he says, he wanted to self-impose fidelity and sobriety, and he thought of marriage as the most effective way of doing that. He felt his life needed stricter guidelines. He wanted to wear the 'family man' tag. He wanted to be a husband, and a father, in the most traditional sense of the word. It was like he wanted to have the title written all over his forehead.

When it came to the actual practicalities of getting married, Angry's proposal to Lindy was not elaborate. In fact, he almost skipped that stage completely. He was so sure about what he was doing that he began planning the wedding before he'd even asked Lindy for her hand. He was determined to make the wedding day special, and one of his priorities was to keep most of the details a secret. That's how he wanted it to be for Lindy...he wanted the day to be a wonderful series of surprises and delights. He had huge plans for everything, from the entertainment to the venue to the food. The only thing he didn't have a huge plan for was the actual proposal. Amongst all his huge visions, he'd basically overlooked the most important step.

Eventually though, after Lindy heard word that a wedding was being planned, Angry pulled it all together and popped the all-important question in bed. He thought that was more appropriate than asking at the dinner table. He says he considered candlelight, or fireworks, or some other extravagance, but settled on a quiet moment in the bedroom.

THE WEDDING DAY. ANGRY AND LINDY WITH ROXY AS FLOWER GIRL. 'HOLDING THE TWO MOST IMPORTANT WOMEN IN THE WORLD'

Angry and Lindy married on 3 January in the Abbey Restaurant, Glebe, Sydney. It was a small wedding, but no expense was spared. Angry wanted the works. He wanted the wedding day to be sensational and unusual, a colourful gypsy-like affair with music and dancers and street performers. He had ideas of a sort of medieval carnival with all the trimmings. As Lindy remembers it, it was a wonderful day. "We had a beautiful wedding. The Abbey was actually a Catholic church and they converted it to a restaurant. We got married in the garden. My mum and dad didn't have to pay for anything because Angry insisted on paying for it all. We had a beautiful silk marquee, we had harps, and people running around with rose petals everywhere. Roxy was flowergirl. We had great entertainment. We had some a cappella singers who had written special songs, one for Lindy Lou, and one for

Angry, and we had can-can girls, and magic and mime artists, and fire throwers. It was wonderful. It was such a good show."

On the morning of the wedding the *Daily Mirror* published a full page article with the headline "Angry Anderson to Wed Longtime Girlfriend". It infuriated Angry. He had trusted the *Mirror's* social writer with the wedding details, and promised exclusivity on the story, on the proviso that nothing would be published until after the event.

It was the only thing that upset Angry on the wedding day. Above all else, on that one day, he wanted privacy. He felt celebrity weddings had become free-for-alls, with the media ruining the solemnity and seriousness of the occasion. They were so intrusive with cameras and reporters that Angry was adamant he was going to keep it private. Security guards were even posted on all the entrances, so when Angry woke up to see the article he was horrified. He'd been forced into a trade-off with the *Mirror*. There was so much media interest in the wedding, Angry felt the best way to keep the situation under control was to offer one group exclusivity, so the other papers and TV shows would be forced to back off. But the social writer betrayed the confidence, so on the morning of the wedding, all the details were out, even the location of the reception.

ANGRY, LINDY AND REYNA (LINDY'S SISTER)

Nevertheless, it was a great day. Angry chose Robbie as his best man, and they both wore white tuxedos with black and white check pants, and mauve ties. The girls all wore antique white. They were married by a celebrant, and they wrote their own vows. As Angry says, "Instead of promising to love, honour and obey, we promised to love, honour and nurture. There was something along the lines of we realised we were individuals, and we'd never stand in each other's way or hold one another down. The vows were all based around that."

Lindy says the day was perfect. Everything was right. "On the actual wedding day, my dad cried, because when me and Angry first got together he wasn't too sure. You know, he kept saying, 'Are you

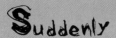Suddenly

I ONLY DREAMED THAT I WOULD FIND
A LOVING HEART, AN OPEN MIND
TO SEE THE REAL ME
AND I HOPED THAT YOU WOULD BE THE ONE.

A CHANCE TO TALK, A CHANCE TO GROW,
I'LL TAKE THE RISK, LET MY FEELINGS FLOW,
I'VE FOUND THE WORDS
I NEED TO SAY.

SUDDENLY YOU'RE SEEING ME
JUST THE WAY I AM
SUDDENLY YOU'RE HEARING ME,
SO I'M TALKING JUST AS FAST AS I CAN,
TO YOU.

SUDDENLY EVERY PART OF ME,
NEEDS TO KNOW EVERY PART OF YOU.
SUDDENLY, OPENLY, YOU'RE ALL I WANT
ALL I NEED YOU TO BE,

SUDDENLY EVERY PART OF ME,
NEEDS TO KNOW EVERY PART OF YOU.
JUST YOU, IT'S YOU.

AND NOW I KNOW YOU ARE MINE,
YOU BRING ME LOVE AND PEACE OF MIND
YOU SEE THE REAL ME
AND I KNOW THAT YOU'RE THE KEY.

certain about this?' They weren't real pleased about it at first, but as the years went by, they sort of learned to love him and see him for what he is."

Angry was still working hard at the time, so they couldn't manage a proper honeymoon immediately. They just had to make do with, in Lindy's words, "A wonderful dirty weekend at the Regent." But, a few months later, they made the most of it and took Roxy up to the Whitsundays for four weeks.

COVER SHOT "SUDDENLY"
- SEEING ME JUST THE WAY I AM

Ironically, the song that's become known as Angry's wedding song, "Suddenly", was not played at his wedding. It had been written and recorded, but it wasn't a hit when they were married. That came later.

"Suddenly" was written in dedication to Lindy. As Angry says, "Lou had always, always said, tongue in cheek, but I knew she meant it...she'd always said 'Why don't you write love songs? You're a romantic person. Why don't you write a song about me.' So one day I wrote it, and we recorded it."

The song was published on the "Beats from a Single Drum" album, but, because it was such a break from the typical Angry Anderson lyric, the record company weren't sure about it. They only really allowed it on the album at Angry's insistence.

Eventually though, the gamble paid off, and "Suddenly" became the biggest hit Angry ever recorded. As soon as it was chosen for the wedding of the century, the "Neighbours" wedding of Kylie and Jason, there was just no turning back. "It was never intended to be sold as a single," says Angry. "The album had been out for a while. Robbie rang me up one day and said, 'Kylie and Jason are getting married', and I said 'Oh, really?', and he said 'Yeah, and they're going to use "Suddenly"'. It was great. I told him to send them congratulations and a bunch of flowers because I knew what it would do for the song."

Angry was even more delighted when he heard that Kylie had chosen the song herself. They spoke one day, and she told him she was an Angry Anderson fan. "The story I got from Kylie was that she heard the song because she had the album, and she said, 'This is the song we're getting married to. End of story.' We did the Bicentennial concert together in 1988, and I was standing around, and Kylie came in. She wasn't anywhere near as big as she is now, and she just walked up and said, 'Hi, I'd like to thank you for the song', and I said 'Well,

THE PROUD FATHER WITH GALEN (MR G)

I'd like to thank you for picking it. You've made it a big hit. It's terrific.' She said, 'Oh, I love the album. You should write more stuff like that, because everyone thinks you're the boogy man'."

"Suddenly" made it to top three in Australia for many weeks, and was only beaten out of the number one position in Britain by a new Cliff Richard single, and Kylie Minogue herself.

Over the years Angry has had many requests to sing it at weddings. Fans write regularly asking for one special performance on their wedding day, but Angry has only done it a couple of times. He has to make a policy of saying no, because otherwise the floodgates would open and he'd be at weddings every Saturday and Sunday.

Although Rose Tattoo, *Mad Max*, and "Midday" have all played a huge part in Angry's life, he maintains it's his family that's really shaped him. The five things he holds most dear in the world are Lindy and the kids. He's the proud patriarch, fussing and clucking over his brood. He says it's a bit like the Waltons or the Bradys or the Cosbys, except that it's real. He's spent years surrounding himself with a big, busy family, so that everywhere he looks he sees happy kids. Sometimes Angry even jokes that one day he might load all the kids into a painted bus and tour the country like the Partridge family or the Von Trapps.

After the disappointment and regret of missing Roxy's birth, Angry made sure he was there for the birth of all his sons. When Galen came along, two years after Lindy and Angry's marriage, Angry was at the hospital doing all the right things. In the months leading up to the birth, he went to the antenatal classes faithfully, and he learned everything so he could be the perfect support partner. He read up on childbirth and became the expert.

As he says now, most of the things he learned went straight out the window as soon as the labour began, but he at least felt confident and secure in his support role. He felt he was prepared for almost every aspect of childbirth, but still says he finds it impossible to describe. "The one thing you're not prepared for, of course, is how you're going to be affected emotionally by a birth. No one could have prepared me for that. You can't explain it. You can say, 'It was the greatest joy of my life', and yes it was, but you can't explain it like that. You can say you're awestruck, but it's more than that too...it's not any one of those things, it's everything. I just wasn't prepared for seeing it."

Angry felt the same brilliant awakening at the birth of all his sons, Galen, Blaine and Liam. He was bowled over every time. All three boys were born within the space of five years. This is Angry Anderson the family man. This is the man he'd always wanted to be.

As a father, Angry places enormous demands on himself. Like many parents, he's his own harshest critic, unforgiving and unsympathetic. When he and Lindy first got together, and Roxy was born, he was so terrified of being a bad parent that he almost didn't go through with it. Parts of him wanted to run so that he'd never have to put himself to the test. He considered leaving Lindy to raise Roxy on her own, because it was almost like he was tempting fate. He didn't trust himself. He was obsessed that he'd inherited many of his father's worst traits, the tempers and the recklessness, so he was haunted with fears that he'd follow in the family line.

"THE ONE THING YOU'RE NOT PREPARED FOR, OF COURSE, IS HOW YOU'RE GOING TO BE AFFECTED EMOTIONALLY BY A BIRTH. NO ONE COULD HAVE PREPARED ME FOR THAT. YOU CAN'T EXPLAIN IT."

In the few instances in his life where he's let himself down as a parent, he's struggled to find his confidence again. "There's a dozen incidents I've never forgiven myself for," Angry says. "It's one of those things. Like the first time you ever smack a child, and smack them hard, you know, so that they cry and there's a red mark on their leg. For that second that you're not in control you say things and do things that are irreparable, because you can't take anything back. It's one of the things that's really, really hard about being a parent, because you will say and do things that you'll regret for an eternity.

"The thing I regret most is that I'm not the perfect father, even though I know I couldn't be as passionate about the children if I wasn't such a passionate person. I think the thing is, you've got to be able to find enough compassion within yourself, for yourself. You have to be constantly reminded that you're a human being. You are going to make mistakes. You've been making mistakes all your life. The one situation where you never even want to make one mistake is with your children, but that's unrealistic. Now, some people have a real problem with that. I do too. It gives me a lot of times for regret because there's been many instances where I shouldn't have been as gruff or as hard."

YOU HAVE TO BE CONSTANTLY REMINDED THAT YOU'RE A HUMAN BEING. YOU ARE GOING TO MAKE MISTAKES. YOU'VE BEEN MAKING MISTAKES ALL YOUR LIFE. THE ONE SITUATION WHERE YOU NEVER EVEN WANT TO MAKE ONE MISTAKE IS WITH YOUR CHILDREN, BUT THAT'S UNREALISTIC.

There is a degree of see-sawing discipline in the Anderson household. Angry says he's too hard on the kids, and Lindy says she's too soft, but they're constantly reassuring and encouraging each other to try and find the balance.

There was one incident with Roxy when she was only three or four years old, where Angry completely lost his temper for a moment. He terrified her. He says it was his worst day as a father, and he still gets upset thinking about it. They were at home alone together because Lindy was in hospital recovering after Galen's birth. Angry was tired and had a short fuse. Roxy had been playing with one of her toys, but she kept doing the wrong thing with it. As Angry says, he made his biggest blunder by trying to teach her a lesson. "Because I was trying to be methodical and educational about the whole thing, I let her keep the toy. I'd already gone through the motions of sitting down with her and explaining why she shouldn't do whatever it was she was doing. But, what I should have done was just pick the toy up, and put it on the bench, and it wouldn't have been an issue. With her attention span she just would have forgotten about it, and walked away, and that would have been the end of the story. But, I don't know, for some reason, I thought I'll persist here because she's got to learn. If she'd been a year or two older I probably could have done that, but she was just too young, and I didn't stop to think about it.

"So, she kept doing it, and I'm falling into the typical trap, thinking this kid is out to get me, because when they look at you when they're a couple of years old, you mistake an innocent expression of playfulness for cunning. So, I picked the toy up, and I just threw it across the room. It hit one of the stools, and it just shattered, and I think that was the second where Roxy realised things weren't quite the way she thought they were, that this wasn't a game.

"She looked at me, and for an absolute millionth of a second, the immediate reaction could have been to burst into laughter, or be the absolute opposite. I looked at her, and she looked up at me, and she was horrified at what she saw. I just turned around and screamed at her, and told her to get upstairs, because I knew there was potential for me to grab her and smack her. She just took off."

Roxy ran up the stairs and hid under her cot. Angry says he's never been able to forgive himself, because although he didn't actually hurt her physically, he really frightened her. As a man whose childhood was full of fear, it bought back a thousand memories. Even when he tried to chase her to apologise, and tell her it was all okay, she was so scared, she wouldn't stand still. All he could see as he ran up the stairs were her little legs, moving as fast as they could to get away from him.

She wouldn't come out from under the cot for ages, and because the area was so small, Angry couldn't quite reach her to get her out. He had to be content to sit there, and wait for her to calm down. He was mortified by what

ON OCCASIONS, ANGRY BELIEVES HE'S SEEN SOME PARTS OF THE MONSTER IN HIS CHILDREN TOO. HE THINKS TO SOME DEGREE, THEY'VE INHERITED HIS TEMPER, SO HE TRIES CONSTANTLY TO HELP THEM LEARN HOW TO DEAL WITH IT.

had happened. His behaviour hadn't been that of a normal angry father. It had been much more than that. He'd actually lost control, and for one tiny moment, Roxanne had seen the monster.

On occasions, Angry believes he's seen some parts of the monster in his children too. He thinks to some degree, they've inherited his temper, so he tries constantly to help them learn how to deal with it. As he says, "Every now and then, I mean it's nothing for them just to explode, and even be destructive. You know, I've seen them when they're trying to do something with a toy and it just won't happen, so they explode and they'll throw it across the room and break it or something.

"BUT, BECAUSE I AM SO SPONTANEOUSLY COMBUSTIBLE, I TRY TO BE REALLY LENIENT AND TOLERANT OF THAT IN THE KIDS. IT DOESN'T ALWAYS WORK OUT THAT WAY. I MEAN SOMETIMES I REACT TO SOMETHING THAT THEY'VE DONE OR SAID IMMEDIATELY, WITHOUT THOSE FEW MILLISECONDS TO PULL IT BACK, AND BEFORE I KNOW WHAT'S HAPPENED, THE LID'S UP, AND THE MONSTER'S OUT."

"But, because I am so spontaneously combustible, I try to be really lenient and tolerant of that in the kids. It doesn't always work out that way. I mean sometimes I react to something that they've done or said immediately, without those few milliseconds to pull it back, and before I know what's happened, the lid's up, and the monster's out. So then there's the effort to reach out and grab it, and put in back in the box and close the lid. Sometimes that takes seconds, if not minutes, and in that time you can end up screaming at the kids, or telling them that they're bloody little nuisances or rotten little kids or whatever, and then you've got to try to repair that later."

Lindy has always been aware of Angry's parenting fears. She's understood his dread. She says he does have to fight to control his temper, and to keep himself in check constantly, or there is a chance he could be just like his father, the man he least respects. As she says, there have been times when he's come very close. "One of his worst fears was that he'd turn out like his dad, but you see, the horrible thing is, he was sort of heading that way slightly. When he realised that, it came as a crushing blow to him. That's when he tried to get some help. Sometimes when he'd smack the boys, he'd say, 'Lou, get them away from me before I lose control', so I'd take the boys away, because he was just so terrified that he'd lose it. He never did. He works really hard to control it."

He says the boys drive him crazy sometimes because of the games they play with him. They love to hide from him, in fun, but sometimes he can become so frantic searching for them, that he comes close to losing his temper. "We've had a collection of a dozen or more times when the kids have hidden from us," says Angry. "When the only thing that keeps your heart in your body is your ribs, where your mind is just in a whirl, and someone's headed for the car to start driving the streets, because you can call and call and call, and you know the child is somewhere in the house, but you can't find them, you immediately think 'Oh, God, they're outside'. Blaine was in a box once under the stairs, and he just sat there while we were in an absolute panic. It didn't make any sense that he could have got out of the house. The front door was locked, the side gate was locked. The only way he could have got out was to climb over the back fence, and so, because that was a thousand to one chance, immediately we thought 'Well, that's what's happened'. When we finally found him, and heard him giggling under the stairs, I was so furious, I couldn't even look at him."

Angry's other great parenting flaw is that he's overprotective. He has great trouble admitting it, but if he could, he'd wrap his children up in cottonwool. His principal aim would, first, be to bundle them up safely so that no one could ever steal them away from him, and second, to protect them from the bad guys of the world so that they could never get involved with anyone like him. When it comes to the kind of friends he wants his children to have, he is his own worst nightmare.

It's like he's turned full circle. For years, he prided himself in being the world's most unappealing prospective son-in-law. Most of the parents of his ex girlfriends were mortified when their daughters bought him home. He was everything they didn't want their girls involved with. Now that Angry's a parent, the situation is exactly the same. Although he's fighting it like mad, if Roxy ever came home with an Angry Anderson as her new boyfriend, it would take all of Angry's strength just to be civil to him. Lindy laughs about it, saying it's because he knows exactly how bad he really was.

Lindy even goes so far as to say that, no matter who Roxy brings home as her first boyfriend, Angry will have trouble dealing with it. "As soon as Roxy gets a boyfriend," she says, "we'll be in more therapy!" The family joke is that to be one of Angry's children, you have to put up with him lavishing attention and affection on you 24

> WHEN IT COMES TO THE KIND OF FRIENDS HE WANTS HIS CHILDREN TO HAVE, HE IS HIS OWN WORST NIGHTMARE. IT'S LIKE HE'S TURNED FULL CIRCLE. FOR YEARS, HE PRIDED HIMSELF IN BEING THE WORLD'S MOST UNAPPEALING PROSPECTIVE SON-IN-LAW.

hours a day. He cannot resist his children. As with most fathers, he wants to hug them and kiss them constantly, although with Angry there's probably also a degree of compensation in his motives. He wants to give his children everything he feels he missed out on, and in doing that, perhaps he can make up for some of what he lost himself.

Once he was talking to a lady in one of the hospitals, and he was holding Liam. As he was listening to the lady talk he was absent-mindedly kissing Liam on the cheek, and after five minutes or so, the lady ended up commenting, "Angry, it's a good thing isn't it, that God made skin so that it never wears out."

As the kids have grown up though, he's had to hold back more and more. When Roxanne reached the age where it's not cool to have your parents anywhere near you, Angry was devastated. The first time she shrugged away from his goodbye kiss outside the school, he found it very hard to take. It was a personal affront, a complete rejection, and he was even more upset when he began to understand that it wasn't just a bad mood. It was actually a phase that was going to last quite some time. As Angry says, "I remember once I came to give her something at lunchtime, and I walked into the schoolyard, and she was just horrified. She came over and said, 'What are you doing here?' She was really abrupt with me. I was very put out by that."

It's different for Angry too, because he's not like any of the other fathers. He doesn't look like the other fathers, and he doesn't sound like them. Even when he hides his tattoos with long sleeves, the broken teeth and bald head give him away. "It's changed," says Angry. "In the last couple of years, I've been cooler. You see, her friends think it's cool for me to be her dad now, but I think in the first couple of years she didn't like the notoriety. When I first told Lou I was really wounded and hurt by the way Roxy had reacted to me, she said she probably would have reacted like that even if I wasn't who I was. She told me, at certain ages, kids just don't like parents, whether they're short and bald or a rock singer on TV or whatever. Kids don't like parents invading their space, unless it's on their terms."

Angry is a strict father. He fought an ongoing battle with Roxanne for about three years over whether she could walk to and from school unaccompanied. All her friends walked to school together

from the third grade, and Roxanne begged and begged to be allowed to walk with them, but Angry just couldn't allow it. When she was in third grade, Angry said she could do it when she was in fourth grade, when she was in fourth grade he said she could do it in fifth grade, and on and on it went. Eventually, after Lindy did some pushing, he was forced to give in. As Lindy says though, he's never been comfortable about it. "She knocks off school at 3.00, and if she's not home at 3.30 sharp, he's out in the car looking for her. She used to complain that he was embarrassing her."

Angry says though, despite the heartache and anxiety, he's enjoyed the tussles with Roxy over the years. He calls it the parent - teenager war, saying that if Roxy has to fight for her rights, and he has to fight for his rights then there's no reason not to use the proper terminology. It's a battlefield, he wins some and he loses some.

"A real moment for all of us," says Angry, "was when Roxy came home from a couple of nights sleep over at a girlfriend's house, and she'd shaved her legs. I mean Lou and I were horrified, and let her know in no uncertain terms. She got into bed, and I said, 'Roxy, you've shaved your legs', and Lou just threw back the covers and screamed 'What?' And Roxy was mumbling and trying to explain. I asked Roxy why she did it, and she said it was because she was hairy. And I said, 'You know, a step like shaving your legs is not something to be done snigger, snigger. Things like shaving your legs and getting a tattoo, they're things you should discuss with your parents.'"

Angry sees no irony in the fact that he's so strict with the kids. He doesn't even accept the argument they could throw it back at him one day. He admits that he hid his own tattoo from his mother, and that he also did a thousand other things that he wouldn't want his kids to do, but to him, it's simple. It's one of the oldest rules in the parenting book - "Do as I say, not as I do". Or perhaps even more the rule in Angry's case - "Do as I say, not as I did".

ANGRY SEES NO IRONY IN THE FACT THAT HE'S SO STRICT WITH THE KIDS. HE ADMITS THAT HE HID HIS OWN TATTOO FROM HIS MOTHER, AND THAT HE ALSO DID A THOUSAND OTHER THINGS THAT HE WOULDN'T WANT HIS KIDS TO DO, BUT TO HIM, IT'S SIMPLE. IT'S ONE OF THE OLDEST RULES IN THE PARENTING BOOK — "DO AS I SAY, NOT AS I DO". OR PERHAPS EVEN MORE THE RULE IN ANGRY'S CASE - "DO AS I SAY, NOT AS I DID".

He's constantly trying not to smother his kids. As he says, "I know you don't protect kids by locking them up. You protect them by making them aware that they have the potential to be better than you. You show them that they should strive to be better than you, with your blessing. In other words, without actually saying 'Hey kids, don't be like Dad', that's exactly what I end up saying."

With the boys, tattoos are the issue. They love Angry's tatts and are always walking around with stick-on dragons and snakes and daggers. Angry's been asked many times how he'll react when he walks into the bathroom, as his own mother did all those years ago, to discover that one of his kids has been 'scarred for life'. He considers the answer for a long time. "I don't want them to come home and show me one. I want them to come home and say, 'I want one, and I want a good one', and then I can tell them who to see. That's if I can't talk them out of it. I don't want them to have tattoos when they're young. I want them to live a bit, and think about it for a while, because having a tattoo is a thing that really affects you. People who aren't tattooed can't ever imagine."

He avoided it for so long, but Angry loves married life. Lindy and Angry are great partners, although their marriage isn't anywhere near perfect. They've had a lot to contend with. As Angry says, during their married life, Lindy has weathered all things. She's weathered the drunkenness in the early years, the neglect while Angry was touring, the tempers, and she's even weathered the infidelity. In the early years of the marriage, it was a real problem. As Angry says, "Lindy is a rock and roll wife, and I don't think there's any rock and roll wife that hasn't had to put up with infidelity to some extent, even if they were unaware of it. I don't think any girl that gets involved with a guy who's in a rock and roll band ever treats herself to the luxury of thinking that while he's away he's a perfect gentleman. I don't think that anyone who gets involved with someone in a band would be that silly. I think they all understand there's a certain amount of adjustment time that guys go through before they realise that fidelity and sobriety and honesty are things that they crave and desire and need and want as much as their wives do. In all fairness, in reality, you can't take something like a tiger,

GRY WITH BELOVED
BULL TERRIER 'STELLA'

and transform it into something else overnight. You've got to make up your mind that it's worth weathering, and I think that's what Lou did. She decided that it was worth weathering and she hung in there through the bad times. She took a colossal risk on me."

There have been a couple of times when Angry and Lindy have been inches from splitting up, but so far, they've managed just to pull through. As Angry says, they work very hard at their marriage. "Lou is that one person in a lifetime. We both do come from less than ideal backgrounds, and we both brought into our marriage, as most people do, the baggage. The good and the bad. I think one of the things that determines the strength and worth of a marriage as a relationship is the ability, or the need and the desire, to want to deal with one another's baggage. You see, I really believe one of the reasons a lot of people get divorced is because they're not prepared to deal with one another's problems. They want the other person to deal with their problems, but they're not willing to take on the same load."

Angry now views marriage as a steady upward climb, where you cross each bridge when you get to it, where you forgive and are forgiven. To him it's an institution where you have to keep learning from your mistakes, and where, if you want the rewards of a fulfilling relationship, you have to take the good with the bad. As he says, "The accepted sense of a good husband and father is too perfect. It's unrealistic. None of us would ever get married because we can't be that perfect. If there's any comfort to be taken in that, it's that all husbands and wives make mistakes, and cause one another pain, disappoint one another, betray one another, let one another down, take one another for granted. The couple that have got a good chance are the people who are willing and able to acknowledge that 'That's life!'."

Over the years, family life has become Angry's greatest joy. He loves being the "Dad". He loves the nights where he has all the kids alone, and he treats them to takeaway and videos. He loves the

I THINK ONE OF THE THINGS THAT DETERMINES THE STRENGTH AND WORTH OF A MARRIAGE AS A RELATIONSHIP IS THE ABILITY, OR THE NEED AND THE DESIRE, TO WANT TO DEAL WITH ONE ANOTHER'S BAGGAGE. YOU SEE, I REALLY BELIEVE ONE OF THE REASONS A LOT OF PEOPLE GET DIVORCED IS BECAUSE THEY'RE NOT PREPARED TO DEAL WITH ONE ANOTHER'S PROBLEMS.

mornings where he ends up with four noisy kids in his bed. He loves bathtime where he's got the same four noisy kids in the bath. He loves almost everything about fatherhood.

As Angry says, "Every time I hear one of my kids, and I must hear it dozens of times a day, every single time one of the kids walks

A TYPICAL ANDERSON SATURDAY MORNING

past and says 'Dad', I just fall apart. It's just the word. You never quite get over it. It's like when you walk in and turn on the TV and, boom, there's one on your right, boom, there's another one on your left, and then there's one crawling up your legs. The novelty never wears off. The effect it has on you never wears off. It's like when you go in, and I've been doing it for ten years with Roxy. The last thing I do every night is go from room to room and check the kids. With Roxy I go in, and I pick up the doona and give it a shake, and put it over her. And, every now and then, she won't even wake up, she'll just reach out and touch me, or she'll be too close to the end of the bed, and I'll just gently move her over, and she'll roll over and just open her eyes a little and say 'Goodnight Dad', and boom, asleep. You never get over that. It affects you so much."

IT'S DIFFERENT FOR ANGRY
TOO, BECAUSE HE'S NOT LIKE
ANY OF THE OTHER FATHERS.
HE DOESN'T LOOK LIKE THE
OTHER FATHERS, AND HE
DOESN'T SOUND LIKE THEM.
EVEN WHEN HE HIDES HIS
TATTOOS WITH LONG SLEEVES,
THE BROKEN TEETH AND BALD
HEAD GIVE HIM AWAY.

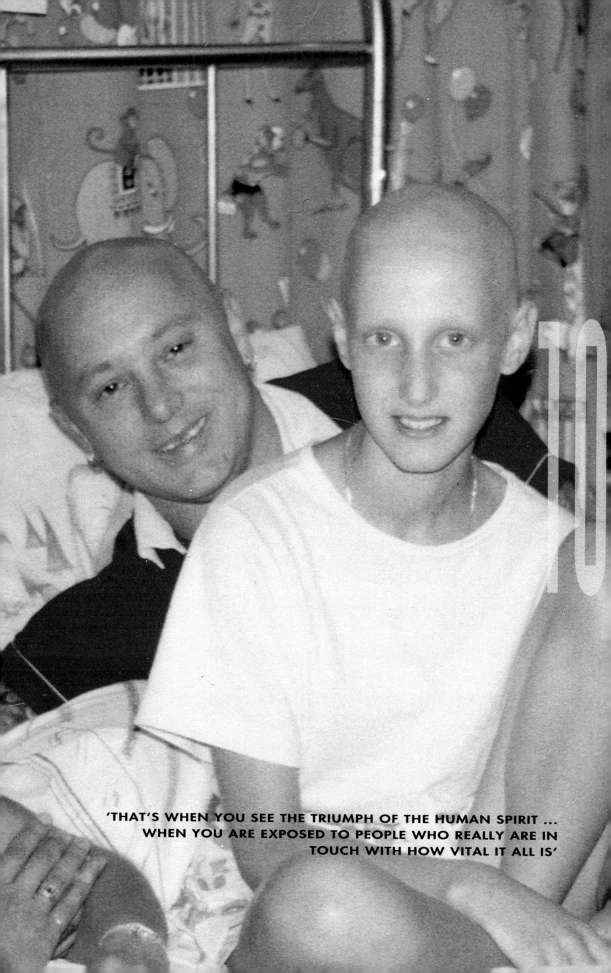

'THAT'S WHEN YOU SEE THE TRIUMPH OF THE HUMAN SPIRIT ... WHEN YOU ARE EXPOSED TO PEOPLE WHO REALLY ARE IN TOUCH WITH HOW VITAL IT ALL IS'

ANOTHER LIFE

Developing the "Midday" profile opened a whole new world for Angry. Instead of having the single focus of a rock singer, people started to understand that he had more scope. Suddenly, he wasn't hearing the same old comments from people on the street. They didn't just come up to him to say "Love your music", or "Hate your music", they actually wanted to talk to him. They wanted to tell him how they felt about certain things, and just as importantly, they wanted to know what he thought too.

Although the TV audience was much, much larger than the audience Angry experienced in the past, it was somehow more intimate. "Midday" viewers seemed to be more inclined to reach out to establish a one-on-one relationship.

THE DRAGON AND THE WITCHING MOON - THE POWER AND THE SPIRIT

Through Channel 9, Angry received letter after letter and phone call after phone call. He thought it was fantastic. People found him accessible, and approachable. His audience had expanded. He was no longer limited to desperado territory - now he had contact with mums and dads and grandparents and everyone in between.

As his confidence grew with the new reporting job, so did his opportunities and slowly he was given a chance to meet some of the people he now considers to be the world's most special.

One of the first stories he did was with a girl called Annie. When he first met her, she was at Prince of Wales Children's Hospital, in the cancer ward. Angry interviewed her as part of a series on teenage cancer patients. She was fresh and honest about her illness, and when Angry did the first interview, her doctors were hoping she'd respond well to treatment and make a full recovery.

Angry and Annie hit it off immediately. They chatted and laughed together in the hospital for hours. They told each other jokes, and Annie talked about her plans to go camping as soon as she was well enough. There was something about Annie, something special. Within the course of one short conversation, Angry and Annie became great friends. They touched something in each other. It was an extraordinary relationship.

A few months after the initial interview, Angry was asked to come back to the hospital, because Annie's condition had worsened. For this interview, Annie looked tired and beaten. She could barely work up a smile. She'd developed three more tumours, and doctors had given her very little chance of survival. Angry just sat with her, cried with her, and tried to laugh with her. When he eventually left the hospital at the end of the day, he felt overwhelmed with emotion.

A few days later, little Annie died. As Angry says, he was devastated. "I don't think I've ever been quite as affected by anything I've ever done as I was by Annie. She was the first one we lost. She was the first person that I actually had a relationship with who died. I couldn't go to the funeral, and I can't watch the story. Every now and then, I'll be looking through a photo album and bang, there's a shot of me and Annie together, and I'll have a little tear. I think it's meant to happen like that to remind me of her, and to remind me of how much she taught me.

"The last time I saw Annie I gave her a doll, and she gave me one back. Can you believe that? She was dying, and she knew it, and all she could think about was other people. That's when you know. That's when you see the triumph of the human spirit...when you are exposed to people who really are in touch with how vital it all is. You and I go about from day to day, and then you run across one of these beaut little people who no longer have the ability or the luxury of taking life for granted, because they know theirs is coming to an end."

Angry's been involved with many kids from Canteen, the kids' cancer group. The relationship usually starts with them declaring themselves fans of Angry Anderson, but almost always ends up with him declaring himself fans of theirs. As Angry says, "I remember once

I walked up to this kid. I walked in and I sat down on the chair, and I said, 'You don't look too good. What's wrong with you?', and he said 'Oh, I'm dying'. You know, if it hadn't sunk in before then, it certainly did that time. I said 'Oh shit', and he said 'Yeah, shit!' He was a teenage kid, and I just reached over and put my hand on his and he said, 'Look, I've known for months now. There's nothing they can do. I'm riddled with it. There's nothing they can do now.' And at the time, I was thinking this kid is a giant. I mean there are not many statements you can make better than that. You know it's like, what can you say after someone makes a statement like 'I'm dying'? What can you say after that? Oh, yeah, well I can fly? I can breathe under water? Do you know what I mean? It's like it's in that category. It's that large.

"It's like that little kid we spoke to. He'd had four different heads of hair after four or five chemotherapy treatments. Like one time he had red hair, which he'd never had before, and another time he had curly hair, then straight black hair. I mean, it was really like he had a remarkable grasp on the whole thing. There was another kid, who was one of the original Canteen group. I saw him on and off for about three years, and every time I spoke to him there was another bit of him missing. In the time that I knew him, he lost his arm from his elbow, and both his legs from the knees. The next time I saw him was up at Canteen camp, and he was alive. That was the thing. It's like, you don't get over those things."

The job also gave Angry an opportunity to get involved with some of Australia's hardest working community welfare groups.

Without even really thinking about it, he became a volunteer - one of the army. Every week he spent hours and hours discussing youth affairs with social workers in the field, and he happily appeared at whatever fund-raising events he could. He talked to street kids and runaways and tried to act as a sort of bridge between them and their guardians.

Perhaps the most important role he played though, was the one

THERE WAS SOMETHING ABOUT ANNIE, SOMETHING SPECIAL. WITHIN THE COURSE OF ONE SHORT CONVERSATION, ANGRY AND ANNIE BECAME GREAT FRIENDS. THEY TOUCHED SOMETHING IN EACH OTHER. IT WAS AN EXTRAORDINARY RELATIONSHIP.

he was paid for. Whenever he thought something needed attention or community focus, he took along a Channel 9 film crew, and it was the public exposure of some of the most traditionally sensitive topics that made the difference. His job at "Midday" put him in an exclusive position. He became a sort of conduit, able to join together the two sides of the community equation - the people in need, and the people with the ability to cater for that need. He was able to represent the people on television who'd always been ignored.

Angry loved his work in the community. It made him feel like he was contributing. As the *Playboy* editor commented, he felt a desperate need to try to make the world a better place, and his work as a volunteer gave him that chance.

In 1986, after only eighteen months with "Midday", Angry was awarded the first of two national medals for his work in youth affairs. He was made the recipient of an Advance Australia award.

On notification of the award, he was astounded. At "Midday", he'd been charging along with a story a week, tackling issues from glue sniffing, to peer group pressure, to prostitution. Although he was proud that he'd made some headway, he just didn't feel that his contribution matched that of the full-time social workers and counsellors he was talking to in the field every week.

He was totally overwhelmed by the acknowledgement. It wasn't the first time he'd received an award - Rose Tattoo had earned a number of silver and gold albums, but it was the first time he'd been recognised for work in the community, and that's what made it special. The gold albums were a monetary thing. They were awarded because the album had sold a certain number of copies, but the Advance Australia award had less tangible criteria. It wasn't so black and white, and at first, Angry had trouble coming to terms with it. He wasn't sure if he was worthy.

He didn't know how to react. He was honoured, but he was confused. People would congratulate him, and he'd change the subject immediately. Newspapers contacted him, but he felt he couldn't comment. He didn't know what to say. He felt almost like a pretender. He couldn't come to terms with the fact that he was only one of twenty people being recognised, yet, out on the streets, he saw

REMEMBER ONCE I WALKED UP TO THIS KID. I WALKED IN AND I SAT DOWN ON THE CHAIR
AND I SAID, 'YOU DON'T LOOK TOO GOOD. WHAT'S WRONG WITH YOU?', AND HE SAID 'OH, I'M
DYING'. YOU KNOW, IF IT HADN'T SUNK IN BEFORE THEN, IT CERTAINLY DID THAT TIME.

IN 1986, AFTER ONLY EIGHTEEN MONTHS WITH "MIDDAY", ANGRY WAS AWARDED THE FIRST OF TWO NATIONAL MEDALS FOR HIS WORK IN YOUTH AFFAIRS. HE WAS MADE THE RECIPIENT OF AN ADVANCE AUSTRALIA AWARD.

evidence of the work of thousands.

It was as if he needed guilt counselling. Everyone was thrilled, and he was plagued. Rosemay thought it was wonderful, Lindy was proud, and at "Midday" the reaction was huge. Ray wanted him to do a whole segment on set with his trophy. It was almost too much for him to take, but after some advice from youth counsellors, he accepted the award in the spirit it was intended.

He was humbled and embarrassed, but he was at least comfortable in the knowledge he was sharing the distinction. As one friend pointed out, he was merely accepting the award on behalf of all the thousands to whom it was owed.

He bought a brand new suit for the ceremony. It was light grey, and he says he still remembers the trip to the shops to buy it. "The dress was lounge wear. You weren't supposed to dress right up. You could if you want, but I mean I don't think they wanted people arriving in tails and medals and shit. A lounge suit was basically what was required so I went out and bought a lounge suit. It was very exciting."

From rock and roll, to movies, to television – to live theatre. That was Angry's next move. Once again the offer came by telephone. In 1989, Robbie Williams received the call inviting Angry to play the role of Vladimir Lenin in *Rasputin*, the musical version of Russian history.

ANGRY ACCEPTING THE ADVANCE AUSTRALIA AWARD

The early word on the production was that Jon English had been approached to play the part of Rasputin, and that Terry Serio was playing the part of the prince. Angry was told there'd be months of rehearsal but the actual production schedule wasn't confirmed. They could have had a two month season, or a three month season, or a four month season, or whatever. The details weren't even set for whether or not they'd tour outside Sydney. It all depended on how the show was received.

Angry was told his role involved a little bit of everything – a bit of acting and delivering lines, a bit of dancing so he'd have to learn steps, and a bit of singing. He was keen to play the role of Lenin. He was fascinated by the character, and flattered that he was first to be considered. Although money wasn't really a huge part of it, the deal being offered by the producers was very good, so from a financial point of view, it was a great opportunity. The other factor was that Angry felt the whole project showed imagination and initiative, and could offer a terrific boost for the Australian industry. He accepted the part, and almost immediately began rehearsing.

The stage was different again for him. In *Mad Max*, Ironbar Bassey had barely said a word, so Angry's experience with the delivery of scripted lines was very limited. It was also the first time he'd performed on stage as someone other than himself. He was Nikolai Lenin, not Angry Anderson, and he had to actually act out the lyrics, rather than sing them. The other major difference was that he had to follow the strict guidelines of a director. On stage for Rose Tattoo he was totally spontaneous. He could move anywhere or do anything he wanted to, but with *Rasputin*, his moves were carefully blocked out, and he had to follow them night after night. It was a whole new experience for him, and he loved it.

FROM ROCK AND ROLL, TO MOVIES, TO TELEVISION - TO LIVE THEATRE. THAT WAS ANGRY'S NEXT MOVE. IN 1989, ROBBIE WILLIAMS RECEIVED THE CALL INVITING ANGRY TO PLAY THE ROLE OF VLADIMIR LENIN IN *RASPUTIN*, THE MUSICAL VERSION OF RUSSIAN HISTORY.

"Getting that part was a matter of being in the right place at the right time. It was a fabulous show. The only thing I regret is that I grew my own beard. I mean, I grew my own beard because I had an allergic reaction to the glue they used to stick the moustache and beard on. I grew my own goatee, and on reflection, I don't think I should have done that. It made me look older. I did TV at the time, and I did photographic shoots."

Angry's vanity speaks up. He hates the fact that people have cold hard evidence of him looking old, with a beard. He regrets that, for a couple of months he went about all his normal business with a goatee that didn't do him any favours. He went to the shops, he did his "Midday" segment, he dropped the kids at school, he did everything as per usual. He allowed the world to see Angry Anderson with hair growing on his chin. As he says, it would be different if he was always in costume as Lenin, so at least the beard would be seen in context, but he now finds the old shots of him in street clothes embarrassing. He says when he wasn't on stage, he looked like a 1990s version of Lenin gone wrong.

As the *Rasputin* rehearsal schedule started to get more hectic, Angry started to get even more carried away. He says, for a little while, he actually started to act and talk like the character. He was just so enthusiastic.

"Once we got into rehearsal," says Angry, "people sent me some books, like the Russian embassy sent me some books, and I think the more that I read about him, the more I got into the part. It was kind of like growing the beard was method acting. I sort of got really into the character. I got absorbed, and I found myself saying things that weren't direct quotes, but I started to really sound like him, you know? There was a stage there where I was willing to grow my hair and just shave the top because Lenin had a horseshoe, and I mean I was inches away from growing my hair instead of wearing a wig. But, there I would have been, looking like Lenin, a balding middle aged man with a goatee. If we were making a movie, I definitely would have done it, but it was a play. We were only doing it at night. I had another life, you know?"

RASPUTIN

The show only played Sydney for three months, and it didn't tour. There were some bad reviews at the beginning, and some internal fighting among the producers and writers about what changes were necessary. As Angry says, the criticism was fair. For the first few weeks the show was clumsy, and it ran too long. He says the whole thing was not cohesive enough. For Angry though, the greatest challenge of the entire job was getting up the courage to go out on stage on opening night.

He was terrified. He was literally pale and shaking. He hung around all day at home, trying not to get distracted so he could focus on the character, but he was almost sick with nerves. "Opening night! It's just, you know, my God, I don't know how many times you have to go through it before you get used to it, but opening nights are just a horror story. There's all this expectation, all this build up, and opening nights are never as good as rehearsal. Jon was right. We rehearsed the bloody thing dozens and dozens of times. There were times there when you do the rehearsal and you think 'Oh, yes, that was great', then you get to opening night, and it's like 'You're kidding? This isn't anywhere near as good as rehearsal', because it just doesn't happen. The only good thing about it was the opening night audience were really supportive. Whether they did it out of sympathy or not, they really supported it. And, let's face it, the majority of people who were there had seen many stage shows before, so they knew what the thing lacked, but they supported it anyway because it was an Australian venture."

BACKSTAGE WITH ROBERT KRUPSKI AND
ONE OF THE CREW MEMBERS

Rasputin wasn't Angry's only experience in stage musicals. In 1992, he was offered an opportunity to take part in another Australian venture, *Jesus Christ Superstar*, the concert. It was one of the biggest line-ups ever put together for an Australian show. All the lead roles were taken by people with successful careers as solo artists. Between them, there'd have been a dozen gold and platinum albums, with John Farnham as Jesus, Jon Stevens as Judas, and Kate Ceberano as Mary Magdalene. Angry accepted the part of King Herod.

It was perfect for him. He got to play the part of the showman...the dancing, singing executioner. The show was staged in the round in the Sydney Entertainment Centre, so every night Angry got to blast out on stage with an interpretation of King Herod that was distinctly his own. He wore a black eight gallon hat, black trousers, a mirrored waistcoat, and an orange and silver striped frock coat. Instead of cowboy boots he wore Doc Martens with chrome toes and a big silver buckle. He looked like a cross between Liberace, Colonel Sanders and a riverboat gambler. He only had one scene, but it was one of the showstoppers.

With *Jesus Christ Superstar*, he had another painful opening night experience, but this time the problems weren't just emotional. He had an accident in one of the final dress rehearsals where he tripped and pulled his calf muscle. It was quite a serious injury, and it left him with a limp. His role required him to tap dance around the edge of the stage, and as he says, his injured leg really held him back. "I had a terrible opening night. I just had a terrible night. I shouldn't have been worrying about my leg. The more I worried about it, the more it detracted from what I was doing. You see, I was physically capable, but I kept thinking about my leg, and you see, that's the wrong place to centre. You know, if my leg stuffs up, then fine…you fall over, and roll in agony, whatever! People will understand and go with you, but they won't understand if you so overcompensate for the injury that it detracts from the performance. That's the mistake I made."

Superstar was like a steam train nobody could stop. Shows were sold out weeks in advance, and the first single released from the concert, "Everything's alright" went straight to number one. The album "Jesus Christ Superstar" went platinum before the program even closed.

As Angry says, he thought the cast were a pretty formidable gang when they got going. He had huge respect for his other cast members, and even though he'd seen the show in rehearsal many times, there were some numbers he just watched over and over again. He hated to miss them, so every night he'd stand backstage and watch the other cast members do their stuff.

He was in awe of John Waters' skill in the part of Pontius Pilate. He loved watching him build the drama. To Angry, he moved the audience like magic. Another of his other favourite parts of the show was Kate Ceberano's version of "I Don't Know How to Love Him". As Angry says "The director kept telling Kate to be flamboyant. You

RASPUTIN WASN'T ANGRY'S ONLY EXPERIENCE IN STAGE MUSICALS. IN 1992, HE WAS OFFERED AN OPPORTUNITY TO TAKE PART IN ANOTHER AUSTRALIAN VENTURE, *JESUS CHRIST SUPERSTAR*, THE CONCERT. IT WAS ONE OF THE BIGGEST LINE-UPS EVER PUT TOGETHER FOR AN AUSTRALIAN SHOW.

know, he'd say 'Don't be a pious converted sinner. Be voluptuous, be sexual'. Her Mary Magdalene was, to me, the way I wanted to see Mary Magdalene. This was a woman that anyone would desire, you know? Even Jesus himself would have wanted to bed this woman! She was a woman who was in touch with all aspects of her being. She was no longer a whore. That's why I was never disappointed in Kate's performance."

Live theatre pushed Angry into a whole new world of review and criticism. Before *Rasputin*, he knew only about rock and roll commentary, but as soon as he took the stage he learned very quickly about the complexities of professional theatre critique. At times he learned the hard way. "I did receive some stinging reviews. I remember in *Rasputin*, one of the critics wrote something like 'Angry Anderson's transformation from rock and roll into live theatre didn't work, it didn't happen, it wasn't worth the effort'. It was along those lines. I know there were a couple of reviews that really, really hurt, but, because I don't like to hurt, I never read them again."

TEN 10

8.00 JESUS CHRIST SUPERSTAR. Entertainment Event of the Year Starring John Farnham, Kate Ceberano, Jon Stevens, John Waters, Angry Anderson. Proudly sponsored by Channel 10.

ten

"With *Superstar*," says Angry, "the review I enjoyed most was the one that said 'predictably Angry Anderson sang flat, but nobody does it better'. I liked that one because that was an accurate appraisal of the performance, but it was complimentary."

Angry learned to accept the reviews as part of the business. He even tried to take the criticism on board and change his performance without taking it too much to heart. As he says, "I suppose, when you get a bad review, you ask the people whose opinion you respect and believe. I mean, you can either turn around and say 'Well, stuff it' or you can say 'Okay, has anyone got any suggestions?' With *Superstar*, I started taking some voice coaching from Lindsay, who is John Farnham's backup singer. He gave me some hints and some pointers. But, I do definitely sing flat. I'm a very undisciplined singer. I can either be very sharp or very flat. One of the things I've enjoyed as a singer is that I have, and I can, and I do improve. The nicest thing ever said is Angry is not so much a singer, he's an interpreter of the lyrics. I place great store in that."

Through all his work in television and on the stage, Angry never gave up on his recording career completely. He still had a contract with Mushroom, and after the huge success of "Suddenly", he was still getting good crowds at live gigs with the Angry Anderson Band.

In 1989, Mushroom decided to have one more go at selling Angry in America. His reputation overseas was huge. It had all been blown way out of proportion in the States, so Mushroom knew that at least they had a profile to work with. It wasn't as if he was an unknown. They made Angry an offer. They asked him to move to Los Angeles with Robbie for a few months, write an album, record it, and test the water. The plan was that if Angry liked Los Angeles, and if the album was received well, Angry and the family could set up a sort of transatlantic lifestyle, living six months in Australia and six months in the US.

"Midday" gave Angry a leave of absence. They were happy to hold the position open for him, and at one stage, even toyed with the idea of using him as a Los Angeles based reporter. There was talk of a new segment, a sort of "Angry Anderson Stateside", but it never happened.

At the first meeting in California, Angry "did breakfast" with the record company executive in charge of his new album. His name was Beau Hill, and he'd met Rose Tattoo years before when they were in England. Beau had always seen a big future for the band, and he particularly liked Angry's style. He was also friendly with a fellow called Michael Slamer, who was an Englishman living in LA. Michael was a guitarist, who in Angry's words played "beautiful guitar", but he was also a songwriter. Beau introduced Michael and Angry, and over the months in LA, the two formed a partnership, writing all their songs together. They had a great deal in common, and Michael ended up playing almost all the guitar pieces for the new album, which was eventually called "Blood from Stone".

By the time Angry moved to America, his brood was only half complete. He had Roxy who was six years old, and Galen who was

"WITH *SUPERSTAR*", SAYS ANGRY, "THE REVIEW I ENJOYED MOST WAS THE ONE THAT SAID 'PREDICTABLY ANGRY ANDERSON SANG FLAT, BUT NOBODY DOES IT BETTER'. I LIKED THAT ONE BECAUSE THAT WAS AN ACCURATE APPRAISAL OF THE PERFORMANCE, BUT IT WAS COMPLIMENTARY."

still a baby. He had no intentions of leaving the family for too long. As soon as he was settled, after a month or so, he wanted Lindy to come over and join him. But the plan went slightly awry.

When Angry and Robbie first arrived in the States, they stayed in the Franklin apartments in the middle of Hollywood. The apartments were owned by Mushroom, and used by a number of their international acts whenever they were commuting backwards and forwards from LA to Sydney. After a few weeks in the apartments, Angry and Robbie moved into a house with a girl who'd been living in Australia for a while. The new house was close to everything, and had great views. The immediate view was over the canyons, and directly in front was the Griffith Observatory. As Angry says, if he stood on his balcony and looked directly left, he could see the huge Hollywood sign on top of the hill.

As soon as they moved into the house, Angry became anxious for Lindy and the kids to fly over. He asked Robbie how the arrangements were going, and he asked Mushroom, but nobody seemed to have any idea what was happening. As far as Angry was concerned, the deal was simple. He believed that as soon as he was settled in a house, the family would be flown over, and they'd all stay together for the six months or so that it took to record the album.

Week after week, they stalled him. He couldn't get anybody to confirm the deal, and as he says, he slowly became more and more frustrated, and more and more annoyed as people evaded his questions. After he'd been overseas for almost four months, he lost his temper. "I just turned to Robbie one day and I said 'Listen, if you don't get my kids over here, I'm going home. You tell Mushroom that I don't care how far along we are with the album, I don't care how much money we've spent, I don't care. Unless my family are here, I'm going home. I just get on the plane and I forget the whole thing. I write it off as four months of my life I'd rather forget.'"

Within a couple of weeks, the problem was fixed. Lindy, Roxy and Galen arrived. From Lindy's point of view, the months of separation had been harder than any other. When Angry was in England there were no kids to worry about, and even when he was on one of the many, many tours, he was at least able to come home occasionally. While he was in Los Angeles, though, the kids asked after him constantly, and it just made Lindy feel more desperate and more lonely.

Angry had found the time interminable. As he says, he couldn't make anyone understand how important his family was to him, and how much he needed them with him. "You see, the thing that unmarried people don't realise is that families are your stability. They can right you in tough water. If I'd had Lou and the kids there right from the start, I could have gone home every day knowing that 'Here's my wife, and here's my kids', and I could have focused right from the start. Instead of going home to an empty bed, and to photos that I had stuck on the wall that I pined for. They don't realise that pining takes away from you. I kept saying 'You've got to realise that I can't live like this. I'm not a rock and roll madman anymore. I'm a rock and roll husband and daddy, and I've got to have those other components because they're more important to me than what we're doing."

As soon as the family were reunited, life in Los Angeles became much more fun. Angry worked during the day, but at night he and Lindy and the kids went sightseeing and star spotting.

The album went well, although Angry was disappointed in its studio sound. He thought it suffered without the live band aspect, and still complains that it sounds sterile.

The trip to America and the last album highlighted many of the problems between Angry and his recording company. Over the years, they'd had plenty of disagreements about the marketing of albums and singles, and about the type of music Angry was releasing. There'd been a long-standing argument about whether Angry's music should be sold under the Rose Tattoo name, or the Angry Anderson name. One of the other major stumbling blocks concerned the timing of some of the singles. Angry disagreed about which songs should be released in which order.

Still, the album was generally a success, and it launched one of

Angry's biggest hits "Bound for Glory". As a single, it made it to the top five on the national charts. It was a big, inspirational song about winning, and so it was chosen as the perfect theme song for the Australian Paralympic Association. That gave it plenty of airplay, and it would now be one of Angry's best known songs.

Although the arguments between Angry and Mushroom didn't seem to affect the sales of the album, they did affect Angry's commitment to recording. He and the family came home from America for the Christmas of 1989, and decided not to return. The whole idea of the permanent transatlantic lifestyle fell by the wayside.

ROXY AND GALEN

Angry resigned from Mushroom a few months after the album was released, and decided just to let the recording industry carry on without him. He'd had enough. He didn't want to stop singing, but he did want to stop his association with record companies and managers and agents. He just called it quits.

As he says, "I've been so hurt and troubled and burnt and disillusioned and frustrated and angered in the last few years, particularly over the last two albums, I just thought 'Well, stuff it. I'll go and sing with a mate's band in a pub on weekends.' So now, I go out for a few bucks a night singing Rolling Stones and Rose Tattoo and AC/DC covers, because that's the music I love, and I'd rather be doing that than signed to a major label, with a manager, having to deal with these people."

11

'IF A HAND COMES OUT OF
THE DARKNESS AND
SOMEONE JUST TOUCHES THE
FINGERS. THEY DON'T EVEN
HAVE TO KNOW WHO'S
TOUCHED THEM, JUST AS
LONG AS SOMEONE DOES.'

ON THE SOAP BOX

If it's possible, Angry Anderson's reaction to his second award for services to the community was even more severe than the first. He was totally overwhelmed. The second distinction was an Australia Medal (AM), and it was presented in 1993. As Lindy says, this time, not only did he refuse point blank to go out and buy a new suit, he was so flabbergasted he didn't want to go to the ceremony at all. He couldn't hold himself together.

Lindy laughs about it now, but she says he was a mess. "He cried for two days before the ceremony," says Lindy. "He didn't feel he deserved it. He didn't want to go. He was in tears the day the governor gave it to him. You know, he burst into tears on stage, up on the platform. I'm saying 'God...Ang, stop crying for a second!' The governor's wife was saying things like 'He's just a big softie isn't he. He's not angry at all. Someone find him a tissue.' You know, they had to give him a cup of tea to calm him down. I can't tell you how proud I am of him. I think of all those people who sat there for years saying 'You'll never amount to anything'. You know, he bombed out at school, had no desire for education. I think a lot of people said that he was never going to make anything of himself. That's why I blow raspberries at the lot of them now, because he's finally made something of himself."

THE LADY

Angry's tears weren't just saved for the ceremony. He cried everywhere. He cried in the green room at Channel 9 when his producer congratulated him before his weekly segment, and he cried again, on air, when Ray congratulated him. It's one of the things the cynics can't make sense of. They suggest the tears are all just part of some theatrical performance, but as Ray knows, and as Angry's friends know, it's just part of his character. It's just the man. He does things in extremes...he's never just happy, he's delirious, he's never just angry, he's outraged, he's never just touched, he's moved to tears. He's a passionate and emotional person, and if it were an act, he'd have exhausted it many years ago.

With the Australia Medal came a whole new level of commitment for Angry. That's how he resolved his confusion. He decided that, even if he wasn't already a worthy AM recipient, he soon would be. "They give you a list of what they expect from members of the Australia Medal club," says Angry. "They say, this is your charter. You have to lead the kind of life that brings honour to your country. So, once I'd become happy with the fact that my name was somewhere on a list, it just gave me a purpose. It gave me somewhere to go. You know, I just thought I will earn this. If I'm unhappy about it now, if I'm uncomfortable with the acknowledgement, if I don't really think I've earned this gong, then I will earn it. I will purposefully, for as long as I can, the way I sit here today, I will earn that medal. I won't let the team down, or I'll try not to."

HE DOES THINGS IN EXTREMES...HE'S NEVER JUST HAPPY, HE'S DELIRIOUS, HE'S NEVER JUST ANGRY, HE'S OUTRAGED, HE'S NEVER JUST TOUCHED, HE'S MOVED TO TEARS. HE'S A PASSIONATE AND EMOTIONAL PERSON, AND IF IT WERE AN ACT, HE'D HAVE EXHAUSTED IT MANY YEARS AGO.

Over the years, Angry's brief with the "Midday Show" slowly changed. He turned himself into much more than a youth reporter, and instead, became a kind of 'odd jobs' man for the program. Whenever there was an issue that didn't fit into the medical segment, or the parenting segment, or the sports segment, or the cooking segment, it fitted into Angry's segment.

His segments covered the whole range of issues. He was able to apply the Angry logic and the Angry touch to every topic. He did in-depth investigations into pollution and immigration. In the studio, he dealt with every subject from bank queues to road safety to unemployment.

One of Angry's proudest moments with "Midday" was also one of his toughest. It was a segment on the Paralympic Games in 1992. Angry rang his producer in a rage one day after he'd attended the launch of the Paralympic appeal. He'd been talking to various officials, and he'd become more and more upset as they'd listed off the disappointments the team had already encountered while trying to find sponsorship and assistance to get to Madrid. By the time Angry got involved, the Paralympic appeal for funds was desperate. It had already reached the stage where officials were concerned that, unless major sponsors came forward, Australia wouldn't be able to field a paralympic team at all.

Angry wasn't just upset with the lack of funds. He was upset with what he saw as a lack of support for the paralympians from the general community. He didn't feel Australian companies were doing all they could to contribute to the team effort. The athletes were flying with British Airways, not Qantas, and Angry thought that was outrageous. Qantas had informed the Paralympic committee that they weren't able to fly the athletes, plus their wheelchairs and equipment, all the way to Spain. Angry wasn't interested in reasons or excuses. He was disgusted that an Australian team couldn't fly with the national carrier. Then, to add to his fury, he heard a report that John Coates, the then head of the able-bodied Olympic committee, had neglected to include the Paralympic athletes in his description of the "true Olympians".

ANGRY, LINDY AND ROXY
AFTER THE AM AWARD CEREMONY

Angry decided he wanted to give the Australian community a blast on air, so in his segment that week, he did just that. In typical Angry fashion though, he went a bit too far. While he was trying to make an appeal for people to come forward and help, he ended up naming a few people he thought were guilty of "incompetence and neglect". Before he'd finished his eleven minute segment, he'd managed to let go a few enormous clangers. He got so carried away that he started abusing the Qantas executive and, in the end, even called John Coates an idiot.

Before the program was off air, the lawyers were on the phone. Angry had defamed people, and he'd given Qantas an unfair public blasting. He was still so hot under the collar when he came off set though, there was nothing that anyone could do about it. They had to wait until he calmed down.

The next week, Angry was forced to make an apology. As he says now though, it wasn't as bad as it could have been. "In a strange sort of masochistic way I even enjoyed eating humble pie. It was a chance for me to explain myself fully, as a person that's fallible, as a person that makes mistakes, as a person who gets emotionally and passionately involved in something, and says and does things irrationally, for the right reasons. And then, when the law of the land, or propriety or just social graces demand that you temper your passion, you can accommodate. You know, as arrogant as I do appear, never would I like people to think I was so arrogant that I couldn't admit when I was wrong, or when I had made a mistake."

'IT WAS A CHANCE FOR ME TO EXPLAIN MYSELF FULLY, AS A PERSON THAT'S FALLIBLE, AS A PERSON THAT MAKES MISTAKES, AS A PERSON WHO GETS EMOTIONALLY AND PASSIONATELY INVOLVED IN SOME-THING, AND SAYS AND DOES THINGS IRRATIONALLY, FOR THE RIGHT REASONS.'

Although Angry's blast had been misguided, it had the right effect. The Paralympic appeal received a sudden boost of funds. Even immediately after the segment, their switchboard was jammed with people trying to find out how they should send their cheques. Angry says he's not proud that he was wrong, but he's proud that the segment made such a difference.

"You see, I never want to become totally disciplined in TV because I think it's so important to keep the essence of who I was when I started out. It's like in a marriage you know…if I'm a wild and crazy guy, and that's what attracted Lou to me, then she should never try to take the wild and crazy guy out of me. She can try to change the behaviour, yes, but not the essence. Ray calls me a loose cannon, and I like that. It's more exciting. I would never want to see myself in ten years with none of that spontaneity, because I think that's what people enjoy about me as a person on television. More importantly, it's what I enjoy about myself as a person on television."

Angry's appeal with the "Midday Show" seems to go across the board. He can't be categorised as a charity worker, or as someone who only appeals to kids, or mums or grandmums. He has fans in every corner. You either love him or you hate him. He gets a reaction almost everywhere he goes, even if it's just a turn of the head.

Angry says he's not sure of exactly what kind of notoriety he enjoys - whether it's fame or infamy. All he does know is that it crept up on him slowly. He says he'd never actually thought about it until he saw himself through the eyes of a Texan guitar player who joined the Angry Anderson Band in 1990.

When Bobby Bath first arrived in Australia, the only thing he knew about Angry was that he'd been front man for one of the biggest, baddest rock and roll bands that ever toured the United States. He'd known Angry in America as an acquaintance, and he'd seen Rose Tattoo perform, so he knew all about the angry Angry. What he didn't know was that Angry had another side, on television, and that his public profile as a champion of causes was almost bigger than his public profile as a rock and roller.

As Angry says, "Bobby was absolutely astounded at how people reacted to me, and it made the rest of us think about it. It was something that we'd taken for granted because of the slow slide up to it. When he saw me talking to kids, six year olds and eight year olds, and then talking to grandmothers that are like 60 years old and 80 years old, it blew his face off, basically. But the thing was, it made me think about it too. I'd never really thought about it in those terms until someone else, who wasn't part of the picture, came in and said, 'Wait a minute. This is really off the wall.' Bobby had no idea what to expect. When he kept gaping and his mouth kept hitting the ground and stuff, the rest of us took a look at me too. You know what I mean? We all stood back and had a look at me, and you know, it really is funny."

ANGRY'S APPEAL WITH THE "MIDDAY SHOW" SEEMS TO GO ACROSS THE BOARD. HE CAN'T BE CATEGORISED AS A CHARITY WORKER, OR AS SOMEONE WHO ONLY APPEALS TO KIDS, OR MUMS OR GRAND-MUMS. HE HAS FANS IN EVERY CORNER. YOU EITHER LOVE HIM OR YOU HATE HIM.

Angry says there was one particular morning where it all came home to him. He tried to stand back, and realised how strange it was. "We pulled into this one town for breakfast, and it had a population of about 400 or something. It was a rail siding, and this bloke at the service station told us that if we really wanted a good breakfast, we should go further into town. So we drove in, and there's this lady behind the counter...a lovely big, robust, typical Aussie with thongs and a floral print dress, short blonde hair, and calling everyone 'Love'. She and her daughters ran the kitchen, and she said, 'Listen Angry, I'll give you half an hour to have your brekkie, but can I ring some people to tell them you're here?' So I say, 'Oh, well, if you really want to.' Minutes later, twenty people turn up. I mean mums and dads, with nannies and kids arrive out the front and sit in cars outside. Now, I mean, we all thought that was hysterical, because that's funny stuff, isn't it? And, it's lovely stuff."

When Angry first went into television, many of his critics said the notoriety had gone to his head. He was canned for being too arrogant, and some of his friends thought he'd changed with the new job. They thought he'd become a television man in television land, and they accused him of believing too much in his own publicity. He says that, although some of that criticism was nothing more than sour grapes from people who didn't like to see him doing so well, he also recognises that some of it was fair comment.

"THERE WAS A TIME IN ALL HONESTY WHERE I DESPERATELY NEEDED TO BE ADORED ... THEN, SOMETHING ELSE TOOK OVER AND I THOUGHT, I WANT TO BE THOUGHT OF AS SOMETHING WORTHWHILE. TO GET TO THE POINT SOMEWHERE IN YOUR LIFE WHERE YOU MAKE THAT DECISION THAT I'M GOING TO BE THE BEST NOBODY /SOMEBODY THAT I CAN BE."

To some extent, he admits, television and its power did go to his head. For a little while, he enjoyed the autograph hunters more than he should. "There was a time in all honesty where I desperately needed to be adored, and to be acknowledged. I wanted people to think of me as something special. Then, something else took over and I thought, I don't want to be thought of as something special. I want to be thought of as something worthwhile. Being somebody. That's everything. To get to the point somewhere in your life where you make that decision that you're going to be as good a human being...husband, father, friend, son, brother, whatever, but I'm going to be the best person. I'm going to be the best nobody /somebody that I can be."

Others in the music industry, however, took Angry's new-found fame with better humour. In about 1988, Angry did a tour with Marc Hunter and Sharyn O'Neil. It was a concept band with a cabaret rock and roll revue where the three lead singers alternated. They just walked on and off stage, singing different solos. They called the tour

"The Good, The Bad, and The Ugly", but after touring for a few weeks with Angry, Marc gave the tour a new name. After watching Angry's effect on the crowds, he decided to make a joke of it and call the tour "The Pope, The Princess, and The Great Pretender".

Marc, Sharyn and Angry were all good friends, and had been for years. They all had their own profile in the music industry - Marc Hunter as lead singer of Dragon, and Sharyn as a solo artist. Marc changed the name of the tour after a humiliating experience one day with an autograph hunter. It was in a little country town, and Angry, Marc and Sharyn were all standing outside a Coles supermarket. After a while, two groups of autograph hunters started to queue - one group in front of Sharyn, and another in front of Angry. Marc was just standing there, so to be polite, Angry asked the first lady in his queue if she'd like Marc's autograph too. She just looked from Angry to Marc, and back again, and with a confused expression said "Why, who is he?"

Angry says it floored Marc, but he took it with good humour. "He made a huge joke out of it. He started calling me the 'Pope', and Sharyn the 'Princess'. He was the 'Great Pretender'. At breakfast from then on, when people would come in, you know, they'd be standing there waiting for us to finish breakfast so they could ask for autographs, and he'd turn around and call out to them to come on over. He'd say 'The Pope's holding audience now. Any children to be healed? Anyone to be blessed? Any christenings to be done?' He used to make mockery of it. It was very funny."

After sitting together on a television set nearly every week for nine years, Ray Martin and Angry Anderson have become firm friends. They're fiercely protective of one another, but they don't always agree. There have been many times when their philosophies have been vastly different. Television writers have often talked about them as the 'odd couple' because they just seem so strangely matched...Ray with his Mr Nice Guy image and dimples, and Angry with his bad boy reputation. Still, something seems to spark between them.

As Angry says, they're almost opposite people, somehow on the same wavelength. "I don't always agree with Ray," says Angry. "I couldn't possibly. We're poles apart. We're on two opposite ends of the stick, but we're joined together. Disagreeing makes the relationship fruitful, and it makes it positive, and productive. Sometimes we can agree, but there are just some things we'll never be able to agree on...like gun control. We do agree that guns cause too many deaths within society, but I don't think removing the guns is going to stop the deaths. In fact, I know it won't. We have to agree to disagree on that issue."

There's a huge respect between them, and despite the disagreements, they have plenty of common ground. They're both devoted fathers and they usually agree on issues involving children. They also both do a lot of work in the community, so they agree on many issues of community concern. From Angry's point of view, the relationship also involves a certain amount of loyalty because he's so grateful to

Ray for opening up a whole new world of opportunity. Without Ray, Angry would never have had a chance in television. He would never have been a reporter, and he would never have developed such a high profile.

At the "Midday Show", Angry's mailbag is full of a mixture of letters from all sorts of people. No two letters are the same, because people seem to write to him about anything and everything. The isolated cases ask for help, but the majority of the letters Angry receives ask for nothing at all. As he says, they're just people who are reaching out.

BRADLEY WOLFE IS PROBABLY ANGRY'S NUMBER ONE FAN. HE SUFFERS FROM CEREBRAL PALSY WHICH DOMINATES HIS BODY TO SUCH AN EXTENT THAT HE IS ONLY ABLE TO COMMUNICATE WITH A COMPUTER.

BRADLEY IS A POET, AND HAS WRITTEN MANY TRIBUTES TO ANGRY. HE STRUGGLED OVER HIS COMPUTER UNTIL 4 AM ONE NIGHT TO WRITE THE FOLLOWING POEM, ESPECIALLY FOR THIS BOOK. AS HIS MUM SHARON WOLFE SAYS, "WRITING DOESN'T COME EASILY TO BRADLEY, ALTHOUGH, READING THE WORDS YOU'D THINK IT DID. HE'S JUST DETERMINED TO LET HIS VOICE BE HEARD, PARTICULIARLY WHEN HE CARES."

Angry Anderson

WHILST WAITING TO BE FREE I DISCOVERED
THE ULTIMATE STAR
AN ORDINARY MAN LIKE YOU AND ME WHO
DREAMS TO HEAL THE DEEPEST SCAR
HE LEFT THE PAST WHERE IT BELONGS YET
LOOKS BACK AS A GUIDE FOR TOMORROW
AND HIDDEN BENEATH HIS HEART OF GOLD
ARE MEMORIES OF GLORY AND SORROW
MANY HAVE BEEN INSPIRED BY THE MUSIC
COMPOSED WITHIN HIS SOUL
FOR FAME WAS DESTINED AND SELFLESSNESS
REWARDED THUS HE REACHED HIS GOAL
VERY FEW WILL EVER TOUCH OUR LIVES AS
RICHLY WITH KINDLY DEEDS
NOR MAKE US GROW FROM WISDOM PLANTED
GENTLY IN THE MIND LIKE SEEDS
IT TAKES A SPECIAL SPIRIT TO GIVE AND
ASK FOR NOTHING IN RETURN
FROM HIM THERE IS AN ABUNDANCE IF
WE ARE WILLING TO ACCEPT THEN LEARN
I'M HONOURED TO HAVE AN UNCONDITIONAL
FRIEND FOR IT MEANS THE WORLD TO ME
AND I KNOW THERE'S A PLACE IN HEAVEN
JUST WAITING FOR YOU ANGRY.

One of the most important letters he ever received was from a boy called Bradley Wolfe. It was early on in his days at "Midday", and at the time, Angry didn't know anything about Bradley. The letter said that he was nine years old, and it included a poem written for Angry. The poem was wonderful, and Angry was so touched he wrote straight back. After a while he got a phone call from a lady called Pam Provost, who had basically set herself up as Bradley's manager cum assistant in Sydney. She explained to Angry that Bradley was a cerebral palsy sufferer whose body was so buckled and twisted that he could only communicate by painstakingly striking the keys of a computer.

ANGRY WITH BRADLEY IN 1993, BEFORE THE START OF THE 'SILENCE ISN'T GOLDEN' CHARITY BIKE RUN

After a few general conversations with Pam, a meeting between Bradley and Angry was arranged. It was to be the first chapter in a great, great friendship. Bradley and Angry hit it off immediately. As Angry says, he was thoroughly impressed with Bradley, with what he'd written, and with the kind of person he was. "Bradley is a remarkable person. He really is. What he can tell the rest of us is that we're all remarkable people, and that we don't need to have cerebral palsy to find that out. The reason we marvel at him is because he's twisted physically, but he has such a huge mind, such a huge capacity to care, and to be able to communicate that."

Angry's mailbag has come to have an enormous influence on his life. Many of the writers don't expect answers. They write to Angry about their problems, but they don't expect him to move mountains for them, it's just as if they're trying to open up the lines of communication.

As Angry says, "There was a couple in Victoria who had huge problems with a block of land. It was a bad sale, they'd mortgaged everything. You know, they were up shit creek, the bank's going to close down on the loan, the husband's working three jobs, they're destitute. All I did was ring them. I just rang, and the lady answered and she broke down, and we had a chat. She said, 'You'll never know what it means just for you to take notice. You read the letter, but you rang'. You know, there was nothing I could do to help them, but she said that ringing was enough. And, the thing that blows me out, is most times, that is enough. Most times that's all it takes. If a hand comes out of the darkness, and someone just touches the fingers. They don't even have to know who's touched them, just as long as someone does. They give you the option. They write, and give you their phone number and address, and you just reach out and touch them."

In 1986, he did receive a fax with a desperate plea. It was addressed simply to Angry Anderson, "Midday Show", and in the middle of the page in huge handwritten letters it just said "PLEASE HELP! WE ARE WATCHING MARK DIE". There was a phone number and address attached, and an accompanying newspaper article and letter explained the whole story. The plea was from a mother in Western Australia, whose sixteen-year-old son was addicted to petrol and glue sniffing. His habit had already reached the point where he'd suffered a degree of brain damage. The mother explained to Angry that she'd sought help from counsellors, hospitals, welfare agencies and drug rehabilitation centres to no avail. She said she felt helpless, and had already been warned by a couple of doctors that she should face facts and prepare herself for the fact that her son would probably kill himself with the addiction.

It was a heartbreaking plea, and Angry followed the story up through "Midday". Angry and his producer talked to the mother, and discovered some of the horrific effects of glue sniffing. Addicts are subject to violent mood swings where they can either abuse themselves or abuse others. Mark's arms were covered in cuts and scars from where he'd tried to hurt himself. He'd gone on mad rampages through the house, and once boarded himself up in his bedroom. His fits had become so bad that his mother had been forced to take out a restraining order to protect herself.

By the time "Midday" did the story, Mark was living on the streets, in a garbage dump. It was a case where Angry could do very little. Mark's mother had already tried everything within her power, and in contacting Angry, she said her principal aim was to make the community aware of the problem. It was one of those cases where everyone was helpless, and for that reason, Angry's never forgotten it.

Angry has never found a way to deal with all his mail. He and Lindy sit together and read through everything carefully. They admit that there have been times when work or family or life has become too hectic, and letters that need answers have gone unattended for months. They could hire a secretary to write responses for them, but Angry won't allow that. He can't resist his two bits worth, so if a secretary tried to respond on his behalf, he'd end up changing all the letters anyway.

Besides, Angry says, it's important that he does answer them himself. "Those letters to me...they're like moments of sanity," says Angry. "They're like my wife, my kids, my friends. They're real people who live real lives and have real problems, and as long as they keep writing to me, I'll know that they think I'm real. They're my saving grace. They let me know that I still belong to the real world, and that they don't see me as such an aloof and unattainable goal. It's like writing to Madonna. You hope and hope and pray that you'll get a letter written back by Madonna, but you just kind of know in the back of your mind that you never will. I'd hate to be thought of like that. In fact, if it got to that point, I'd like to think that I'd be able to say, this is fucked. I don't need this. If this is what I've become, or if this is what it's making me into, forget it. I don't need that, you know. Where I came from wasn't always a bed of roses, it wasn't always the beaut life, but it's real, it's committed, it's what happens. You see, I don't think those people will ever know how grateful I am. I don't think they'll ever know. There is no way that I can ever repay what they've given me just by writing 'Dear Angry'."

WHERE I CAME FROM WASN'T ALWAYS A BED OF ROSES, IT WASN'T ALWAYS THE BEAUT LIFE, BUT IT'S REAL, IT'S COMMITTED, IT'S WHAT HAPPENS. YOU SEE, I DON'T THINK THOSE PEOPLE WILL EVER KNOW HOW GRATEFUL I AM. I DON'T THINK THEY'LL EVER KNOW. THERE IS NO WAY THAT I CAN EVER REPAY WHAT THEY'VE GIVEN ME JUST BY WRITING "DEAR ANGRY".

In 1993, the producers of the "Midday Show" introduced a new segment that suited Angry perfectly. It was his soapbox. Every month Angry would come in to the studio, take his position on top of a wooden box, and talk for 30 seconds about whatever topics Ray threw at him. Not only did the segment afford Angry the luxury of talking

about almost every issue under the sun, it also afforded the producers the luxury of a loud, persistent buzzer. As soon as the clock struck thirty, the buzzer would sound, as stubborn and tenacious as Angry, forcing him into silence. It was like a miracle for the program producers, because they suddenly found a way to control their loose cannon. Segments that had blown out to sixteen or seventeen minutes were contained to an action-packed eight minutes.

Although at first Angry hated the soapbox and buzzer he slowly began to enjoy the challenge. It was great discipline for him, trying to get his point across to an audience in less than thirty seconds. He gave his opinion on everything from breastfeeding in public, to the Australian flag, to housework for men. As the clock moved closer and closer to the zero, Angry's voice would get louder and louder, until he was eventually shouting over the countdown. He could never beat the buzzer though, and was always left mid-sentence.

Angry lists his years at "Midday" as some of his best. As he says, "Midday" was sort of like my debut...my coming out. It was the revealing of the real picture. I think it's just like I wrote in the words of "Suddenly": Suddenly you're seeing me, just the way I am/Suddenly you're hearing me, so I'm talking just as fast as I can. Of course, television helped me discover certain things about myself. That's only natural. But, more importantly, other people discovered things about me too. I was no longer perceived to be the boogy man that hid under the bed, or the troll that lived under the bridge. People started to see me as more than that."

Angry has many heroes. From childhood he worshipped the outlaws and bad boys of the screen. He always imagined himself as the James Dean type - brooding, dangerous, reckless. He loved that image. As he says, when he owned his first motorbike, it was Marlon Brando he was desperate to resemble. But, over the years, his heroes have changed. He'd now place Sir Bob Geldof at the top of his list of champions.

Like Angry, Geldof is an improbable good guy...a prolific community worker with some very rough edges. As Angry says, "I would have loved to have interviewed Bob Geldof because he is a modern-day hero to me. I mean I loved him even before he changed history. There's very, very few people in anyone's lifetime who can affect people like that. I mean, I would have loved to interview John Lennon too, but I don't think there's too many people on the planet that wouldn't. But Bob Geldof is a real live, living inspiration. I worship the guy. Bob Geldof changed history for several countries and several million people. He had a profound effect on the globe. His contribution to humanity is far greater than many other people who are more revered than him."

Angry did manage to meet Geldof one day on the set of "Midday", but, for what must be the first time in his life, he was too taken aback to actually identify himself as a fan. There he was, the same guy who calls people forward to the front of the autograph line saying 'Come on, don't be frightened. I don't bite,' completely overwhelmed in the presence of his own hero - another person who presumably doesn't bite.

Aside from Geldof, most of Angry's other heroes are of the cartoon variety. With some imagination and insight, Angry believes in the cartoon format, the storyteller can create the perfect hero. As he says, "I mean the Phantom now he's my favourite. the Phantom is not like the Lone Ranger. I mean, I never related to the Lone Ranger. I

HEROES

used to watch it on TV, but I just thought that Tonto got a raw deal, you know. But, I loved the Phantom. He's the ghost who walks. He's the legend. He represents good, the triumph over evil. You know, his family were slaughtered by pirates, and he devoted his life to fighting evil wherever he found it. He lives in deepest, darkest Africa and he's got a horse named 'Hero' for Christsake. Do you know what I mean? He's got a horse, and a dog and a terrific looking girlfriend, you know, and it's amazing that he goes everywhere with sunglasses and a hat and a coat, and no one knows it's him. It's ludicrous, but it works because it's just fantasy."

In Angry's mind the Phantom beats any superhero. Batman, Wonderwoman, even Superman. As he says, "Superman is terrific because he's from another planet and all that stuff, but the Phantom, now he really is the boy. He's strong, he's big, he's a dead shot, you know, don't mess with this guy. He could outfight, outshoot, outpunch anybody, yet he's this really, really sensitive guy. He's a butch bloke, yet his whole life is based around love and compassion and sensitivity. I love those heroes."

HEROES

Angry's even a fan of the most modern cartoon characters – the sensitive new age heroes of the 1990s. As he says,"The kids were watching the TV the other night, and they were watching 'Captain Planet', the ecological hero, and I think he's like a 1990s Tarzan. I think Edgar Rice Burroughs was a greenie when he wrote Tarzan. I think he was a man who loved his environment, who loved the temple that the world is, and the religion that life is, and I think he wanted to create a hero that represented all that.

"I was watching 'Captain Planet' with the kids...and I mean they love 'Captain Planet.' They sing the song, they pretend they're him, because he's a good guy. He's got muscles on muscles, you know how they draw those characters? I mean he's got the most exaggerated chest and thigh muscles. There's a ripple on every inch of his body. And, I kept looking at him thinking 'Yeah, he's like the Phantom, he's like Tarzan'. He's not a little wimp, he's a Schwarzenegger."

As far as Angry is concerned the celluloid heroes of today are trapped in a web of their own making. They're the Rambos, the big-gun heroes. Audiences expect their movies to be packed with action and violence, and they won't let them pull back an inch to soften the image. No one is interested in a gun toting hero with heart. "These guys, the Stallones and the Schwarzeneggers, can't make 'nice' movies. Their 'nice' movies have all flopped. Unless they kill 68 people in twelve seconds, nobody goes to the cinema. It's a shame because there should be more to them. I mean, the Phantom kills people too, but only when he's absolutely forced to. I mean, he usually just shoots people's guns out of their hands, then leaves them tied up for the police."

HEROES

READING MATTERS

If you ask Angry Anderson for a list of his favourite books, you're asking for trouble. He can try, time and time again, to narrow down the field, but he actually finds it impossible. He's passionate about books, and he has a habit of reading the same book up to eight or nine times. He likes to keep them on his shelf so he can refer to them later when he feels he's gained some new insight to the author's message. He also says he wants to make sure his children have an opportunity to read the books he's loved, not just because he loved them, but because, "great books are timeless". As he says, "I've kept some particular books so that my kids can discover the same truths that I discovered."

BOOKS

Here are some of Angry's favourites:

SPARTACUS: "Do you know the story of Spartacus? You know... sold into slavery to the Romans, rescued as a young man, and taught to become a gladiator - to fight for sport. After he fought some duels, he started to rebel. He argued that free men, born of free spirits should not have to kill themselves like cattle, and allow themselves to be slaughtered for the pleasure of other human beings. In other words, he stood for dignity. He led a revolt saying to other slaves and peasants and gladiators 'Hey, just because you were born into slavery doesn't mean that's your lot in life. You're a human being so don't accept this hokey-pokey story that you were born into slavery, and that's where you have to stay.' So, what it represented to me, apart from all the romance of the time, was exactly what I needed to hear in those early days. It said that no matter how you start, no matter how damaged you might be, no matter how they label you, you can rise above that. It's a book that gave me courage. I've seen the film twenty times, and I kid you not, I enjoy it every time. I could recite the bloody thing. It's just a wonderful story, and it says things about people...about what we should be, and what we can be, and how we can aspire."

MOBY DICK: "It's as much about the folly of obsession as it is about anything. To me, it's basically a tragic tale. It taught me that your life force can't be about obsessive vengeance. You can't dedicate your life to negative things. Ahab loses his leg to the whale, and becomes obsessive as a whaler, trying to hunt and kill the white whale. His obsession was revenge, because he thought the only way to purge the pain of losing his leg was to kill the object of his hate.

BOOKS

LUST FOR LIFE: " Vincent van Gogh's biography. I fell in love with the title. I cried most of the time. I kept picking up the book thinking, I'm going to cry, it's going to hurt me, I'm going to be sad, I'm going to be angry for this guy, but you fall in love with him. You fall in love with the way he looked at life, and what he did about it. I mean he lived in pain. Pain gave us van Gogh."

SEVEN PILLARS OF WISDOM : "It's the story of Lawrence of Arabia. I've read it over and over again, and I just finished reading it again the other day. The reason I love the book is because it's such a terrific expression of a man's battle and struggle with his own life. He's a master of the English language, so he's able to capture it all in the book. It's all there. The book inspired me and gave me hope. He was a quirky person, in charge of a quirky organisation and I suppose I identify with that. He writes at the end of the book 'Beware the dreamers, for they are dangerous men, for they might dream, and then say one day, "I'm going to make this happen". And he says 'This I did'. That's not quite verbatim, but I really love that quote."

Almost every week for two years 'The Midday Show' put Angry on his 'SOAPBOX'. He'd stand tall on a painted wooden box and give thirty second opinions on whatever topic Ray Martin fired at him.

This is Angry with thirty seconds on:

THE GENERATION GAP - 'Probably one of the most used and abused terms. I think it's a way of describing something that most people really don't understand. I think there is a distance between parents and kids, but I don't think it exists in the terror form that the media suggests. I think there is a distance, and it needs to be there. I think it's a distance that needs to be acknowledged and respected by both sides. And, no, I don't think we can ever bridge the gap ... I don't think we're meant to. The gap is there to teach us something.'

SOAPBOX

BREAST FEEDING IN PUBLIC - 'It's a thing I love to see, because I appreciate what breast feeding really is. It's much more than nourishment ... it's an incredible communication between mother and child. When I see a woman breast feeding in public, I think it's a step back towards civilisation. It's a step back towards true civilisation where womanhood and motherhood are revered, and not pushed into a corner.'

CHILDHOOD FANTASIES - 'Fantasies are an incredible part of life. I've just found that out. I think parents who deny their children's fantasies could be doing irreparable damage. You hear parents say stuff like 'Oh Junior, grow up! You haven't got a little friend who sleeps under the bed.' The parents who say things like that aren't doing justice to their kids. They should try to help their kids enjoy their fantasies because the fantasy world is so important.'

SUPERSTITIONS - 'I've never really been superstitious. My mother on the other hand is completely superstitious. I walk under ladders, break mirrors, ignore black cats, but if my mother drops a knife, it'll stay on the floor for months because she thinks it's bad luck to pick it up. She has another quaint superstition which I think is really amusing - she will never put a new pair of shoes on a chair or table. I don't know why that's supposed to be bad luck. It could be a Mauritian superstition. Who knows?'

THE SENSITIVE NEW AGE GUY (SNAG) - 'Ahh...(hands on head)...that's an interesting one. I don't really like the term. It irks me. I mean, I'm a 'bloke'. We've established that. I'm not a sensitive new age guy in the way I look at things. I am a sensitive *old-fashioned* guy, or at least, I'm trying to become more of a sensitive old-fashioned guy as time goes on.'

TOY GUNS - 'I think that in the largest of all pictures and in the best of all worlds we wouldn't have them. That's all I have to say on that.'

TABLE MANNERS - 'Any child that does not have good table manners is not welcome at our house. Manners of all description and shape and size are a big thing in the Anderson family. I've had discussions with people who say manners restrict children and put too much of a burden on their young thinking, and I think that's rubbish. I think you've got to teach kids good manners. I don't think you've got to make kids behave like robots or anything, but it's important for them to behave well.'

FATE - 'I'm not a big fan of destiny. I don't believe in fate because it eliminates the human component. Destiny is something that you can have a hand in, but fate is in the hands of the gods. In other words, if you believe in fate you believe you have no control over your life regardless of what you do or think, and that's rubbish.'

TATTOOED WOMEN - 'I love seeing women tattooed...but I hate seeing them with masculine tattoos displayed in a fashion that detracts from their femininity. I think good tattoos on ladies are as attractive as good tattoos on men...and bad tattoos are just as unattractive.'

PEER GROUP PRESSURE - 'We were talking to kids outside the schools once, asking them how they felt about certain issues, and one of the girls told us she thought peer group pressure was really over-rated. I agree with her. I think it is over-rated. I think it is a real thing, but I don't think it's responsible for all the things the media makes out. I give kids more credit than that. I mean, I don't think kids are all mindless morons where if one says let's jump off the bridge, they all do it.'

PRIDE - 'What a burden pride is, don't you think? It's a child of ego. I think you've got to be proud to a degree. I think you have to be proud of who you are and what you've done, in a *quiet* way. But I think there are people who wear pride round like a badge ... it's a vanity-based, ego type, preening sort of thing and I'm not comfortable about that. That's why I like the term foolish pride, because it's so apt.'

SOAPBOX

SCHOOL UNIFORMS - 'I love seeing kids in school uniforms. I think that uniformity is a very instructive and constructive thing, and I think you learn a lot about yourself by having to adhere to a uniform or a dress code. There's a school of thought that says uniforms inhibit personality and creativity, but I don't think kids really need to have free rein during school years. I think there's just as much character building and personality growth in situations where kids wear uniforms.'

TALENT - 'Everybody has a talent for something. Most of us have the potential, or the talent, to be good people...to be good parents, or good partners, or good friends. We all, at least, have the talent to be good human beings. But talent is so neglected. Even the people who recognise their talents never seem to do enough with them.'

'IF YOU HAVE THE RAGE IN YOU,
YOU CAN MANIFEST THE ENERGY. YOU CAN TAME IT.
YOU CAN GIVE IT A PURPOSE. IN OTHER WORDS, YOU
ARE THE MASTER OF YOUR OWN DESTINY.'

12

STILL ANGRY

Angry Anderson turns fifty on 8 August 1997. He expects the celebrations to be very low key, just as they have been for all his most recent birthdays. Basically, he dares anyone to mention the date or its significance, but Lindy and the kids always break the rules. As Angry sees it, he has no problems with age. He won't mind turning fifty. He still has a couple of years to prepare for it, so that's no problem. He only objects to birthdays because he feels they're used as measuring sticks and he doesn't want to spend one day a year adding up how much he's earned, or how many of his dreams he's realised, or how much he's achieved. He just wants to keep on moving slowly.

THE PHOENIX
WITH THE POWER
TO RECREATE ITSELF
IN ITS OWN FIRE

He thinks of himself as a work in progress. No matter how much he succeeds, he's constantly aware of the fine line he's walked. He has the firm belief that he narrowly missed life as a car thief, or a drunken maniac, or a drug addict. He recognises that it would only have taken one more wrong move, or one piece of bad luck, and he'd have been any or all of those things.

From childhood, he was steered in the wrong direction, but over the years he's developed an almost superstitious fear of admitting that, by some miracle, he managed to stay on track. Just as no one ever wants to say "This is my favourite wallet, I've never lost it", Angry doesn't want to jinx anything. He doesn't ever want to think that perhaps he spoke too soon. Whenever he talks about his achievements it's like he wants to put a "touch wood" at the end of each sentence for safe measure.

He's had an extraordinary life, yet as he says, when he looks back, he recognises so many familiar patterns. "My case is so cliched," says Angry. "It's so text book, but the thing about it is that there's so many of us that we do fall into the cliched category. The reason there are textbooks written about people like me is because there are so many of us."

"TEMPER IS A BEAST. YOU GIVE IT LIFE SO YOU CAN TAKE IT AWAY. AS LONG AS YOU DON'T GIVE IT A SHAPE AND A SIZE AND A NAME, IT CAN ALWAYS BE THIS MYSTERIOUS THING ... GIVE IT A NAME, GIVE IT A SHAPE, GIVE IT A SIZE, THEN YOU CAN STAMP IT OUT. THEN YOU CAN DEAL WITH IT."

Angry hasn't seen or heard from his father since the day of the divorce when he unknowingly sat near him in the courtroom. He hasn't wanted to make any contact, because he still finds it so difficult to deal with the problems of his childhood. As he says, he doesn't know where his father is now, and he doesn't care.

As his family would agree, it was Angry, with his mum, who bore the brunt of his father's madness. He's also the one who bore the grudge. He's black and bitter about his years as a child. He says the greatest task in therapy is to forgive and forget. Not to forgive his father, because he says he will never have the heart to do that, but to forgive the mistakes, and the pain, and put them truly behind him.

The one breakthrough he has made, though, is to decide that he no longer hates his father. He no longer despises him, or the memory. As he says, "You see I haven't seen the man for most of my life. I haven't had any physical contact with him for more than half my lifetime, so what possible reason is there to keep alive something which has no purpose? I don't fear him anymore, you know, and I lived in fear of him the whole time we lived together because I was physically afraid that he'd hurt me or that he'd hurt Mum. There was a reason for me to actively despise him...actively absolutely hate the mere mention of his name. But now, there's no physical reason to hate him any more. There's nothing physical that's happening any more. I don't fear him. I don't have to fear him...he's old. He's in his 70s. He's an old man. I can't fear him, but I can't forgive him either."

In many ways Angry has been able to turn most of his rage and bitterness around. He's been able to use his street knowledge and his brawler instinct in positive ways. He's still volatile, because he can never really break free of that, and he is still, in his own words, potentially violent. But, for the most part, he has his temper under control. He says the most important steps he's taken are the steps to recognise his own ferocity, and face it.

He says it is a matter of making the rage work for you...investing in something constructive rather than surrendering to it. "If you have a rage in you, you can manifest the energy. You can tame it. You can give it a purpose. In other words, you are the master of your own destiny. You can make from life what you want out of life. We are what we want to be. I really believe that. If we're failures and we're drug addicts, and we're badly done by, then, that's what we wish for ourselves. Not in the front part of our mind, but in the back part, the dark part. It's the part that we won't even recognise, the part the church and other people have taught us to fear. The reason it causes us so many problems is because we fear it. You can be worried or concerned, but you shouldn't fear yourself, and you shouldn't fear those parts of yourself. You see, my rage and my anger, I don't think I'm ever going to be over it. So, if I'm never going to be over it, then I'd better learn to deal with it. You can turn yourself into the master, not the victim. You can say to yourself, 'Yes, I have this rage or this sadness and then you can deal with it."

YOU CAN MAKE FROM LIFE WHAT YOU WANT OUT OF LIFE. WE ARE WHAT WE WANT TO BE. I REALLY BELIEVE THAT. IF WE'RE FAILURES AND WE'RE DRUG ADDICTS, AND WE'RE BADLY DONE BY, THEN, THAT'S WHAT WE WISH FOR OURSELVES.

In doing the interviews for the early chapters of this book, Angry found it tough. Sometimes he cried, and sometimes he waved his arms around madly trying to get his point across. He rarely talks about his real father. The only time he ever uses the word dad is in reference to Bert Roach, his mother's second husband.

He's also never talked before about details of his childhood, particularly the sexual assaults. But, as with everything else in his life, he has strong opinions about bringing sexual abuse into the open, so in a sense, it is simply a matter of "practise what you preach". As he says, he's well and truly aware of the fact that he is not alone. "You know, outing now as a sexually abused child has become the butt of stand-up comedy because so many people have just 'discovered' they were abused as a child. But, it's not like they're jumping on the bandwagon.

Psychologists say that a lot of people in show business are there to give themselves an alter ego, another personality. They can express themselves in ways that they haven't been allowed because they've been abused or neglected or repressed as children. The same can be said of kids who steal or break into cars or whatever. It's tragic that they have to break the law, but it's a way for them to have notoriety. It's a way for them to get control, and another way for them to express themselves. Many kids can't see themselves finding notoriety in Angry Anderson terms...you know becoming a rock star or a person on television, so they can only see one way of making people pay attention to them, of getting control."

Angry would be the first one to admit he is a classic psychologist's case...that he entered show business primarily to give himself an alter ego and another personality. It was precisely that kind of outlet he was looking for when he found Rose Tattoo.

In many ways, Rose Tattoo was the greatest club Angry ever belonged to. It was tailor-made for him. In his wildest dreams he couldn't have imagined anything to suit him better. It was a lifeline to him, because it gave him such purpose. It kept him off the streets, literally. With Rose Tattoo, Angry was able to take all the best parts of his character and the worst parts of his character and roll them into one. He was able to concentrate, and he was given a glimpse of something that was way beyond his shady life in the suburbs.

With the band, Angry and the boys made their own rules. In a way they created their own society. It was larger than life, anything goes. It was macho, and ugly, and loud, and dangerous, and it was everything Angry was looking for. He believes wholeheartedly in the birds of a feather philosophy. As far as he's concerned, the members of Rose Tattoo were all bent and desperate in their own ways. They were all misfits, performing for misfit crowds. There was just something in their chemistry that made them special. They were dynamic as a team, and unique as a band.

In spite of their reputation, Angry defends the Rose Tattoo image passionately. He doesn't even attempt to argue that they weren't drunks, or that they weren't reckless, or that they weren't out of control... they were all those things. But he argues they had a well-earned credibility with their audience, and they managed to establish something that goes beyond a punk fad or a moment of audience madness. As Angry says, "We didn't think of kids just as potential record buyers because we were such a grassroots band, such a street level band. We were really in touch with the kids. We really had a good relationship with them. That's why it still amazes me when kids come up and recognise me, and tell me Rose Tattoo was such a great band. It wasn't just the fashion, because that's come and gone. It was more than that. It still gives me a kick when a sixteen year old runs up to me in the street to say 'Hey man, I was at the Gunners gig.' You can see it it their eyes. They just don't relate to the fact that you're fat and forty. It's what you do, and what you did that's important to them."

Every now and then, when he's walking down the street, or sitting in a restaurant, or giving a speech in a school or a conference, Angry will be confronted with his past. Kids will sometimes quiz him on his history. They're tactless, but they make their point. They'll ask him if he took drugs, they'll ask him if he drove dangerously, they'll ask him how he broke his teeth. Whenever he repeats the slogan from the campaign against alcohol abuse, "Don't get off your face", they ask him how often he got drunk. It's like they're putting out a warning. They're telling him that they're prepared to listen, but they don't want to hear a hypocrite.

Angry encourages the questions because he wants to explain. He wants kids to examine his arguments more closely, and demand explanations. As he says, "I don't think kids should just mindlessly worship rock and roll stars. They shouldn't just excuse their idols if they're not good. I can understand kids wrestling with my past."

Angry admits all his mistakes. He lays himself at the mercy of his accusers, and as he says, they're more forgiving than he'd have imagined. They understand what he's trying to say. He has a real knack with young people that comes from his bluntheadedness. He's so laid back in his approach, he makes people drop their guard. He has a sneer that says "Take me or leave me", and much to the disappointment of some of his critics, he truly couldn't care which option they choose. He is secure enough with his image now, and confident enough about his friends and fans, that to strike a few enemies occasionally doesn't faze him.

As the years wear on, it's unlikely there'll be much more than an inch of Angry's body unillustrated. The only stretch of skin that's certain to remain untouched by the tattooist's needle is his head. It's his promise to his mother. He's always told her, that no matter what else he does, his scalp will remain skin coloured.

AS THE YEARS WEAR ON, IT'S UNLIKELY THERE'LL BE MUCH MORE THAN AN INCH OF ANGRY'S BODY UNILLUSTRATED. THE ONLY STRETCH OF SKIN THAT'S CERTAIN TO REMAIN UNTOUCHED BY THE TATTOOIST'S NEEDLE IS HIS HEAD. IT'S HIS PROMISE TO HIS MOTHER.

When it comes to his tattoos, there's one other vow Angry hopes never to break. At the moment, on the scroll of women's names on his upper arm the name "LOU" doesn't appear. That's the way Angry would like to keep it. As he says, "The tattoos were all in memorial basically. I didn't tattoo anyone's name on my arm until after we'd broken up. I guess it was just a way of marking history. It's funny though because there's a few girls who I've had really good relationships with who possibly think they deserve a slot too, but I guess there was just something about those particular girls at those particular times. I've never really thought that I'd have to remember Lou by having her name tattooed on my skin. I've just always thought she'd be there."

Angry's very big on second chances. He's big on support and encouragement. As he says, "Lou has never condoned or approved of the way I've conducted some of my life, but she wasn't there as a critic. She was there as a supporter, so she was critical of some of my excesses, but supportive. In other words, she didn't just say, 'You're a drunken loser'. She gave me the chance to prove there was more to me. She stuck with me through the drunken years, through the infidelities, through a certain amount of emotional abuse and neglect. I was never really abusive, but I was abusive of the situation, and Lou stuck by me. Whether we survive as a marriage or not, I will always have the highest respect and love for her because of that."

Angry will always work. He'll always have some interest or

project, basically because he believes retirement is such a dangerous business. As soon as television and music and theatre and movies have had enough of him, he wants to move into a new field. Painting is his dream, or writing. He says he imagines himself one day living in the country with Lindy, in some house on top of a hill with a painter's palette and an easel.

He sometimes toys with the idea of going into politics, and doesn't even rule it out completely. He's just not sure whether he has the discipline. The one thing he is sure of, is that in the future, he'll become a much more focused campaigner. He wants to keep working with charity groups, but not so much on the ground level. He sees himself as moving into the lobbyists' arena, trying to get bigger and better things done on a grander scale.

People sometimes jokingly ask him if he'll ever make a push to become prime minister. In typical form, Angry loves the idea of running the country, but believes there's really only one way he could ever do it. He laughs and says he'd need a very loud, very public call to power. In his own words, it would have to be "a sort of Camelot experience. You know, the people would have to carry me down the street on their shoulders saying 'We must have this man'. It would have to be that sort of thing."

Angry's a passionate person, and he hasn't lost any of his drive, but he's now moving toward midlife with a calmness he's never felt before. For years, the person known as Angry Anderson, the maniacal rocker, was just a cover for an unheard of person known as Gary Anderson. Now, the two people are one and the same.

Angry's motto to life is simple. He's a believer in giving everyone a fair go, and in trying to see the real people hiding behind the masks. As he says, "It's like something I used to tell the crowd when I was on stage. I'd be philosophising the way I always have, and I'd say, 'Well folks, all you've got to remember is that there's a little bit of evil in the so-called best of them, and there's a little bit of good in the worst'."

ANGRY'S A PASSIONATE PERSON, AND HE HASN'T LOST ANY OF HIS DRIVE, BUT HE'S NOW MOVING TOWARD MIDLIFE WITH A CALMNESS HE'S NEVER FELT BEFORE. FOR YEARS, THE PERSON KNOWN AS ANGRY ANDERSON, THE MANIACAL ROCKER, WAS JUST A COVER FOR AN UNHEARD OF PERSON KNOWN AS GARY ANDERSON. NOW, THE TWO PEOPLE ARE ONE AND THE SAME.

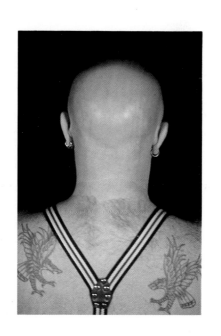